Marcus Radetzki, Marian Radetzki, Niklas Juth
Genes and Insurance: Ethical, Legal and Economic Issues
978 0 521 83090 4

Ruth Macklin
Double Standards in Medical Research in Developing Countries
978 0 521 83388 2 hardback   978 0 521 54170 1 paperback

Donna Dickenson
Property in the Body: Feminist Perspectives
978 0 521 86792 4

Matti Häyry, Ruth Chadwick, Vilhjálmur Árnason, Gardar Árnason
The Ethics and Governance of Human Genetic Databases: European Perspectives
978 0 521 85662 1

Ken Mason
The Troubled Pregnancy, Legal Wrongs and Rights in Reproduction
978 0 521 85075 9

Daniel Sperling
Posthumous Interests: Legal and Ethical Perspectives
978 0 521 87784 8

Law, Legitimacy and the Rationing of Healthcare
A Contextual and Comparative Perspective

Keith Syrett argues for a reappraisal of the role played by public law adjudication in questions of healthcare rationing. As governments worldwide turn to strategies of explicit rationing to manage the mismatch between demand for and supply of health services and treatments, disappointed patients and the public have sought to contest the moral authority of bodies making rationing decisions. This has led to the growing involvement of law in this field of public policy. The author argues that, rather than bemoaning this development, those working within the health policy community should recognise the points of confluence between the principles and purposes of public law and the proposals which have been made to address rationing's 'legitimacy problem'. Drawing upon jurisprudence from England, Canada and South Africa, the book evaluates the capacity of courts to establish the conditions for a process of public deliberation from which legitimacy for healthcare rationing may be derived.

DR KEITH SYRETT is a Solicitor and Senior Lecturer in Law at the University of Bristol.

Cambridge Law, Medicine and Ethics

This series of books was founded by Cambridge University Press with Alexander McCall Smith as its first editor in 2003. It focuses on the law's complex and troubled relationship with medicine across both the developed and the developing world. In the past twenty years, we have seen in many countries increasing resort to the courts by dissatisfied patients and a growing use of the courts to attempt to resolve intractable ethical dilemmas. At the same time, legislatures across the world have struggled to address the questions posed by both the successes and the failures of modern medicine, while international organisations such as the WHO and UNESCO now regularly address issues of medical law.

It follows that we would expect ethical and policy questions to be integral to the analysis of the legal issues discussed in this series. The series responds to the high profile of medical law in universities, in legal and medical practice, as well as in public and political affairs. We seek to reflect the evidence that many major health-related policy debates in the UK, Europe and the international community over the past two decades have involved a strong medical law dimension. Organ retention, embryonic stem cell research, physician-assisted suicide and the allocation of resources to fund health care are but a few examples among many. The emphasis of this series is thus on matters of public concern and/or practical significance. We look for books that could make a difference to the development of medical law and enhance the role of medico-legal debate in policy circles. That is not to say that we lack interest in the important theoretical dimensions of the subject, but we aim to ensure that theoretical debate is grounded in the realities of how the law does and should interact with medicine and health care.

Law, Legitimacy and the Rationing of Healthcare

A Contextual and Comparative Perspective

Keith Syrett

CAMBRIDGE
UNIVERSITY PRESS

CAMBRIDGE UNIVERSITY PRESS
Cambridge, New York, Melbourne, Madrid, Cape Town, Singapore, São Paulo,
Delhi

Cambridge University Press
The Edinburgh Building, Cambridge CB2 8RU, UK

Published in the United States of America by Cambridge University Press,
New York

www.cambridge.org
Information on this title: www.cambridge.org/9780521674454

First published 2007

Printed in the United Kingdom at the University Press, Cambridge

A catalogue record for this publication is available from the British Library

ISBN 978-0-521-85773-4 hardback
ISBN 978-0-521-67445-4 paperback

To the memory of my father and of my mother

Contents

Table of Cases

3.   European Court of Human Rights

4.   South Africa

Acknowledgements

I would like to thank those with whom I have worked both at the University of Bristol and at the University of East Anglia for their friendship, encouragement and advice in the years leading up to the publication of this book. Particular thanks are due to Caroline Ball, Dave Cowan, James Davey, Bronwen Morgan, Jill Morgan, Tony Prosser, Oliver Quick, Mike Radford, Claudina Richards and Mark Stallworthy.

My understanding of the Canadian perspective was enormously enhanced by a research trip to the country in 2005, funded by Foreign Affairs Canada. I would especially like to thank Colleen Flood and Rebecca Cook of the University of Toronto, and Martha Jackman of the University of Ottawa, both for their helpful advice and for their generous hospitality towards me.

I have also benefited immensely from discussions with Charles Ngwena of the University of the Free State and Marius Pieterse of the University of the Witwatersrand in South Africa.

Last, but certainly not least, I thank Paula for her help, support and love. I could not have written this book without her.

The law is stated as of 1 January 2007.

1   Introduction

Towards the end of 2005, a major news story broke in the British media. Under headlines such as 'NHS denies woman life-saving drug to treat breast cancer',[1] 'Why can't I have breast cancer drug now?'[2] and 'Bureaucracy threatens cancer sufferers' lives',[3] it was reported that a number of Primary Care Trusts (PCTs) and health boards, whose responsibility it is to commission provision of healthcare services for their local populations, had refused requests to provide funding for a new 'wonder drug', Herceptin, for the treatment of early stage breast cancer. Journalists and commentators cited evidence that there were geographical variations in access to the treatment (an example of the so-called 'postcode lottery' in the provision of care),[4] reported dissatisfaction with 'bureaucratic' regulatory processes which were perceived as delaying access to the treatment,[5] and noted that a number of disappointed patients were threatening to make use of the courts in an attempt to overturn decisions to deny access to the treatment.[6]

Across the globe, similar incidents are occurring as health systems of all types come under significant strain from the increasing demands placed upon them. Decisions on the allocation of resources for healthcare represent some of the most pressing and controversial choices faced by modern governments. Yet, this was not how it was supposed to be. For example, in the United Kingdom (UK), the belief was that the establishment of the National Health Service (NHS) would reduce the demand for healthcare services and thus offset the requirement to establish priorities

---

[1] *The Independent*, 9 November 2005.
[2] *BBC News Online*, 19 October 2005, available at http://news.bbc.co.uk/1/hi/health/4355950.stm (accessed 8 January 2007).
[3] *Daily Mail*, 14 November 2005.
[4] See e.g. 'Scots get Breast Cancer "Wonder Drug"', *The Scotsman*, 17 February 2006; 'Postcode Lottery for Cancer Wonder Drug', *Daily Mail*, 10 April 2006.
[5] See e.g. *Daily Mail*, above n. 3, 'Life or Bureaucracy?', *The Times*, 16 February 2006.
[6] See e.g. 'Nurse Sues for Right to Have Breast Cancer Drug', *Sunday Times*, 18 September 2005; 'Mother's legal fight for life', *Daily Express*, 9 November 2005.

for expenditure. Put simply, 'the assumption in 1948 was that there existed a finite amount of ill-health in the land, that this could be reduced by improved healthcare and that thereafter the maintenance of the good health of the population would be a relatively simple matter'.[7] Today, with the hindsight afforded by more than half a century of growing pressure on a publicly funded health service which has been described as existing in a state of 'almost perpetual crisis',[8] such a view seems almost astonishingly naïve.

Nevertheless, demanding as it is, the policy problem arising within health systems is not 'simply' the need to manage the mismatch between the demand for healthcare and the supply of available resources. Disappointed individuals who have been denied access to treatment seem increasingly unwilling to accept such decisions without question. The process of allocative decision-making in healthcare is thus strongly marked by volatility. As an eminent commentator notes: 'suspicion, distrust and even resistance [will] often greet efforts to set limits on access to medical services'.[9] Accordingly, there is a need to undertake steps to address the systemic instability which tends to be generated by the 'rationing' of healthcare resources.

The most straightforward reading of the increasing readiness to resort to litigation in cases of this type would suggest that this is a symptom of such instability. It follows that those policy-makers and academic commentators who are concerned to find means to resolve this problem will tend to regard the involvement of the law with disapproval. This book seeks to propose an alternative perspective, which provides the basis for a more positive evaluation of the role of law, and particularly of the courts, in this field. However, working from the premise that a proper appreciation of the function of law cannot be developed in isolation from the socio-political environment in which it operates, it is necessary also to attain an understanding of the character of allocative decision-making in healthcare and of the nature of the difficulties which arise. In this respect, the Herceptin episode affords an instructive illustration, and examination of it in more depth therefore offers a useful starting-point for analysis.

---

[7] B. Salter, *The Politics of Change in the Health Service* (Basingstoke: Macmillan, 1998) at 17.

[8] R. Klein, 'Self-Inventing Institutions: Institutional Design and the UK Welfare State' in R. Goodin (ed.), *The Theory of Institutional Design* (Cambridge: Cambridge University Press, 1996) at 243.

[9] N. Daniels, 'Accountability for Reasonableness in Private and Public Health Insurance' in A. Coulter and C. Ham (eds.), *The Global Challenge of Health Care Rationing* (Buckingham: Open University Press, 2000) at 89.

Herceptin and the NHS: a case study of the rationing of treatment

Herceptin (the brand name of the drug trastuzumab) is a targeted treatment for breast cancer. It takes the form of a monoclonal antibody which attaches itself to those cancer cells containing large amounts of the HER2 protein which functions as a growth factor receptor, stimulating cancer cells to grow and multiply. It has been used on its own and in combination with chemotherapy for advanced breast cancer for a number of years, and guidance issued by the National Institute for Clinical Excellence (NICE, an independent agency whose responsibilities include the appraisal of the clinical and cost-effectiveness of new medical technologies)[10] in May 2002, recommended that it be made available on the NHS in England and Wales for certain categories of patient suffering from the disease in its advanced state. Subsequently, three major international clinical trials on patients with early-stage breast cancer reported preliminary results which suggested that treatment with Herceptin significantly improved response rates, with the cancer returning in half as many cases as those in which treatment took the form of chemotherapy alone.[11] However, the drug is very expensive, with a standard 38-week course of therapy costing £15,500 per patient, as distinct from the cost of £2.39 per month for Tamoxifen,[12] currently regarded as the 'gold standard' anti-hormonal agent for breast cancer.

Unsurprisingly, once the results of the clinical trials started to emerge, pressure began to mount upon the British Government to make the drug available on the NHS for those suffering from early stage breast cancer. A campaign group, Women Fighting for Herceptin, was established in July 2005 and it subsequently organised a march on Downing Street, presenting a petition of more than 30,000 signatures demanding access to the treatment.[13] The media campaigned for the drug to be made available.[14]

[10] For further discussion of the Institute (now renamed the National Institute for Health and Clinical Excellence), see below Chapters 2 to 4.

[11] See M. Piccart-Gebhart, M. Proctor, B. Leyland-Jones et al., 'Trastuzumab after Adjuvant Chemotherapy in HER2-positive Breast Cancer' (2005) 353 New England Journal of Medicine, 1659; E. Romond, E. Perez, J. Bryant et al., 'Trastuzumab Plus Adjuvant Chemotherapy for Operable HER2-Positive Breast Cancer' (2005) 353 New England Journal of Medicine, 1673; R. Dent and M. Clemons, 'Adjuvant Trastuzumab for Breast Cancer: We Need to Ensure that Equity Exists for Access to Effective and Expensive Treatments' (2005) 331 British Medical Journal. 1035.

[12] See 'Live or Die? Your Postcode Decides', The Guardian, 6 October 2005.

[13] See 'Breast Drug Campaign Frustration', BBC News Online, 22 September 2005, available at http://news.bbc.co.uk/1/hi/health/4270548.stm (accessed 8 January 2007); also 'Herceptin Group Takes to Streets', BBC News Online, 13 November 2005, available at http://news.bbc.co.uk/1/hi/england/staffordshire/4430036.stm (accessed 8 January 2007).

[14] 'Breast Cancer Campaign', The Sun, 30 September 2005.

The issue was also regularly raised in both Houses of Parliament,[15] was discussed in Select Committee[16] and was the subject of both a private members' debate in Westminster Hall[17] and an Early Day Motion sponsored by the shadow Health Secretary.[18]

Such pressure prompted a political response. The Government announced that all women with early stage breast cancer were to be tested to ascertain whether they could benefit from the drug,[19] indicated that PCTs and health authorities should not refuse access to the treatment on cost grounds alone,[20] and promised that the drug would be 'fast-tracked' for appraisal of its clinical and cost-effectiveness by NICE as soon as a marketing licence had been issued by the European Medicines Agency (EMA).[21] More broadly, concern over delay in accessing this and other treatments, given the usual length of a NICE technology appraisal, prompted the Institute to review its decision-making processes, leading to the introduction of a Single Technology Appraisal which would issue recommendations within eight weeks, in contrast to the 54-week average length of the existing process. Herceptin was identified as one of the first treatments scheduled for appraisal via the new process, once implemented.[22]

In certain parts of the UK, the response to these developments was to make Herceptin immediately available for early stage breast cancer patients for whom it had been recommended.[23] However, elsewhere, a number of other PCTs became embroiled in controversy over decisions to deny access to the treatment. Such refusal was justified primarily on the basis that regulatory processes should not be circumvented by permitting access to the treatment prior to its evaluation by EMA and NICE. This enabled the argument to be made that the safety and effectiveness of the

---

[15] See e.g. *House of Commons Debates*, vol. 439, col. 2268W (24 November 2005); vol. 440, cols. 398W and 403W (29 November 2005); *House of Lords Debates*, vol. 674, col. WA33 (10 October 2005).

[16] Health Committee, *Public Expenditure on Health and Social Services*, HC 736-ii (2005–06) qs. 271–281.

[17] *House of Commons Debates*, vol. 438, col. 185WH (1 November 2005).

[18] EDM 1020, 14 November 2005 (A. Lansley).

[19] See 'Breast Cancer Drug Test for All', *BBC News Online*, 5 October 2005, available at http://news.bbc.co.uk/1/hi/health/4311140.stm (accessed 8 January 2007).

[20] Department of Health, Chief Executive Bulletin No. 294, 4–10 November 2005.

[21] Department of Health Press Release 2005/0263 (20 July 2005).

[22] NICE Press Release 2005/027 (3 November 2005).

[23] See e.g. 'Herceptin Decision "Breakthrough"', *BBC News Online*, 18 October 2005, available at http://news.bbc.co.uk/1/hi/england/cornwall/4354448.stm (accessed 8 January 2007) (Devon and Cornwall); 'Minister in N.I. Cancer Drug Move', *BBC News Online*, 11 November 2005, available at http://news.bbc.co.uk/1/hi/northern_ireland/4426816.stm (accessed 8 January 2007) (Northern Ireland).

drug was as yet unproven. However, it was apparent that cost also played an important part in the thinking of PCTs, notwithstanding the injunction of the Secretary of State for Health that financial factors should not be the sole considerations underpinning decisions to deny access. Thus, one PCT argued that 'the evidence of [Herceptin] as a cost-effective use of the finite health resources available for [the PCT's] patients is not confirmed. It would therefore be premature to agree to introduce it as a routine treatment. To do so could seriously affect the availability of care to other patients, including those with other cancers.'[24] Financial concerns were exacerbated by the need for PCTs to allocate funding for any provision of Herceptin from their existing budgets, as the Government refused to provide any additional resources to pay for the treatment.[25]

For those patients who were refused access to Herceptin, two avenues of challenge were available. Initially, challenges were mounted through the PCT's *internal appeal process*. Here, the patient would appeal against the decision which had been reached under the PCT's 'Commissioning Exceptions Policy' (which covered cases in which treatment was not normally funded – for example, because there was insufficient evidence of effectiveness – but where individual clinical circumstances warranted an exception being made) to a Commissioning Appeals Panel. In some instances, this proved successful, as PCTs reversed the original decision.[26] However, in other cases, patients sought, or threatened, *judicial review* of the refusal to make the drug available. In two such cases, the threat of legal proceedings (coupled, in the second instance, with significant political pressure) prompted the PCT concerned to reverse its initial decision and to make the drug available, citing the patient's 'exceptional circumstances' as justification.[27] In a third case, the Court of Appeal (reversing the decision of the court at first instance) found that Swindon PCT had acted unlawfully in operating a policy which purported to allow for the provision of Herceptin upon proof of exceptionality but under which it was, in practice, impossible to envisage any

[24] North Stoke Primary Care Trust, Press Release, 8 November 2005.
[25] See *House of Commons Debates*, vol. 439, col. 1361 (22 November 2005) (J. Kennedy).
[26] For an example, see 'Cancer Woman Can Appeal Drug Ban', *BBC News Online*, 3 November 2005, available at http://news.bbc.co.uk/1/hi/england/manchester/4403614.stm (accessed 8 January 2007) and 'Cancer Patients Win Herceptin Bid', *BBC News Online*, 18 November 2005, available at http://news.bbc.co.uk/1/hi/england/manchester/4449966.stm (accessed 8 January 2007).
[27] See 'Breast Cancer Sufferer Wins Fight for Wonder Drug', *The Times*, 3 October 2005; 'Health Chiefs Avert Court Clash over Cancer Drug', *The Times*, 10 November 2005. In the latter case, the Secretary of State had sought an urgent meeting with the PCT to discuss the refusal: see 'Hewitt Steps in to "Wonder Drug" Cancer Row', *The Times*, 8 November 2005.

exceptional circumstances which would justify provision of funding for one patient and denial for another.[28]

Finally, in August 2006, NICE issued guidance recommending that Herceptin be made available on the NHS for women with early stage HER2-positive breast cancer, except where concerns existed as to cardiac function.[29] However, controversy continued to surround the treatment, with cancer specialists pointing out that cuts in other services would be required to fund provision of the drug.[30]

What conclusions may be drawn from the Herceptin episode? First, it is apparent that any decision to 'ration' the provision of healthcare will only emerge after engagement with a complex interplay of various factors, including those of a clinical, financial and political nature. This is significant because, while the development of more explicit methodologies and mechanisms for the allocation of resources in healthcare has served to render more publicly visible the necessity of making 'hard choices' in this field of public policy, the inherent 'messiness' of this form of decision-making can readily generate incomplete or confusing – and possibly, deliberately misleading – explanations for rationing decisions. For example, North Stoke PCT, as cited previously, purported to justify its initial refusal to provide Herceptin to a patient on the grounds of the insufficiency of evidence of the safety and *relative* cost-effectiveness of the drug.[31] Upon reversing the decision, it sought to refute media suggestions that the *absolute* cost of the treatment had been a factor (albeit that this claim was perhaps somewhat undermined by the PCT's simultaneous observation that it had no budget to provide for Herceptin in the current financial year and that it would cost £700,000 to provide in the following year).[32] The apparent confusion between these two arguments suggests that the PCT's reasoning was not fully understood by the public or by the patient, who were likely to perceive the decision indiscriminately as being 'about money'.[33] It might therefore be argued that decision-making in

---

[28] See *R (on the application of Rogers)* v. *Swindon NHS Primary Care Trust and Secretary of State for Health* [2006] 1 WLR 2649, discussed in Chapter 6 below.

[29] NICE Press Release 2006/038 (23 August 2006).

[30] A. Barrett, T. Roques, M. Small *et al.*, 'How Much Will Herceptin Cost?' (2006) 333 *British Medical Journal*, 1118.

[31] See above n. 24 and accompanying text.

[32] North Stoke Primary Care Trust, Press Release, 9 November 2005.

[33] See e.g. A. d'Argue, quoted in 'Woman Waits for Herceptin Ruling', *BBC News Online*, 2 November 2005, available at http://news.bbc.co.uk/1/hi/england/manchester/4398588.stm (accessed 8 January 2005): 'It is an NHS lottery and it always will be and however they dress it up the bottom line is it's about money'; A. M. Rogers, quoted in 'Doctors "Prescribing Herceptin"', *BBC News Online*, 3 February 2006, available at http://news.bbc.co.uk/1/hi/health/4677538.stm (accessed 8 January 2007): 'I think it's down to money and I think they put money before life'.

this field continues to be somewhat opaque and that mechanisms should be devised through which those responsible for allocative decisions can be called to provide reasoned explanations and evidence for the choices which have been made, in a manner which is comprehensible both to those directly affected and the broader public. As will be argued subsequently in this book, such a development can benefit decision-makers as well as those subject to the decision, in that the process of justification should enhance public understanding both of the need for, and the criteria relevant to, limit-setting choices in healthcare. In turn, this can stimulate a process of democratic debate upon healthcare rationing.

The tendency for explicit rationing decisions to be socially and politically unstable is also amply demonstrated by the Herceptin case. Notwithstanding attempts to 'depoliticise' the process of resource allocation in healthcare through the establishment of technocratic modes of decision-making which draw upon scientific and social-scientific evidence to reach 'rational' conclusions upon priorities for expenditure (as reflected in this instance by the roles fulfilled by the EMA and NICE regulatory agencies),[34] this field of public policy remains strongly characterised by 'classic' pluralist politics. This takes the form of extensive interest group lobbying, direct government intervention and activation of internal and external mechanisms for appeal and review. Indeed, perhaps paradoxically, the techniques of 'evidence-based medicine' actually served to fuel the controversy in this instance, in that the campaign to make Herceptin available on the NHS for those suffering from early-stage breast cancer was largely stimulated by the results of the three major international clinical trials. This appears to reinforce the view that, while 'sometimes defining issues as questions of technique or evidence masks the underlying political disputes ... the political issues are still there, even when they are addressed indirectly using the language of technique and evidence. Battles over income, turf, and the goals of medicine and policy lie just below the surface. Under these circumstances, evidence becomes an instrument of politics rather than a substitute for it.'[35]

As well as being prone to political instability, it is readily apparent that decisions on the rationing of healthcare resources provoke a significant clash of ethical perspectives. Once again, this is clearly evident from the

---

[34] For discussion, see K. Syrett, 'A Technocratic Fix to the "Legitimacy Problem"? The Blair Government and Health Care Rationing in the United Kingdom' (2003) 28 *Journal of Health Politics, Policy and Law*, 715.

[35] M. Rodwin, 'The Politics of Evidence-Based Medicine' (2001) 26 *Journal of Health Politics, Policy and Law*, 439. See also Barrett, Roques, Small *et al.*, 'How Much Will Herceptin Cost?' at 1119.

events surrounding the availability of Herceptin. PCTs, such as that serving North Stoke, were apt to supplement explanations as to the need to avoid circumvention of the regulatory process by reference to utilitarian arguments:

> Primary Care Trusts strive to make good use of the resources entrusted to them in order to meet the requirements of their population in accordance with their statutory duties and to maintain and improve the health of their population to the greatest possible extent. North Stoke PCT is required to fund treatments (or preventative measures) of proven effectiveness for many groups of patients with well-recognised healthcare needs. In doing so it is necessary to make difficult choices about which services represent the best use of a finite resource.[36]

On the other hand, for their part, affected patients (and their supporters and advisors) would typically posit powerful individualistic claims based upon clinical need and human rights. Thus, Elaine Barber, the woman involved in the North Stoke case, argued that 'I need this drug to help me survive – without it I will die',[37] and remarked that 'I can't believe that I have been put through all this just so the health authority can balance the books. Human life cannot and should not be measured in pounds',[38] while her solicitor indicated that the threatened legal challenge would be based upon an alleged violation of the right to life under the Human Rights Act 1998. Statements such as these suggest that individualistic and community-based ethical perspectives on the fair distribution of scarce healthcare resources may ultimately be incommensurable. This presents a very significant political problem for a government which seeks to set priorities for expenditure in a manner which is publicly regarded as legitimate.

The final – and for the purposes of this book's central theme most significant – issue raised by the Herceptin episode relates to the proper place of law in the rationing of healthcare resources. It is interesting to note that those patients who chose to invoke the threat of legal proceedings in their efforts to obtain treatment claimed to be doing so with considerable reluctance, arguing that they had been forced to act in such a way out of 'sheer desperation',[39] and that 'the last thing that

---

[36] Above n. 24.

[37] See 'Mother Refused Breast Cancer Drug', *BBC News Online*, 8 November 2005, available at http://news.bbc.co.uk/1/hi/england/staffordshire/4417076.stm (accessed 8 January 2007).

[38] See 'Woman Gets Cancer Drug in U-Turn', *BBC News Online*, 9 November 2005, available at http://news.bbc.co.uk/1/hi/england/staffordshire/4421570.stm (accessed 8 January 2007).

[39] B. Clark, quoted in 'Dying Nurse Sues NHS for Denying Her Cancer Drug', *The Observer*, 18 September 2005.

[the patient] wants to do is to go to court'.[40] This suggests both that the legal process (or, to be more precise, public law adjudication) is regarded as being somewhat marginal to decision-making on the allocation of healthcare, and further, that it is perceived in largely negative terms. It is seen as an obtrusion into the work of those responsible for setting priorities, which should only be employed as a means of last resort. Nonetheless, it is clear from the statements cited in the preceding paragraph that both the allocative choices made by PCTs and the challenges which were raised to these by individual patients were conceived, at least in part, in terms of the relevant legal framework: hence the reference to the 'statutory duties' of the PCT,[41] in addition to the more self-evident deployment of the Human Rights Act 1998 by frustrated patients. It appears extremely likely, therefore, that law will become involved to some degree in rationing choices such as that which was at issue in the case of Herceptin. Indeed, the probability of such engagement has increased significantly in recent years. This is in part because trends such as a more litigious citizenry and the rise of a 'rights culture', coupled with declining deference to the judgment of professionals and the greater availability of information, have made it more likely that individuals will look to the law when seeking to obtain treatment which has been denied to them. However, it is also submitted that the evolution by governments of strategies and institutions through which priorities for healthcare expenditure can be *explicitly* established has brought this field of public policy firmly within the ambit of *public law*, which may broadly be defined as law relating to the exercise and control of governmental power and relationships between the individual and the state.[42]

Objectives, structure and scope of this book

It is this interface between public law and the rationing of healthcare resources which forms the subject-matter of this book. In keeping with its subtitle, the analysis which is offered reflects both a contextual and comparative approach, albeit one which is, in places, particularly informed by the author's British perspective.

---

[40] Y. Amin (solicitor), quoted in 'My Fight for Life', *ThisisWiltshire.co.uk*, 19 December 2005, available at www.thisiswiltshire.co.uk/display.var.663185.0.my_fight_for_life.php (accessed 8 January 2007).

[41] See above n. 36 and accompanying text.

[42] See e.g. A. Bradley and K. Ewing, *Constitutional and Administrative Law* (London: Longman, 14th edn, 2006) at 9–10.

Chapters 2 and 3 seek to provide the reader with an understanding of the *policy context* against the backdrop of which public law adjudication on healthcare rationing has evolved. As such, they may primarily be of interest to those with relatively little knowledge of recent policy developments within health systems who wish to comprehend the nature of the issues confronted by the courts in this area. The discussion will consider what it means to speak of the 'rationing' of healthcare, why rationing takes place, the extent to which it is both inevitable and of growing significance, which individuals or institutions should have responsibility for undertaking rationing choices, and the varying strategies (both implicit and explicit) which have been deployed in an attempt to manage the mismatch between demand and supply in this area.

By contrast, Chapters 4 and 5 focus primarily upon the *theoretical context*. Drawing upon recent academic analyses of health policy and, more broadly, upon theories of democracy, Chapter 4 will seek to explain why rationing (in particular, the explicit variant) has generated a problem of legitimacy for those who must make decisions on the allocation of scarce healthcare resources. It will also consider the proposals which have been put forward to address this problem. In Chapter 5, the emphasis will switch to law. Perceptions of the appropriate role for law (and, especially, for public law litigation) in this field will be examined in light of concerns as to the competence of the judiciary to adjudicate upon disputes centred upon the rationing of healthcare. It will be noted that, while objections to judicial engagement remain highly pertinent, those working within the fields of health policy and public law share a common interest in the legitimation of public power and advance similar prescriptions for alleviating any deficiencies in institutional legitimacy which might serve to impair the pursuit of collective state goals.

It is the central contention of this book that, given these significant points of confluence, those concerned with resolving the 'legitimacy problem' to which the rationing of healthcare gives rise should reassess the contribution which may be made by the courts in this area of public policy. The nature of that contribution will be examined in Chapters 6 to 8, by means of a *comparative analysis* of the public law jurisprudence on questions of the allocation of scarce healthcare resources and the financing of healthcare in three jurisdictions: England, Canada and South Africa. In view of the growing involvement of the legal process in this arena of public policy, a characteristic which is readily apparent from the Herceptin example, such an analysis appears crucial to the development of a full understanding and critique of this form of allocative decision-making. However, Chapters 6 to 8 do not set out to offer an exhaustive account of the statute and case law relating to the allocation of scarce healthcare resources in any individual jurisdiction, and readers with an interest in such analysis are advised to look elsewhere.[43]

Rather, the intention is to present a critical reading of public law adjudication which emphasises the *facilitative* capabilities of legal principles, values and processes to assist in resolution of problems of legitimation. It will be argued in Chapter 9 that the outlines of this perspective can best be identified by reference to the role played by courts in this field in South Africa which, although to some degree peculiar to that social, political and constitutional context, nonetheless might be relatively easily adapted to form a model for public law adjudication in other jurisdictions. In acknowledging the instrumental possibilities of public law litigation in spite of its inherent limitations, the book accordingly seeks to present a modest case for a more positive attitude towards the engagement of the courts with decision-making of this type, in contrast to the widely held view that law is an irritant which should, so far as possible, be excluded from intrusion upon allocative decision-making in the healthcare context.

It follows from the above that the discussion of the legal framework which is offered here is necessarily selective. In particular, this text considers only the role of *public law*, notwithstanding that issues relating to scarce healthcare resources may well arise in private law, most self-evidently in cases of medical negligence.[44] The rationale for this choice of focus lies in the emphasis, shared by health policy analysts and public lawyers and explored in Chapter 5, on the identification and resolution of problems of legitimacy which, it is claimed, afflict those who must reach decisions on priorities for healthcare expenditure. In addition, a leading commentator on medical law has claimed that 'it can be confidently predicted that in the future the importance of public law regulation of healthcare provisions is going to come to the fore',[45] citing as justification for this view the growing visibility of decision-making at a macro- and micro- provision level as a result of increased managerial involvement in the allocation of healthcare resources.

The legal analysis in Chapters 6–8 is also restricted as to its geographical scope, focusing as it does upon the position in just three jurisdictions. The choice of a limited number of jurisdictions for discussion should not be taken to imply that problems relating to the allocation of limited

---

[43] For example, for an excellent account of the English legal framework, see C. Newdick, *Who Should We Treat?* (Oxford: Oxford University Press, 2nd edn, 2004).

[44] See *ibid.*, especially Chapters 6 and 7.

[45] A. Grubb, 'Problems of Medical Law', in S. Deakin, A. Johnston and B. Markesinis, *Markesinis and Deakin's Tort Law* (Oxford: Clarendon Press, 5th edn, 2003) at 263.

healthcare resources are not present elsewhere. The mismatch between the demand for, and supply of healthcare resources which is analysed in Chapter 2 presents a political (and increasingly, a legal) challenge to governments and other decision-makers across the globe.[46] Thus, it has been argued that 'pressure on health resources is an international dilemma. It is probably the most significant driver of healthcare reform in the world'.[47]

Rather, in addition to responding to practical considerations of space, the decision to focus solely upon the position in English, Canadian and South African law reflects certain beliefs in the value of comparative analysis. These are twofold. First, it is argued that comparisons are of greatest utility when the systems under consideration *share sufficient common features* such that approaches and principles which have evolved in one may be readily understood and, where appropriate, 'transplanted' to another. Here, the greater part of the populations of all three countries receive publicly funded healthcare; public law in all three systems is dominated by common law principles and reasoning; and all three systems have witnessed (at least to some extent) the engagement of public law adjudication with allocative decision-making. On the other hand, *sufficient distinctions* between the systems should exist for comparative analysis to play an instrumental role in informing the further development of law and policy in directions which have not as yet been fully explored, given that this book seeks to amount to more than a simple exercise in identification of the intersection of existing legal norms. In this regard, a particular theme which will emerge in the analysis contained in Chapters 6 to 8 is the implication of adjudication upon questions of healthcare rationing as matters of human rights, as distinct from judicial review of the legality of administrative decisions and actions. This aspect of the discussion may therefore be regarded as a contribution to the literature on the relationship between law, human rights and healthcare.[48]

---

[46] For discussion, see Coulter and Ham (eds.), *The Global Challenge of Health Care Rationing*; C. Ham and G. Robert (eds.), *Reasonable Rationing* (Buckingham: Open University Press, 2003).

[47] W. Edgar, 'Rationing in Health Care – a New Zealand Perspective on an International Dilemma' (2001) 81 *Schweizerische Ärztezeitung*, 190 at 193.

[48] See e.g. I. Kennedy and A. Grubb, *Medical Law* (London: Butterworths, 3rd edn., 2000) at 6: 'In our view . . . medical law is a subset of human rights law', although note that these authors understand the latter to extend more widely than protection of rights through legal instruments with constitutional significance, such as the Human Rights Act 1998 in the UK. For further discussion of the rights dimension, see e.g. J. Mann, S. Gruskin, M. Grodin *et al.* (eds.), *Health and Human Rights: a Reader* (New York: Routledge, 1999).

This book's focus upon mechanisms of public law, coupled with the selective geographical coverage which has been adopted, means that the distinctive legal and policy problems which arise from the rationing of healthcare in market-based systems and those in the developing world will not be comprehensively addressed here. In health systems in which funding is predominantly of a private nature, such as the United States, decisions to limit the availability of care may be less systematic and visible to the population as a whole than in systems which are publicly funded. It has been argued that 'the American way of rationing is to decentralize (in political terms, hide) the choices: the result is rationing through an accumulation of narrow public policies, private decisions and luck'.[49] As a consequence of this lower level of public awareness, the policy debate in such systems may differ somewhat from those in which rationing is more explicit, as noted in Chapter 4, and processes of *private law* will assume greater significance in regulating rationing decisions. As for health systems in developing nations, it has been claimed that 'priority-setting in the developed countries often takes on problems and methods that are somewhat removed from those usually addressed by developing countries'.[50] These include deficiencies in the availability of clinical and health economics data upon which decisions on the allocation of resources may be based,[51] the particular need to allocate priority for certain treatments (such as antiretroviral drugs for HIV/AIDS) in order to address specific public health problems from which their populations may suffer, and difficulties caused by political instability and weak governmental institutions which tend to mean that rationing takes place in an ad hoc manner and that resources earmarked for healthcare are frequently diverted into other sectors.[52]

Instead, the book's primary concern is with the intersection between public law and the rationing of resources in *publicly funded healthcare within the developed world*. That said, the thesis which is advanced should provide a workable starting-point for those who wish to extend the discussion to other systems. In particular, much of the theorising upon health policy which provides the context for analysis of the appropriate role for public law (discussed primarily in Chapter 4) originates in the United States, and to

---

[49] J. Morone, 'The Bias of American Politics – Rationing Health Care in a Weak State' (1992) 140 *University of Pennsylvania Law Review*, 1923 at 1933.

[50] J. Bryant, 'Health Priority Dilemmas in Developing Countries', in Coulter and Ham (eds.), *The Global Challenge of Health Care Rationing* at 64.

[51] See e.g. G. Mooney and V. Wiseman, 'Burden of Disease and Priority-Setting' (2000) 9 *Health Economics*, 369 at 371.

[52] K. Khan, 'Public Health Priorities and the Social Determinants of Ill Health', in Coulter and Ham (eds.), *The Global Challenge of Health Care Rationing* at 80.

this extent the book's argument that the function of law in this context merits fresh evaluation is as applicable to that system as to the others surveyed, albeit that analysts of the system will be obliged to consider the role of private, as well as public, law. As regards the problems of rationing which arise within health systems in developing nations, the inclusion of South Africa as one of the jurisdictions examined allows for some consideration both of the distinctive difficulties (such as ensuring equitable access to potentially life-saving treatments for public health problems such as HIV/ AIDS) and opportunities (in particular, the implications of constitutional protection of rights of a socio-economic nature, which are frequently given primacy in such jurisdictions) which exist within such systems, even though South Africa itself is not generally classified as a 'developing' nation.[53]

Consequently, while the argument presented in this book will undoubtedly have greatest resonance within the publicly funded healthcare sector (and particularly within the three jurisdictions surveyed), it is intended that it will serve as a stimulus to the critical rethinking of the appropriate role for public law in *all* systems in which issues of the allocation of scarce healthcare resources present a legal and political challenge. To this end, the conclusions which are drawn from the comparative analysis presented in this book can be regarded as representing a contribution, however small, to a process of 'policy learning' (also known variously as 'policy transfer', 'emulation' and 'lesson drawing'). This refers to 'a process in which knowledge about policies, administrative arrangements, institutions *etc.*, in one time and/or place is used in the development of policies, administrative arrangements and institutions in another time and/or place'.[54] It is submitted that such an undertaking is likely to prove of particular value in this field, as it has been observed that 'public policy-making [in healthcare] appears to be an extraordinarily imitative process'.[55]

---

[53] South Africa is classified as an 'upper middle income' nation by the World Bank, based upon its Gross National Income per capita. See http://web.worldbank.org/WBSITE/ EXTERNAL/DATASTATISTICS/0,,contentMDK:20420458~menuPK:64133156~ pagePK:64133150~piPK:64133175~theSitePK:239419,00.html (accessed 8 January 2007).

[54] D. Dolowitz and D. Marsh, 'Who Learns What from Whom: a Review of the Policy Transfer Literature' (1996) 44 *Political Studies*, 343 at 344.

[55] H. Leichter, *A Comparative Approach to Policy Analysis: Healthcare Policy in Four Nations* (Cambridge: Cambridge University Press, 1979) at 272. For application of this concept in the context of healthcare rationing, see K. Jacobs and P. Barnett, 'Policy Transfer and Policy Learning: a Study of the 1991 New Zealand Health Services Taskforce' (2000) 13 *Governance*, 185, especially at 203–5; and, more generally, C. Ham, 'Priority-setting in Health Care: Learning from International Experience' (1997) 42 *Health Policy*, 49; C. Ham and A. Coulter, 'Explicit and Implicit Rationing: Taking Responsibility and Avoiding Blame for Health Care Choices' (2001) 6 *Journal of Health Services Research and Policy*, 163.

2   Why 'Ration' Healthcare Resources?

This chapter seeks to explain what is meant by the 'rationing' of health-care resources, and to analyse why such a strategy might prove necessary within a health system. It will be seen that these issues are interconnected, with the consequence that the task of definition and explication is not as straightforward as might at first appear to be the case. For example, the extent to which rationing is regarded as an inevitable feature of a health system will turn upon the precise meaning which is attached to that term. It has been noted that this area of public policy is characterised by 'confusing linguistic threads',[1] and, to this end, it will be necessary to explore the political implications of the discourse of 'rationing' and the more neutral expression which is frequently (but arguably mistakenly) used as its synonym, 'priority-setting'. The chapter will also seek to analyse the key determinants of healthcare expenditure in order to ascertain whether pressures for cost-containment are growing, rendering rationing an increasingly fundamental characteristic of modern health systems.

The meaning of 'rationing'

In common parlance, 'rationing' refers to allocation in fixed quantities or the provision of a fixed allowance, especially of food.[2] As Klein, Day and Redmayne note, the word is a cognate of 'rationality', and thereby connotes a distribution based upon the exercise of reason, which is carried out fairly and even-handedly.[3] This is the understanding of the term which is emphasised within economics, the fundamental concern of which might be described as 'the study of the allocation of scarce resources among competing ends'.[4] From this perspective, it may be regarded

[1] P. Ubel, *Pricing Life: Why It's Time for Health Care Rationing* (Cambridge, Mass: MIT Press, 2000) at 16.
[2] *Oxford English Dictionary* (Oxford: Oxford University Press, 2nd edn, 1989).
[3] R. Klein, P. Day and S. Redmayne, *Managing Scarcity* (Buckingham: Open University Press, 1996) at 7.
[4] A. Maynard, 'Rationing Health Care: an Exploration' (1999) 49 *Health Policy*, 5 at 5.

as 'rational' for those who control limited resources to establish priorities for expenditure,[5] thus enabling the achievement of the utilitarian objective of the maximisation of community welfare. In view of the fact of scarcity, undertaking this task will necessarily carry the consequence that some individuals will only secure access to the resource in question after others have already done so, and may not obtain access at all if the resource has already been exhausted.

Although this appears superficially straightforward, there is nonetheless 'tremendous variation in what people mean when they talk about healthcare rationing'.[6] In this regard, a useful exercise in typology has been developed by Ubel and Goold, who have divided discussions of rationing in the healthcare context into three categories.[7] First, there are definitions which focus upon the *explicitness* (or otherwise) of the decision to allocate limited resources. For example, Aaron and Schwartz refer to 'the deliberate and systematic denial of certain types of services, even when they are known to be beneficial, because they are deemed too expensive'.[8] Such definitions focus upon administrative decisions to limit access to resources, connecting to the popular imagery of government-imposed maximum consumption levels in periods of national crisis.[9] Other accounts, however, regard more *implicit* modes of allocation, such as that undertaken by clinicians exercising expert medical judgment, as also constituting rationing.[10]

An important issue which arises from this first definitional categorisation is whether a restriction on access to health treatment and services which is based upon the ability of the patient to pay can be said to amount to 'rationing'. Not surprisingly, this question is debated most comprehensively in the American literature and, in view of this book's focus upon publicly funded healthcare, it is merely of tangential relevance here. Nonetheless, it may be noted that there is disagreement on this matter. For example, Havighurst seeks to distinguish between the provision of medical care and the means by which this is financed, arguing that 'rules restricting the availability of healthcare financing . . . ration only healthcare

---

[5] See M. Loughlin, 'Rationing, Barbarity and the Economist's Perspective' (1996) 4 *Health Care Analysis*, 146 at 148.

[6] P. Ubel and S. Goold, '"Rationing" Health Care: Not All Definitions Are Created Equal' (1998) 158 *Archives of Internal Medicine*, 209 at 214.

[7] *Ibid.* at 210.

[8] H. Aaron and W. Schwartz, 'Rationing Health Care: the Choice Before Us' (1990) 247 *Science*, 418 at 418.

[9] See L. Locock, 'The Changing Nature of Rationing in the National Health Service' (2000) 78 *Public Administration*, 90 at 92.

[10] See M. Hall, 'The Problems with Rule-Based Rationing' (1994) 19 *Journal of Medicine and Philosophy*, 315.

financing, not medical care itself. Thus, a service that is deemed to fall outside a patient's coverage is not necessarily denied to the patient. It may still be provided at the patient's personal expense or at the expense of the provider'.[11] Others, while pointing to the value of the distinction drawn within economics between 'price rationing' and 'non-price rationing',[12] maintain that allocation of healthcare through the mechanisms of the free market amounts to a form of rationing, given that the necessity for individuals to be able to access certain services invests them with a significance (or, to use a philosophical principle which is explored in greater depth in Chapter 4, a 'special moral importance') which does not attach to the majority of goods distributed through the marketplace. Thus, Ubel and Goold claim that 'some healthcare services are so important that limiting their distribution by ability to pay can result in a type of deprivation and hardship commonly associated with rationing'.[13] The significance of these conflicting views lies in the fact that acceptance of the first view – and the consequent reluctance to admit that rationing is taking place at all except in cases of explicit denial of treatment (which, in the case of the insured population in the United States, have been relatively few)[14] – tends to close off debate upon the criteria which should underpin the allocation of healthcare resources within market-based systems, a phenomenon which was remarked upon in Chapter 1.[15]

Ubel and Goold also classify definitions of healthcare rationing into those which turn upon the absolute scarcity of a resource, and those which do not. Accepting the former view would entail categorising only those decisions which relate to the distribution of resources the amount of which is fixed (at least in the short term) – such as organ transplantations – as 'rationing' choices, while those which relate to the apportionment of relatively scarce resources, such as the number of intensive care beds or paediatric specialists, may be better regarded as 'allocation' decisions.[16] As

[11] C. Havighurst, 'Prospective Self-denial – Can Consumers Contract Today to Accept Health Care Rationing Tomorrow?' (1992) 140 *University of Pennsylvania Law Review*; 1755 at 1759.

[12] See especially U. Reinhardt, 'Rationing Health Care: What It Is, What It Is Not and Why We Cannot Avoid It' in S. Altman and U. Reinhardt (eds.), *Strategic Choices for a Changing Health Care System* (Chicago: Health Administration Press, 1996).

[13] Ubel and Goold, '"Rationing" Health Care: Not All Definitions Are Created Equal' at 211.

[14] Uwe Reinhardt has estimated that access to 'about one per cent' of procedures is denied by managed care organisations in the United States, with the consequence that 'for most Americans we do not really ration yet at all': 'Healthcare Crisis: Who's at Risk?', available at www.pbs.org/healthcarecrisis/Exprts_intrvw/u_reinhardt.htm (accessed 8 January 2007).

[15] See above, Chapter 1, n. 49 and accompanying text.

[16] See e.g. R. Evans, 'Health Care Technology and the Inevitability of Resource Allocation and Rationing Decisions' (1983) 249 *Journal of the American Medical Association*, 2208.

the authors note, this distinction is problematic, since 'allocation' decisions (how much of a particular resource is provided within a system) will necessarily impact upon 'rationing' decisions (how that resource is distributed between those who demand access to it). Put simply, if the number of intensive care beds is limited, then there will be insufficient to meet the needs of all of those who might require access. Both of these types of decision may be labelled as 'tragic' in the terminology famously coined by Calabresi and Bobbit[17] and it is thus somewhat misleading to attempt to separate them. That said, the distinction has some utility in that it draws attention to the different levels of decision-making at which rationing may take place, an issue which is pertinent to the discussion of the meaning of the alternative discourse of 'priority-setting' which is offered below.

Thirdly, definitions of rationing may turn upon the degree of necessity of access to the treatment or service in question. For Hadorn and Brook, rationing amounts to 'the withholding of necessary services' and refers to 'societal toleration of inequitable access (for example based on ability to pay) to services acknowledged to be necessary by reference to necessary care guidelines',[18] while Fleck states that 'rationing means that government will deny one of its citizens life-sustaining medical care on the basis of an arbitrary budgetary limit'.[19] Other understandings of the term treat the medical service as a less imperative requirement for the individual concerned and thus embrace many more decisions which must be taken within a given health system. Thus, Brown argues that rationing means 'the deliberate, systematic withholding of beneficial goods or services from some elements of the population on the grounds that society cannot afford to extend them',[20] and Dougherty defines it as 'the denial of services that are potentially beneficial to some people because of limitations on the resources available for healthcare'.[21] However, terms such as 'necessary' and 'beneficial' are far from unambiguous. As Ubel and Goold note, both denote relative, rather than absolute, states of affairs and will therefore necessitate the making of value-laden judgments by some individual or organisation.[22]

---

[17] See further below Chapter 4.

[18] D. Hadorn and C. Brook, 'The Health Care Resources Allocation Debate: Defining Our Terms' (1991) 266 *Journal of the American Medical Association*, 3328 at 3331.

[19] L. Fleck, 'Just Health Care Rationing – a Democratic Decision-Making Approach' (1992) 140 *University of Pennsylvania Law Review*, 1597 at 1605.

[20] L. Brown, 'The National Politics of Oregon's Rationing Plan' (1991) 10 *Health Affairs*, 28 at 30.

[21] C. Dougherty, 'Setting Health Care Priorities: Oregon's Next Steps' (1991) 21 *Hastings Center Report*, Supplement: 1 at 3.

[22] See Ubel and Goold, '"Rationing" Health Care: Not All Definitions Are Created Equal' at 213.

It will be noted that these definitions are drawn from the American literature, perhaps reflecting the relative lack of familiarity of a readership in a market-based health system with the concept, for the reasons which have been previously identified. Definitions of 'rationing' within systems which are primarily publicly funded are, in general, somewhat more broad than those cited above, suggesting a greater willingness to engage with the issue as a problem of public policy. Thus, Maynard states that 'rationing takes place when an individual is deprived of care which is of benefit (in terms of improving health status, or the length and quality of life) and which is desired by the patient';[23] Locock observes that 'it is arguable that *all forms* of resource allocation, whether through the market or not, constitute rationing',[24] thus making clear that modes of allocation which are explicit and implicit and those which are and are not based upon ability to pay are equally encompassed; and, in similar vein, Klein merely equates rationing with the allocation of scarce resources.[25] These definitions are much more closely akin to the meaning of the term as a matter of economics,[26] an understanding which is well captured by Mechanic's claim that rationing is 'no more than a means of apportioning, through some method of allowance, some limited good or service'.[27] Nonetheless, the restriction proposed by Maynard – that it is only meaningful to speak of the 'rationing' of healthcare in instances where the treatment in question is beneficial and desired by the patient – should be regarded as an indispensable component of any definition for, as Klein, Day and Redmayne observe, 'if the NHS decides not to provide snake oil on prescription, there would be no talk about rationing'.[28]

It is submitted that these broader definitions of rationing, and particularly that advanced by Maynard, are to be preferred to those which seek to limit the term by reference to particular characteristics of the decision,

---

[23] See Maynard, 'Rationing Health Care: an Exploration' at 6.
[24] See Locock, 'The Changing Nature of Rationing' at 92. Emphasis in original.
[25] See R. Klein, 'Priorities and Rationing: Pragmatism or Principles?' (1995) 311 *British Medical Journal*, 761 at 761.
[26] See especially Reinhardt, 'Rationing Health Care: What It Is, What It Is Not' at 68.
[27] D. Mechanic, 'Cost Containment and the Quality of Medical Care: Rationing Strategies In an Area of Constrained Resources' (1985) 63 *Millbank Quarterly*, 453 at 457.
[28] R. Klein, P. Day and S. Redmayne, 'Rationing in the NHS: the Dance of the Seven Veils – in Reverse' (1995) 51 *British Medical Bulletin* 769 at 770. Restriction of the definition of the term to treatments and services which are of benefit to the patient also captures the distinction between 'need' and 'demand', for which see further below. However, as observed above, n. 22 and accompanying text, ascertainment of 'benefit' to the patient will necessitate the making of value judgments, raising the issue of who should make rationing decisions, which is explored in Chapter 3.

of the resource, or of the degree of the patient's need for the service. This approach has been adopted in part because the book's focus upon publicly funded healthcare necessarily inclines towards acceptance of those understandings which have greatest currency in such a context. However, there is a further, more apposite reason for preferring a broad meaning of the term. The argument posited in Chapter 4 of this book, drawing upon the work of key health policy theorists, is that a process of public deliberation on the need for the rationing of healthcare and the criteria which should underpin allocative decisions can serve to alleviate the problems of legitimacy which arise when limitations are placed on access to healthcare resources. A broader understanding of the nature of rationing connects to such a process, providing 'a more useful starting point for debates about healthcare policy and healthcare priority-setting' than the more restricted meanings.[29] This is because such an understanding emphasises the ubiquity of such choices within health systems, however funded, with the consequence that 'rationing is not defined as *de facto* inappropriate',[30] but rather as an inevitable concomitant of scarcity (an issue which is explored further below). It therefore becomes possible – indeed, arguably imperative – to engage in an open and public debate upon the need to make allocative choices in healthcare, rather than sidestepping the issue by means of narrow definitions which can easily lead to the conclusion that this policy problem either does not exist, or that it can be easily resolved.

'Rationing' and 'priority-setting' – the importance of language

The terms 'rationing' and 'priority-setting' are frequently treated as synonymous. For example, Ham and Coulter explain that they use the expressions 'interchangeably',[31] while Mullen simply refers indiscriminately to 'rationing or priority-setting'.[32] For his part, Maynard, as befits the broad definition of the word which he adopts – influenced by

---

[29] Ubel and Goold, '"Rationing" Health Care: Not All Definitions Are Created Equal' at 213.

[30] *Ibid.* at 214.

[31] C. Ham and A. Coulter, 'Explicit and Implicit Rationing: Taking Responsibility and Avoiding Blame for Health Care Choices' (2001) 6 *Journal of Health Services Research and Policy*, 163 at 163. See also A. Coulter and C. Ham (eds.), *The Global Challenge of Health Care Rationing* (Buckingham: Open University Press, 2000) at 2; S. McIver and C. Ham, 'Five Cases, Four Actors and a Moral: Lessons from Studies of Contested Treatment Decisions' (2000) 3 *Health Expectations*, 114.

[32] P. Mullen, 'Is It Necessary to Ration Health Care?' (1998) 18 *Public Money and Management*, 52 at 52.

understandings drawn from the economics literature – equates 'rationing' with 'resource allocation'.[33]

Others, however, seek to develop a more nuanced understanding of the terminology. Klein, Day and Redmayne utilise the two terms to distinguish between the various levels at which resource allocation decisions take place. They define the 'macro' level, at which national decisions are taken as to the budgets which are to be allotted to various departments of government and where ministers establish priorities for the distribution of the resources allocated, and the 'meso' level, where agencies of central government (such as PCTs) determine which services and treatments should be given precedence, as constituting 'priority-setting'. They reserve the word 'rationing' for the 'micro' level, 'where those responsible for providing services or making payments decide on who is to get what within the budgetary limits which have been set'.[34] The authors note, however, that these levels of decision-making are interconnected, especially in so far as decisions to limit or 'de-prioritise' expenditure at the first two levels will determine what may be provided at the point of service delivery, thereby constraining – but not altogether eradicating – the discretion to provide an individual patient with a particular treatment or service.[35] Rationing decisions may therefore be viewed as points on a continuum rather than discrete choices, isolated from the broader financial context.

A further, and valuable, explanation of the distinction between 'rationing' and 'priority-setting' is offered by Tragakes and Vienonen in work carried out for the World Health Organization.[36] Defining rationing as 'a way of distributing scarce goods when there is no market to perform the task', the authors point out that this necessarily achieves the objective of allocating scarce healthcare resources among competing uses. Priority-setting, which they argue 'refers to a process whereby governments or public authorities or clinicians make decisions about the relative ranking (priorities) to be attached to different programmes, services or types of patients', also fulfils the same function, given that 'the assignment of relative priorities to different activities necessarily results in a

---

[33] Maynard, 'Rationing Health Care: an Exploration' at 6.

[34] Klein, Day and Redmayne, *Managing Scarcity* at 7–10.

[35] It should be noted that the taxonomy adopted by Klein, Day and Redmayne is subject to slight variations in other accounts of healthcare rationing. For example, Hunter identifies *four* levels of decision-making: decisions about allocation to broad sectors or client groups; decisions about allocation to specific interventions and treatments; decisions about how to prioritise access to treatment between different patients; and decisions about how much to invest in individual patients once access has been granted: D. Hunter, *Desperately Seeking Solutions* (London: Longman, 1997) at 25.

[36] E. Tragakes and M. Vienonen, *Key Issues in Rationing and Priority-setting for Health Care Services* (Copenhagen: WHO, 1998) at 2–3.

corresponding allocation of resources among the competing activities'. However, this may not be the only way to accomplish the task of allocating scarce resources between competing goods: thus, rationing might also entail strategies such as deflection or deterrence (which are discussed below), neither of which involve the creation of 'ranking lists' of priorities for expenditure. The authors thus maintain that there is a 'clear conceptual distinction' between the terms, but concede that they 'often become muddled because of the ambiguous ways in which priority-setting is defined'. To this end, it would appear that they would prefer to follow Klein, Day and Redmayne in assigning the latter term to those decisions which involve a process of ordering of preferences for expenditure, rather than decisions on the provision and withholding of treatments to individual patients taken at the 'micro' level.

While teasing out the precise meanings of 'rationing' and 'priority-setting' is therefore not a simple task, it would appear to amount to more than a mere exercise in 'semantic pedantry'.[37] As Tragakes and Vienonen note, notwithstanding the similarities in the function performed by the two processes, they carry 'very different emotive connotations', which they view as being negative and positive respectively.[38] Similarly, Klein, Day and Redmayne also view 'rationing' as 'an emotion-laden word',[39] while Ubel and Goold remark that 'healthcare rationing is a morally charged term, suggesting difficult decisions with potentially tragic consequences'.[40] By contrast, 'priority-setting' is seen as a 'less stark notion'[41] and 'a more neutral term'.[42]

The differing overtones of the two terms are relatively easily outlined. 'Rationing' connects to a popular imagery of national emergency, being especially associated in the UK with wartime privation, and thus its usage in the healthcare context implies that a health system is in a state of unprecedented crisis. The word connotes deprivation and forced choice: hence, 'public attitudes towards rationing are likely to be coloured by its association with unwelcome cuts in resources and the fact that it conjures up images of people being denied life-saving treatments'.[43] For its part, 'priority-setting' may be viewed as an active, rational exercise in making

[37] Klein, Day and Redmayne, *Managing Scarcity* at 7.
[38] Tragakes and Vienonen, *Key Issues in Rationing* at 3.
[39] Klein, Day and Redmayne, *Managing Scarcity* at 7.
[40] Ubel and Goold, '"Rationing" Health Care: Not All Definitions Are Created Equal' at 210.
[41] R. Maxwell, 'Why Rationing is on the Agenda' (1995) 51 *British Medical Bulletin*, 761 at 761.
[42] Klein, Day and Redmayne, *Managing Scarcity* at 2.
[43] C. Bryson and B. New, 'Health Care Rationing: a Cut Too Far?', in R. Jowell, J. Curtice, A. Park *et al.*, *British Social Attitudes: the Seventeenth Report* (London: Sage, 2000) at 21.

informed choices between alternatives with the goal of using societal resources effectively and thereby promoting community welfare. Far from being a mark of crisis, it implies that the decision-maker has control of the situation.[44] Thus, Loughlin argues that the term is more attractive than 'rationing' because:

talking in this way enables us to focus on that which is achieved, rather than dwelling on failures. Our intellectual starting point becomes not a highly developed complex service already providing many forms of care, but rather we begin by thinking of a blank sheet, a scenario in which nothing is provided...Then, instead of deciding which services have to be cut, we think about which to provide. Against this benchmark, any provision at all becomes an achievement. The implicit comparison with a single, rational creature deciding which goals to set itself, helps us to forget that the 'deprioritised' services are not simply goals which we (the 'rational community') have – temporarily or permanently – decided prudently to give up, but that they represent depriving some individuals of the means of a bearable existence, and sometimes of life itself.[45]

Reading the two terms as modes of discourse in this manner makes apparent that these are not, first and foremost, terms of art which signify differing types and levels of decision-making on the allocation of scarce healthcare resources. Rather, the choice of one over the other amounts to a political strategy. Put simply, in adopting the language of 'priority-setting', politicians and others who are responsible for making resource allocation decisions seek to avoid the negative connotations attached to the 'rationing' of healthcare resources and the consequent electoral unpopularity which will ensue from being seen to deny treatment to individuals. This may be seen as a component of broader strategies of 'blame avoidance' and 'blame diffusion' which have particularly characterised the National Health Service in the UK, but which are highly likely to be present in all health systems operating under conditions of scarcity.[46] Conversely, those who wish to engage in critique of government policy on healthcare financing tend to employ the language of 'rationing' precisely because of its 'distasteful' implications.[47]

---

[44] See Tragakes and Vienonen, *Key Issues in Rationing* at 3.

[45] Loughlin, 'Rationing, Barbarity and the Economist's Perspective, at 148.

[46] For discussion of these strategies in an international context, see C. Ham and A. Coulter, 'Conclusion – Where Are We Now?', in Coulter and Ham (eds.), *The Global Challenge of Health Care Rationing* at 233. In respect of the UK, see R. Klein, *The New Politics of the NHS* (London: Prentice Hall, 4th edn, 2001) at 66–7.

[47] See Bryson and New, 'Health Care Rationing: a Cut Too Far?' at 21: 'The word "rationing" is particularly avoided [by senior politicians while in government], with preference being for terms such as "priority-setting" or "resource allocation". However, such distaste for the word is not shared by commentators, journalists and opposition politicians.'

Thus, commentators on the NHS have observed that 'the Secretary of State continues to reject the term rationing',[48] and warn that 'denial [of the fact of rationing] is not an option. If ... the Secretary of State for Health continues to ban the word from the ministerial vocabulary it will only make him look foolish and undermine his credibility'.[49] In this regard, it is noteworthy that although an apparent partial reversal of this position occurred in 1999, when minister Alan Milburn stated that he was 'going to break with convention as a Secretary of State for Health and talk about the issue of rationing', he then proceeded to deny that 'each patient only gets a fixed "ration" of healthcare, regardless of their personal need and circumstances in a way somehow reminiscent of Second World War limits on rashers of bacon, eggs and butter' (a statement with which, it is submitted, any commentator on healthcare rationing would concur), and then to effect a demotion of the term while redefining the issue in the more acceptable terminology of priority-setting:

Of course no health system in the world has ever provided all the healthcare it might theoretically be possible to provide but to call that rationing is in practice meaningless. Because even if the whole of UK GDP was spent on healthcare, and the whole of the British economy was turned into one giant hospital, some people would still claim there would be 'rationing' on this definition. What is true, is that the NHS, just like every other healthcare system in the world – public or private – has to set priorities and make choices.[50]

Speaking in debate in the House of Commons, the Secretary of State was not even prepared to take this small step. Thus, in answer to an Opposition motion which called for the acknowledgement of the existence of rationing within the NHS, Milburn stated that:

the National Health Service has always faced hard choices. That is the reality of life in the NHS. It is the reality for clinicians on the ground, and it is the reality for those of us who are charged with running the service. There has always been priority-setting in the National Health Service, and there always will be. The issue is how priorities are set. We believe that priorities should be set on the grounds of effectiveness and what works ... It is not about rationing: it is about rational decisions.[51]

---

[48] Maxwell, 'Why Rationing is on the Agenda' at 761.

[49] R. Klein, 'Puzzling Out Priorities' (1998) 317 *British Medical Journal*, 959 at 959.

[50] A. Milburn, 'Modern Services, Modern Choices: Tackling the Lottery of Health Care', speech to NICE Conference, 8 December 1999, available at www.nice.org.uk/oldsite/conf/sos_speech.htm (accessed 8 January 2007). For similar language, see *The NHS Plan* (London: HMSO, 2000 (Cm. 4818-I)) at para. 3.31.

[51] *House of Commons Debates*, vol. 336, cols. 878–9 (26 October 1999).

Moreover, other officials involved in resource allocation in healthcare have been similarly opaque. Thus, the Chairman of NICE has argued that 'the notion that the NHS has ever 'rationed' healthcare is a gross misuse of the English language',[52] and that 'the NHS has never been about rationing, that's what insurance services do. What a national health service has to do is look at priorities'.[53]

These discursive strategies are of considerable significance for the thesis pursued in this book. The consequence of the political emphasis on 'priority-setting' over 'rationing' is that the implications of the allocative decisions which are being taken – that is, that these are potentially 'tragic choices' – are obfuscated, at least in part. This inhibits the development of a broad public debate upon the need for allocative choices in healthcare and, in particular, upon the ethical value judgements which must underpin these. Moreover, denial of the true nature of the decisions being taken may, contrary to political intention, in some cases serve to *exacerbate* public dissatisfaction with the provision of healthcare services. This may lead to challenges to the moral authority of the body which is responsible for denying or delaying access to treatment. Interestingly, such an outcome was foreseen by Enoch Powell, Minister of Health in the UK in the early 1960s, whose recognition of the existence of rationing within the NHS was arguably unprecedented given both his political function and the absence of discussion on the matter at that period.[54] Powell wrote of 'the political convention that the existence of any rationing at all must be strenuously denied', arguing that:

... the public are encouraged to believe that rationing in medical care was banished by the National Health Service, and that the very idea of rationing being applied to medical care is immoral and repugnant. Consequently, when they, and the medical profession too, come face to face in practice with the various forms of rationing to which the National Health Service must resort, the usual result is bewilderment, frustration and irritation.[55]

The contention advanced in Chapter 4 is that it is crucial to engage in a public debate upon the rationing of healthcare in order to secure legitimacy for allocative choices, especially in so far as the political, social and moral questions raised by resource allocation will never prove susceptible to simple, 'rational' solutions through some form of technocratic

---

[52] M. Rawlins, 'In Pursuit of Quality: the National Institute for Clinical Excellence' (1999) 353 *Lancet* 1079 at 1082.
[53] M. Rawlins, 'Building a Reputation', *Primary Care: NHS Magazine* (September 2004).
[54] See Klein, Day and Redmayne, *Managing Scarcity* at 40.
[55] E. Powell, *A New Look at Medicine and Politics* (London: Pitman Medical, 1966) at 38. For similar arguments see below Chapter 3.

decision-making process. However, the discourse of 'priority-setting', with its rationalist connotations, tends to deflect attention away from such a strategy, encouraging the view that decisions on access to scarce resources in healthcare can somehow be resolved through the exercise of expert judgment and the application of 'technical' criteria. It is for this reason that 'rationing' is to be preferred to 'priority-setting', and, wherever possible, it will be employed throughout this book. Support for this position can be derived from the work of Ubel and Goold, who argue for the wider use of the former term, understood in a broad sense as the denial of beneficial healthcare services, because:

Difficult judgments about whether to offer these benefits will no longer be made to look like scientific judgments about whether the benefits are truly necessary. Instead, people will recognise the need to make value judgments about whether specific beneficial services can be offered to everyone...we can use the word's negative connotations to draw attention to difficult moral decisions about which benefits are worth pursuing. By focusing attention on our inability to offer beneficial services to all who need them, we can highlight morally questionable healthcare policies that create inequitable access to beneficial healthcare.[56]

Given the evident difficulty of generating the necessary public debate through conventional political channels, reflected in the resolute adherence of senior government politicians to rhetoric which both conceals the character of the decisions being taken and which implicitly defines them as questions upon which it is most appropriate for expert judgment to be brought to bear, it may prove necessary to explore other avenues through which such a debate can be stimulated. The argument advanced subsequently in this book is that the courts may have a useful role to play in this regard.

Why is the rationing of healthcare resources necessary and is it inevitable?

The broader the definition of 'rationing' which is employed, the more obvious is the explanation as to why it takes place in the healthcare context, especially in the publicly funded sector. From an economic perspective, non-price rationing 'refers to distribution under conditions where a supply that is limited by considerations of cost confronts a demand that is not constrained by considerations of price'.[57] An

---

[56] Ubel and Goold, '"Rationing" Health Care: Not All Definitions Are Created Equal' at 213.

[57] Tragakes and Vienonen, *Key Issues in Rationing* at 2; see also Klein, Day and Redmayne, *Managing Scarcity* at 9.

alternative way of expressing the equation is to observe that resources for the delivery of healthcare (supply) are finite – both the funds used to finance it and the physical resources needed (hospitals, medical staff, equipment etc.) are limited – but that the demand for access to care is, at the least, highly elastic and potentially infinite. Some mechanism is therefore necessary to bring demand into line with supply. In market-based systems, equalisation is achieved through monetary criteria: the inability of certain individuals to pay for treatment has a dampening effect on the demand for services. In publicly funded systems, the same function is performed by a number of strategies which will be considered in the next chapter, but the criterion of medical 'need' is especially significant in reducing excess demand by determining who accesses care. On the basis of the broad definition adopted earlier in this chapter, both of these situations would amount to the 'rationing' of healthcare.

It is important to recognise that the 'demand' for healthcare is not synonymous with the criterion of 'need'. The relationship between the concepts may be expressed as follows:

The 'need' for medical care must be distinguished from the 'demand' for care and from the use of services or 'utilisation'. A need for medical care exists when an individual has an illness or disability for which there is an effective and acceptable treatment or cure. It can be defined either in terms of the type of illness or disability causing the need, or of the treatment or facilities for treatment required to meet it. A demand for care exists when an individual considers that he has a need and wishes to receive care. Utilisation occurs when an individual actually receives care. Need is not necessarily expressed as demand, and demand is not necessarily followed by utilisation, while, on the other hand, there can be demand and utilisation without real underlying need for the particular service used.[58]

A number of implications, of differing degrees of controversy, may be drawn from this analysis. It appears relatively straightforward to argue that an individual who believes him/herself to be ill and who wishes to receive medical care will not necessarily satisfy the 'need' requirement, and will therefore not access care if (s)he is not, in fact, suffering from an illness or disability at all. On the other hand, it may be regarded as much more contentious to argue that the definition of 'need' which is adopted here raises 'the possibility that someone may even be seriously ill without there being a reasonable prospect . . . of medical care effectively changing their characteristics for the better. In such cases, whatever else they "need", they do not "need" the sort of health or medical services that

---

[58] G. Matthew, 'Measuring Need and Evaluating Services' in G. McLachan (ed.), *Portfolio for Health* (Oxford: Oxford University Press, 1971) at 27.

might be available.'[59] This brings into question the issue of the 'effectiveness' of medical care or treatment, which will be addressed below.

'Need' acts as a principle of distributive justice, especially at the 'micro' level of allocation to individual patients, in that it functions as a criterion for selection between differing allocations of resources on grounds of equity. Thus, 'justice requires that people with equal needs should receive equal treatment, with greater need trumping lesser need'.[60] However, this apparently simple statement masks the fact that there are a number of differing ways in which 'need' may be defined, which have been analysed by Cookson and Dolan.[61] First, 'need' may be assessed in terms of ill health, with principles (derived from the 'rule of rescue') which provide that immediate threats to life should take priority over the enhancement of life, and/or that those in immediate pain and suffering should take precedence over those who are not yet in this position.[62] Secondly, 'need' may be defined in relation to 'benefit' – thus connecting with the definition of 'rationing' put forward by Maynard[63] – so that resources are allocated in relation to the individual's capacity to gain from the healthcare which is provided. Those who would gain most from the provision of care will be treated in preference to those whose capacity for benefit is less, and an absence of gain (for example because the treatment in question is wholly ineffective) would give rise to no access to healthcare resources at all.

Whichever meaning of 'need' is selected, it is apparent that, if the principle is to function as a criterion through which the rationing of resources within a health system can be achieved, some assessment of need must take place and that, if a distinction is to be drawn between this concept and 'demand', such assessment cannot be left to the individual

---

[59] A. Culyer, 'Need: the Idea Won't Do – but we still need it' (1995) 40 *Social Science and Medicine*, 727 at 727. Note that Williams acknowledges that the definition of 'effectiveness' may need to be broadened beyond a medical understanding, in that 'a treatment, known to be ineffective in relation to the patient's physiological condition, may still be given as a demonstration (to him or his loved ones) that someone cares, and this may give satisfaction to them and, indeed, to other members of the community unknown to the patient who sympathise with the plight of the sick generally, so that the treatment may be quite 'effective' in this broader sense': A. Williams, 'Need as a Demand Concept (with Special Reference to Health)' in A. Culyer and A. Maynard (eds.) *Being Reasonable about the Economics of Health* (Cheltenham: Edward Elgar, 1997) at 180.

[60] Klein, Day and Redmayne, *Managing Scarcity* at 25.

[61] R. Cookson and P. Dolan, 'Principles of Justice in Health Care Rationing' (2000) 26 *Journal of Medical Ethics*, 323.

[62] For discussion, see J. McKie and J. Richardson, 'The Rule of Rescue' (2003) 56 *Social Science and Medicine*, 2407.

[63] See n. 23 and accompanying text. See also Williams, 'Need as a Demand Concept' at 181.

patient concerned. This raises the important question of *who* should determine access to healthcare, which is examined at length in Chapter 3. For the present, the issue to be explored here is whether, in light of the meanings of 'demand' and 'need' which have been offered, rationing is, as is generally claimed, inevitable where healthcare is publicly funded.

Mullen advances the argument that there is 'no absolute case that healthcare need/demand will always outstrip supply – and that rationing is inevitable'.[64] She offers four justifications for this view. First, it is claimed that rationing would not be necessary if health services were to be more generously funded: as Klein, Day and Redmayne put it, that 'government parsimony is to blame'.[65] This, however, appears implausible. Taking the NHS as an example, while its relatively low levels of funding may exacerbate the need for rationing, it is readily apparent that strategies for the management of expenditure through the restriction of access to care have been adopted in countries which spend a much higher proportion of GDP on the financing of healthcare.[66] Moreover, increases in spending which have occurred under the Labour Government since 1997[67] have not 'resolved' the mismatch between demand and supply in the NHS: this may, in part, be explained by the nature of healthcare as a labour-intensive service, meaning that there is a high rate of labour-cost inflation.[68] And, even though a much higher level of expenditure on healthcare may be sustainable,[69] it seems unlikely that this would be politically acceptable in the long term, given competing demands on the public purse. It therefore seems unrealistic to view increased expenditure as a panacea: as Tragakes and Vienonen state: 'no country has ever allocated enough resources to statutory healthcare provision to provide

---

[64] Mullen, 'Is It Necessary to Ration Health Care?' at 57.

[65] Klein, Day and Redmayne, *Managing Scarcity* at 97.

[66] Thus, the other two jurisdictions discussed in this text spend more on healthcare than the United Kingdom: Canada at 9.6% of GDP and South Africa at 8.7%, compared with 7.7% for the UK (figures for 2002), but – as the discussions in Chapters 7 and 8 make clear – rationing of care occurs in both systems. See World Health Organization, *The World Health Report 2005* (Copenhagen: WHO, 2005) at 196.

[67] Health expenditure in the UK has increased from 6.8 per cent of GDP in 1997 to 7.7 per cent in 2003: see World Health Organization, *The World Health Report 2002* (Copenhagen: WHO, 2002) at 208; *OECD Health Data 2005* (Paris: OECD, 2005).

[68] For a comparable analysis, see Klein, Day and Redmayne, *Managing Scarcity* at 102. Approximately 60 per cent of the NHS budget is spent upon staffing and pay costs: see Department of Health, *Chief Executive's Report to the NHS: December 2005* (London: Department of Health, 2005) at 16.

[69] It has been calculated that the UK could afford to spend 30% of its GDP on the NHS in 2055, assuming annual growth in the economy of 2% per year and in NHS spending of 5%: see J. Appleby and A. Harrison, *Spending on Health Care – How Much Is Enough?* (London: King's Fund, 2006) at 64.

comprehensive and universal coverage of every possible healthcare need'.[70]

The second and third grounds for doubting that the rationing of healthcare resources is inevitable are the associated claims that the eradication of inefficiencies in the administration of the health system may offset the need for the rationing of the services provided, and that elimination of ineffective, non-beneficial and harmful treatments would preclude the need to limit access to those which are effective and beneficial. These arguments have had a significant impact upon the development of recent policy on the delivery of healthcare, particularly in the NHS.

Here, the creation of the 'internal market' in the early 1990s represented an attempt to grapple with supply-side problems. Notable amongst these were the so-called 'efficiency trap', whereby the existence of a fixed financial allocation based upon the needs, mortality and morbidity of a population offered hospitals no incentive to reduce unit costs, and the problem of 'moral hazard', which meant that clinicians tended to over-treat patients as they had no direct interest in controlling costs in the absence of mechanisms which required account to be given of these.[71] Accordingly, health authorities were required by the Department of Health to 'demonstrate that resources were being used more efficiently' and to 'achieve greater efficiency and effectiveness through ... use of resources and organisational development'.[72] These objectives remain highly pertinent to the Labour Government's vision of the NHS,[73] notwithstanding its view that incentives for improved NHS performance had been 'too narrowly focused upon efficiency and squeezing more treatment from the same resources', to the detriment of 'quality, patient responsiveness and partnership with local authorities'.[74] However, such policies have clearly not put an end to the rationing of treatments and services, as the instances of public law litigation examined in Chapter 6 demonstrate. Indeed, as will be explained in the next chapter, the *visibility*

---

[70] Tragakes and Vienonen, 'Key Issues in Rationing' at 4.

[71] For discussion of these issues, see C. Newdick, *Who Should We Treat?* (Oxford: Oxford University Press, 1st edn, 1995) at 41–3.

[72] Klein, Day and Redmayne, *Managing Scarcity* at 52–3, citing respectively NHS Management Executive, *Priorities and Planning Guidance for the NHS for 1992–93* (London: Department of Health, 1991 (EL(91) 103)) and NHS Management Executive, *Priorities and Planning Guidance for the NHS for 1994–95* (London: Department of Health, 1993 (EL(93) 54)).

[73] See *The NHS Plan* at 4, which, as elements of one of the 'NHS Core Principles', states that 'the NHS will work continuously to improve quality services and to minimise errors', and that 'the NHS will continuously improve its efficiency, productivity and performance'.

[74] *Ibid.* at para. 2.21.

of rationing – if not necessarily the frequency of its occurrence – has increased as a result of the implementation of strategies such as the institution of a purchaser/provider split in the delivery of healthcare.

Similar conclusions may be reached in respect of measures taken to eliminate ineffective forms of treatment and services from the NHS. As described in Chapter 3,[75] in line with a broad epistemological shift within the medical profession towards the application of 'evidence-based' approaches (such as the randomised controlled trial and meta-analysis) for determination of clinical effectiveness,[76] coupled with the growing impact of the tools of health economics (notably, the Quality-Adjusted Life Year) as means of assessing cost-effectiveness,[77] the UK Government has established NICE with a brief to issue guidance to the NHS in England and Wales on 'best practice' in clinical practice, use of medical technologies and promotion of good health. The work of this agency clearly has an impact upon resource allocation in the NHS, especially given that NICE recommendations on technologies carry a mandatory funding obligation for purchasing Primary Care and Hospital Trusts.[78] However, despite a net *increase* in NHS expenditure of £800 million as a result of the implementation of NICE guidance,[79] it is apparent that rationing continues to take place. This occurs not only where NICE itself refuses to recommend a treatment for routine use on the NHS,[80] but also where health authorities delay provision of a treatment pending the issuing of guidance by NICE,[81] and where priorities for expenditure on other treatments are re-arranged to accommodate the extra spending necessary to fund the implementation of NICE guidance.[82] These outcomes suggest that the deployment of scientific and

---

[75] See below, Chapter 3, n.128 and accompanying text.
[76] See e.g. S. Straus, W. Richardson, P. Glasziou *et al.*, *Evidence-Based Medicine: How to Practice and Teach EBM* (Edinburgh: Churchill Livingstone, 3rd edn, 2005).
[77] For further discussion, see below, Chapter 4.
[78] See below, Chapter 3, n. 130 and accompanying text.
[79] See Audit Commission, *Managing the Financial Implications of NICE Guidance* (Wetherby: Audit Commission, 2005) at para. 23.
[80] Notable examples have included beta-inteferon for multiple sclerosis (which was subsequently made available to 20,000 patients through an arrangement reached between government and manufacturers): see NICE Press Release 2002/007 (4 February 2002), and donepezil, rivastigmine, galantamine and memantine for Alzheimer's disease: see NICE Press Release 2006/048 (11 October 2006).
[81] As was the case for certain PCTs in relation to the provision of Herceptin for early stage breast cancer: see above Chapter 1.
[82] For discussion, see R. Cookson, D. McDaid and A. Maynard, 'Wrong SIGN, NICE Mess: is Guidance Distorting Allocation of Resources?' (2001) 323 *British Medical Journal*, 743; Health Committee, *National Institute for Clinical Excellence*, Second Report, HC 515-I (2001–02) at paras. 77–81.

social-scientific methodologies cannot in itself obviate the need for the rationing of healthcare resources. This is a conclusion which corresponds to views that evidence on effectiveness is frequently ambiguous,[83] with relatively few treatments being totally non-beneficial for *any* patient and thus uncontroversial targets for withdrawal from a health system.

The fourth argument advanced by Mullen against the inevitability of healthcare rationing contests the view that demand for healthcare is infinite,[84] and that supply of resources is finite. She argues that 'commonsense would suggest that we do not all wish to consume healthcare simply because it is there',[85] that the costs associated with factors leading to increased demand (such as an ageing population and advances in technology, which are examined in more detail in the next section of this chapter) are exaggerated, and observes (in an argument closely related to that turning on underfunding) that 'any limit on total healthcare expenditure in the UK is a matter of choice, not economic necessity. How much, in total, should be devoted to healthcare is not a given.'[86]

On one level, these points appear uncontentious. Demand for healthcare services may indeed cease when marginal utility falls to zero; new drugs may prove more cost-effective than existing ones and the cost of treatment of the elderly may have been over-estimated; and it would clearly be possible for society to divert more resources than is presently the case to the provision of healthcare services. To this extent, Mullen's analysis serves the avowed purpose of identifying 'a rather pessimistic or defeatist thread [which] can be detected running through a number of arguments' and which leads to the conclusion that measures such as the elimination of ineffective treatments, or increasing funding of health services, are 'either not worth pursuing or should be relegated to a secondary position behind the "hard choices" of explicit rationing'.[87] One might even accept the argument that the terms 'infinite' and 'finite' are ill chosen when referring to the demand for, and supply of, healthcare resources, given that an

[83] See M. McKee and A. Clarke, 'Guidelines, Enthusiasms, Uncertainty and the Limits to Purchasing' (1995) 310 *British Medical Journal*, 101 at 101, criticising evidence-based medicine for resulting in 'the imposition of a spurious rationality on a sometimes inherently irrational process'; and further, Klein, Day and Redmayne, *Managing Scarcity* at 102–8.

[84] Mullen's argument is somewhat undermined by her equation of 'demand' with 'need', the distinction between which she considers to be 'not central to the argument here': Mullen, 'Is It Necessary to Ration Health Care' at 53. This leads her to argue that need is not infinite, a conclusion which is self-evident if 'need' is, as here, viewed as a rationing criterion which functions to enable priorities to be set in conditions of scarcity. It does not follow from this that 'demand' is finite, as Mullen appears to claim.

[85] *Ibid.*   [86] *Ibid.* at 55.   [87] *Ibid.* at 56.

economic model *could* be constructed which contradicted such assumptions. However, it must surely be conceded, at the very least, that – *given current political and popular preferences for public expenditure* (and, most likely, even if expenditure was to be increased) – the demand for healthcare will continue to outstrip the available supply and that some form of rationing is therefore necessary to bring the two into (or closer to) equilibrium. Indeed, Mullen herself appears to acknowledge this. From her statement that 'rationing/priority-setting in the presence of a generous resource allocation, *mutatis mutandis*, is likely to be far less painful – will need fewer "hard choices" – than rationing/priority-setting in the face of severely constrained resources',[88] one can draw the inference that conditions of scarcity *will* always exist – and thus that rationing *is* inevitable – but that the frequency and difficulty of the necessary choices may be diminished if expenditure on health services is increased.

It is therefore submitted that the correct view of the rationing of healthcare resources is expressed in statements that it is 'unavoidable', 'ubiquitous',[89] a 'truism',[90] and 'a fact of life'.[91] Indeed, the necessity of rationing appears to be accepted by the public, at least in the UK,[92] notwithstanding continued opposition to the principle of restricting access to health services.[93]

---

[88] *Ibid.*

[89] D. King and A. Maynard, 'Public Opinion and Rationing in the United Kingdom' (1999) 50 *Health Policy*, 39 at 40, 43. These authors express the tongue in cheek view that 'anyone who doubts that rationing in the NHS is universal and has existed always is in need of psychiatric care!': *ibid* at 40.

[90] D. Hunter, 'Rationing Health Care: the Political Perspective' (1995) 51 *British Medical Bulletin*, 876 at 877.

[91] Maxwell, 'Why Rationing is on the Agenda' at 765.

[92] See Bryson and New, 'Health Care Rationing: a Cut Too Far?' at 25–6, reporting that 72 per cent of those surveyed for *British Social Attitudes* agreed with the statement that 'due to lack of funds the NHS will have to cut down or cut out certain types of treatments'. Interestingly, however, the authors note that there is considerable sensitivity to question wording on this issue, with only 41 per cent agreeing with the statement that 'as demand on the NHS grows, it will have to ration some treatments': *ibid.* at 26. This would seem to reinforce the argument as to the negative discursive connotations of the term 'rationing' which was posited above, and to point to the need for 'more information about the role and consequences of rationing before a wider and more meaningful debate can take place': *ibid.*, a conclusion which accords with the central theme of this book.

[93] Bryson and New, 'Health Care Rationing: a Cut Too Far?' at 25, report that eight in ten of those surveyed were of the opinion that 'the NHS should never cut down or cut out any types of treatment'. Similar figures have been reported for Canada: 76 per cent of a survey population of 1,200 members of the public opposed restriction of the range of healthcare services on offer if government could not cover all healthcare costs: see *Health Care in Canada Survey 2003* at 11, available at www.mediresource.com/e/pages/hcc_survey/pdf/2003_hcic.pdf (accessed 8 January 2007).

Is the rationing of healthcare resources becoming increasingly necessary?

A further question which merits examination is the matter of whether expenditure on healthcare is likely to continue to rise, placing increasing pressure on budgets and thus rendering the rationing of access to healthcare resources an ever-growing policy imperative.

While patterns of growth in healthcare expenditure within OECD countries have been uneven across the decades since the Second World War, there has been significant growth in spending since 1990, with public expenditure on healthcare as a percentage of GDP rising by approximately 21 per cent by 2003.[94] Recent studies have projected a continuation of this growth. It has been estimated that, in the absence of any policy action to deal with this issue, public spending on health, coupled with that on long-term care, will virtually double across OECD countries by 2050, and that even if measures are taken to control costs, there could be an average increase of 3.5 percentage points of GDP over the same period.[95] Similar projections have been made for health expenditure in the UK in an influential independent review of the long-term resource requirements of the NHS commissioned by the Treasury (the 'Wanless Report'). Depending upon the manner in which the major drivers of cost develop in the future, the review estimates that total spending on the NHS may need to increase from £68 billion in 2002–3 to between £154 billion and £184 billion in 2022–3, if high quality clinical standards are to be delivered and the rising expectations of those who use the NHS are to be met.[96] Given figures such as these, it is little wonder that the OECD has identified spending on healthcare as a 'first-order policy issue',[97] and that strategies to curtail costs – including the rationing of resources – have been widely adopted by governments globally. But why has the increase in spending been so dramatic? What are the determinants of rising expenditure on healthcare?

The key demographic factor would appear to be the ageing of the population. In the UK, life expectancy increased by over twenty-five years during the course of the twentieth century, with the consequence that the population aged 65 and over rose from 7.4 million in 1971 to 9.2

---

[94] See *OECD Health Database 2005* (Paris: OECD, 2005).

[95] See OECD, *Projecting OECD Health and Long-term Care Expenditures: What are the Main drivers?* (Paris: OECD (ECO/WKP(2006)5), 2006) at 7.

[96] See D. Wanless, *Securing Our Future Health: Taking a Long-term View* (London: HM Treasury, 2002) at para. 5.10.

[97] OECD, *Projecting OECD Health and Long-term Care Expenditures* at 5.

million in 1998.[98] A comparable trend can be observed across OECD countries, with an average gain in life expectancy of 8.4 years between 1960 and 2001,[99] and projections that the ratio of people over 65 to those aged between 20 and 64 could double by 2050.[100] A rising proportion of older people might be expected to increase healthcare costs, both because the ageing process results in biological degeneration, increasing vulnerability to disease, and as a result of cumulative exposure to the risks associated with environmental and lifestyle factors. The consequence is that there has been a shift in the burden of disease from the infectious diseases which were prevalent in the nineteenth and early twentieth century, to chronic diseases whose prevalence tends to increase with age, with utilisation of health services following suit. The impact upon expenditure is exacerbated by the fact that advances in medical technology – the significance of which will be examined in more detail below – have the potential to transform the nature of some diseases such as certain cancers, from acute terminal illnesses into chronic conditions, with the consequent necessity for longer-term care of the affected patient.

However, notwithstanding an apparently strong correlation between healthcare expenditure and age, it would appear that surprisingly little of the increased spending which has been witnessed in health systems in recent years can, in fact, be attributed to this factor. The Wanless Report estimates that only 15 per cent of the growth in healthcare expenditure in the NHS between 1965 and 1999 can be accounted for by the ageing of the British population,[101] and projections of the impact of demographic factors on health expenditure across OECD countries up to 2050 also suggest that the effect will be fairly small.[102] A possible explanation for this seemingly counter-intuitive outcome is that a significant proportion of healthcare expenditure on an individual is concentrated at the end of life,[103] with the consequence that there is a close association between the level of healthcare expenditure and proximity to death. Since the cost of dying at

---

[98] See D. Wanless, *Securing Our Future Health: Taking a Long-term View: Interim Report* (London: HM Treasury, 2001) at paras. 3.22, 3.24.

[99] OECD, *OECD Factbook 2005* (Paris: OECD, 2005) at 190–3.

[100] See J-P. Cotis, 'Population Ageing: Facing the Challenge' (2003) 239 *OECD Observer* (Paris: OECD, 2003).

[101] Wanless, *Securing Our Future Health: Interim Report* at para. 3.25.

[102] See OECD, *Projecting OECD Health and Long-term Care Expenditures* at 16, estimating that the increase in expenditure between 2005 and 2050 which can be attributed to demographic factors is 0.6 percentage points of GDP.

[103] The Wanless Report estimates that 'more than a quarter of all acute healthcare costs are incurred in the last year of life': Wanless, *Securing Our Future Health* at para. 9.16.

age ninety is no greater than the cost of dying at age forty,[104] an increase in life expectancy alone cannot account for an increase in health expenditure. Rather, the impact of an ageing population is simply to shift a larger proportion of healthcare expenditure to an older age cohort, with the overall per capita level of spending remaining unchanged.[105] Such a conclusion rests, however, upon acceptance of the assumptions of the 'compression of morbidity' thesis, that is, that an increase in life expectancy translates into a reduced percentage of an individual's lifespan spent in ill health.[106] If, in contrast, the 'expansion of morbidity' thesis is correct,[107] and greater longevity *increases* the proportion of life during which ill health is suffered (in particular, because of an enhanced susceptibility to chronic conditions, as previously discussed), then healthcare costs will tend to increase as the population ages *even if* proximity to death is accepted as an important driver of expenditure. In fact, it is unclear which of these hypotheses presents the more accurate picture, although the Wanless Report reports evidence that 'while levels of very serious ill health are falling, older people are experiencing more minor health problems'.[108]

There is, therefore, a degree of uncertainty as to the impact which demographic changes are having on healthcare expenditure, although it appears to be generally accepted that an ageing population is not the sole, nor indeed the major, determinant of increased spending.[109] It is therefore necessary to consider the relevance of non-demographic factors.

A significant focus of the literature on healthcare expenditure has been upon the role played by changes in individual and national income. It has been argued that healthcare is a 'luxury' good, with an income elasticity greater than one, which means that expenditure will rise disproportionately to income.[110] Put simply, 'as people become richer, they are willing to pay more for a given improvement in health'.[111] Since the rate of increase in expenditure exceeds that of income, cost-containment

---

[104] See *ibid.* at para. 9.17; OECD, *Projecting OECD Health and Long-term Care Expenditures* at 11.

[105] See P. Zweifel, S. Felder and M. Meiers, 'Ageing of Population and Health Care Expenditure: a Red Herring?' (1999) 8 *Health Economics*, 485.

[106] See especially J. Fries, 'The Compression of Morbidity' (2005) 83 *Milbank Quarterly*, 801.

[107] See e.g. E. Grunenberg, 'The Failure of Success' (1977) 55 *Millbank Memorial Fund Quarterly*, 3; E. Schneider and J. Brody, 'Ageing, Natural Death and the Compression of Morbidity: Another View' (1983) 309 *New England Journal of Medicine*, 854.

[108] Wanless, *Securing Our Future Health* at para 9.30.

[109] See OECD, *Projecting OECD Health and Long-term Care Expenditures* at 10; Wanless, *Securing Our Future Health* at para. 3.25.

[110] The classic exposition of this argument is contained in J. Newhouse, 'Medical Care Expenditure: a Cross-National Survey' (1977) 12 *Journal of Human Resources*, 115.

[111] Appleby and Harrison, *Spending on Health Care* at 5.

measures, such as rationing, become necessary. Similarly, as a country's GDP increases, so it tends to spend more on healthcare.[112] From this perspective, it is possible to make the observation, which 'is not particularly new and may even border on the obvious', that 'the amount spent on healthcare is determined by the amount available to spend rather than the amount of disease'.[113]

Nonetheless, such a conclusion appears counter-intuitive if allocation of healthcare resources is regarded as determined, at least to some extent, by 'need': the very nature of the latter concept suggests that healthcare cannot, by definition, be a 'luxury'.[114] Thus, 'if the per-unit cost of care and the incidence of illness are similar across populations, a poor population would be expected to devote a higher share of its income to healthcare than a rich one. This is also the pattern that emerges when data on healthcare spending by families and individuals within a country are related to family or individual income.'[115] Clearly, this is likely to be particularly true for health systems which are primarily publicly funded or those which are heavily subsidised,[116] but even in market-based systems such as that of the United States, the existence of publicly financed programmes (such as Medicare and Medicaid) should function to diminish the strength of any link between individual or family income and spending on healthcare.[117]

Considerations of this nature have led to challenges to the 'conventional wisdom' that healthcare is a 'luxury good'.[118] Some commentators have questioned the methodologies used in earlier studies, arguing that they inappropriately relied upon the application of microeconomic analysis to macroeconomic data,[119] and that small sample sizes and use of data from a specific year rather than across time have resulted in a failure to control for the impact of time-specific shocks (such as a pandemic) across all countries, or for country-specific effects such as policy

---

[112] See Wanless, *Securing Our Future Health: Interim Report* at para. 3.28.

[113] T. Getzen, 'Health Care is an Individual Necessity and a National Luxury: Applying Multilevel Decision Models to the Analysis of Health Care Expenditures' (2000) *Journal of Health Economics*, 259 at 268.

[114] A. Culyer, *Health Care Expenditures in Canada: Myth and Reality; Past and Future* (Toronto: Canadian Tax Federation (Paper No. 82), 1988) at 20.

[115] A. Blomqvist and R. Carter, 'Is Health Care Really a Luxury?' (1997) 16 *Journal of Health Economics*, 207 at 208.

[116] See L. Di Matteo, 'The Macro Determinants of Health Expenditure in the United States and Canada: Assessing the Impact of Income, Age Distribution and Time' (2005) 71 *Health Policy*, 23 at 24.

[117] See Blomqvist and Carter, 'Is Health Care Really a Luxury?' at 208.

[118] D. Parkin, A. McGuire and B. Yule, 'Aggregate Health Care Expenditures and National Income: Is Health Care a Luxury Good?' (1987) 6 *Journal of Health Economics*, 109 at 109–12.

[119] *Ibid.*

changes.[120] Others have sought to refine the analysis by observing that there has been a failure to distinguish between income elasticity at the *individual* level (the effect of private or public health coverage being to minimise or eliminate the influence of cost of care on decisions of whether/ how much care is required, thus spending on healthcare is not sensitive to income) and at the level of a *national health system* (where total expenditure is limited by income, corresponding to the 'luxury good' analysis).[121] In view of these critiques, the most that can perhaps be said is that 'whether healthcare is a luxury or a necessity is still an unsettled issue'.[122]

Alternative rationales for the widely observed positive relationship between national income and aggregate expenditure on healthcare must therefore be sought. One possible explanation relates to the fact that provision of health services is labour-intensive, and the relative price of labour-intensive commodities tends to rise with income.[123] However, the determinant which is generally regarded as having had the most signifi-cant impact upon health expenditure is technological change.[124]

A leading study by Newhouse postulates that technological change may account for up to 75 per cent of the increase in healthcare expenditure,[125] and the hypothesis that this is a major contributory factor is supported by subsequent research which indicates that real aggregate healthcare expenditure per capita responds to expenditure on research and develop-ment of medical technologies.[126] It appears to be clear, therefore, that medical advances, such as those which have occurred in respect of

[120] See A. Sen, 'Is Health Care a Luxury? New Evidence from OECD Data' (2005) 5 *International Journal of Health Care Finance and Economics*, 147.
[121] See Getzen, 'Health Care is an Individual Necessity'.
[122] OECD, *Projecting OECD Health and Long-term Care Expenditures* at 73.
[123] See Blomqvist and Carter, 'Is Health Care Really a Luxury?' at 209. The Wanless Report cites this as a determinant of rising health expenditure in the NHS: Wanless, *Securing Our Future Health: Interim Report* at para. 3.26, and notes that over the past twenty years, NHS staff costs have increased by two percentage points a year more than inflation in the wider British economy: *ibid.* at para. 11.10. Similar arguments have been advanced in the Canadian context: see L. Di Matteo and R. Di Matteo, 'Evidence on the determinants of Canadian provincial government health expenditures: 1965–1991' (1998) 17 *Journal of Health Economics*, 211.
[124] In a survey of leading American health economists conducted in 1995, 81 per cent agreed with the statement that 'the primary reason for the increase in the health sector's share of GDP over the past thirty years is technological change in medicine': V. Fuchs, 'Economics, Values and Health Care Reform' (1996) 86 *American Economic Review*, 1 at 8.
[125] See J. Newhouse, 'Medical Care Costs: How Much Welfare Loss?' (1992) 6 *Journal of Economic Perspectives*, 3. DiMatteo, 'The Macro Determinants of Health Expenditure' at 40 estimates that technological change accounts for a maximum of 66 per cent of the increase in real per capita health expenditures.
[126] See A. Okunade and V. Murthy, 'Technology as a "Major Driver" of Health Care Costs: a Cointegration Analysis of the Newhouse Conjecture' (2002) 21 *Journal of Health Economics*, 147.

equipment (e.g. computer tomography scanners and magnetic resonance imaging systems), pharmaceuticals (such as statins for coronary heart disease, beta interferon for multiple sclerosis and taxanes for cancer) and diagnostic and surgical procedures (e.g. invasive cardiology, transplantation and renal dialysis), have had a significant impact upon healthcare spending.[127] Moreover, there appears to be every likelihood that medical advances will continue into the foreseeable future. The developments which are likely to have the most direct impact upon health expenditure include the evolution of technologies which permit the treatment of conditions which are currently acute in nature as chronic, an increasing focus upon prevention and treatment of risk rather than disease (by means of screening and treatment with drugs for the population which is at risk), and advances in genetics and stem cell technology which offer the prospect of identifying patients who are at risk, creating individualised drug regimes and replacing faulty genes and dead or dying cells, thereby treating many conditions which are presently incurable.[128]

Two effects of the introduction of new technologies upon the provision and financing of healthcare may be identified.[129] First, the new technology may be regarded as simply *substituting* for the old: in this respect, the unit cost may increase or decrease as a result of its introduction, although health outcomes should improve as this is the objective of the process of researching and developing medical interventions. Unit costs may also diminish in the longer term, as competitor technologies enter the marketplace.

However, irrespective of whether the new technology is cheaper or more expensive than that which is being replaced, its introduction is also likely to have a *treatment expansion* effect. This occurs in a variety of ways. First, a new technology may open up the possibility of treatment in areas where this was previously unsafe or impossible. For example, it has been hypothesised that a large increase in NHS expenditure on newborn babies and the elderly relative to other age groups may be explained by the availability of interventions to respond to conditions which were previously untreatable.[130]

---

[127] Pharmaceuticals alone account for greater than 10 per cent of all health expenditure in all but two OECD countries for which figures are available, and more than 20 per cent in ten countries (figures for 2003): OECD, *OECD Health Data 2005*. During the 1990s, real per capita pharmaceutical expenditure exceeded growth in total health expenditure in eleven of sixteen countries: see OECD, *Competition and Regulation Issues in the Pharmaceutical Industry* (Paris: OECD, 2001 (DAFFE/CLP (2000) 29)) at 25.

[128] For discussion, see Wanless, *Securing Our Future Health: Interim Report* at paras. 10.51–60.

[129] See D. Cutler and M. McClellan, 'Is Technological Change in Medicine Worth It?' (2001) 20 *Health Affairs*, 11 at 14.

[130] See A. Harrison, J. Dixon, B. New and K. Judge, 'Funding the NHS: can the NHS Cope in Future?' (1997) 314 *British Medical Journal*, 139 at 140.

Secondly, medical research may also result in the redefinition of treatment thresholds, increasing the number of potential patients: recent
examples of this phenomenon include diabetes[131] and hypertension.[132]
Thirdly, a new technology may have an impact both upon clinical diagnosis (with physicians being more willing to prescribe drugs or utilise
surgical procedures if these are safer and more effective) and upon patient
uptake – as the Herceptin case outlined in Chapter 1 demonstrates, the
publicising of new technologies tends to stimulate demand and patients
are likely to show greater knowledge of their condition and willingness to
seek medical assistance if they are aware that an effective treatment
exists.[133] Finally (and notwithstanding the doubts as to the impact of an
ageing population which were expressed above), the impact of medical
innovation may simply be to replace short-term treatment for acute conditions with longer-term treatment for chronic diseases, with a consequent increase in costs as patients receive medical care for longer periods.
The potential for new medical technologies to permit acute conditions
such as cancer to be treated as chronic illnesses has already been noted,
but the effect has also been felt in changes in the burden of disease, from
infectious illnesses to chronic conditions. As Weisbrod and LaMay note,
perhaps somewhat unsympathetically: 'the use of antibiotics to prevent
deaths from infections can cause people to live longer and hence to die
from heart disease or cancer, which typically entail even greater costs'.[134]

The overall effect of new medical technologies would thus appear to be
to place upward pressure on aggregate healthcare expenditure.[135]
Nonetheless, two important qualifications to this apparently pessimistic
conclusion should be noted. First, medical advances may have beneficial
consequences elsewhere in the public sector (e.g. by reducing the need for
long-term social care) and the wider economy (e.g. enabling individuals
to work longer as a result of greater longevity and compression of morbidity).[136] Secondly, the impact of new technology upon health expenditure
can, to some degree, be managed, unlike some of the other determinants
discussed here (such as demographic change). In particular, health technology assessment, a research activity which provides a systematic

---

[131] See WHO, *Definition, Diagnosis and Classification of Diabetes Mellitus and its Complications: Report of a WHO Consultation* (WHO: Geneva, 1999 (WHO/NCD/NCS 99.2)).
[132] See D. Wanless, *Securing Good Health for the Population: Population Health Trends* (London: HM Treasury, 2002) at paras. 4.16–17.
[133] See Cutler and McClellan, 'Is Technological Change in Medicine Worth It?' at 14.
[134] B. Weisbrod and C. LaMay, 'Mixed Signals: Public Policy and the Future of Health Care R & D' (1999) 18 *Health Affairs*, 112 at 116.
[135] See Wanless, *Securing Our Future Health: Interim Report* at para. 10.11.
[136] See *ibid.* at para. 10.12, and, more generally, Cutler and McClellan, 'Is Technological Change in Medicine Worth It?'.

evaluation of the short and long-term consequences of a health technology from a wide variety of perspectives, including clinical effectiveness, social and ethical considerations and cost-effectiveness, may be useful in assisting decision-makers in reaching judgments on the affordability of new technologies.[137]

The final driver of increasing health expenditure to be discussed here is the role played by changing patient expectations of health services. To a degree, this may connect to rising income levels, considered previously. As individuals become more affluent, so they might be expected to demand a wider range of higher quality services, with the consequence of increasing pressure on healthcare spending.[138] However, the issue extends much more broadly than this. The 'marketisation' of publicly funded healthcare, reflected in the introduction of forms of managed competition such as the divide between purchase and provision of healthcare in the NHS in the early 1990s, has been accompanied by at least a partial redefinition of the individual as a 'consumer' of health services. In the UK, this was embodied by the Patient's Charter of 1991, which set out the standards which users of the NHS could expect to receive, and which sat within a network of targets and mechanisms for inspection and audit of the delivery of healthcare. In such an environment, rising patient expectations – and the voicing of complaints if these were not satisfied – were intended to function as a quality assurance mechanism, driving up standards and achieving efficiency *within* existing resources.[139]

However, once stimulated, patient and public expectations of what a health service should achieve may be difficult to restrain, contributing to the upward pressure on health spending. Thus, the Wanless Report, drawing upon research commissioned to predict future patient expectations of the NHS, concludes that there will be continued expectations of safe, high quality clinical treatment, fast access, an integrated system, comfortable accommodation and patient-centred care.[140] Meeting such expectations and ensuring the quality of treatment are postulated as 'the most expensive cost drivers' of future NHS expenditure.[141] The additional costs of reducing inpatient and outpatient waiting times to two

---

[137] For a useful general discussion, see E. Jonsson, 'Development of Health Technology Assessment in Europe: a Personal Perspective' (2002) 18 *International Journal of Technology Assessment in Health Care*, 171.

[138] See Wanless, *Securing Our Future Health: Interim Report* at para. 3.26.

[139] For discussion of the objectives and achievements of the Charter, see e.g. C. Farrell, R. Levenson and D. Snape, *The Patient's Charter: Past and Future* (London: King's Fund, 1998).

[140] Wanless, *Securing Our Future Health: Interim Report* at para. 7.28.

[141] *Ibid.* at para. 5.23.

weeks, improving clinical governance[142] and implementing National Service Frameworks[143] to secure best practice in the treatment of the key areas of cancer, coronary heart disease, mental health, diabetes and renal disease, have been estimated at £10 billion, £1.4 billion and between £7.5 and £9 billion respectively by 2022–3.[144]

Two further generic social trends, closely linked to the above, may be seen to contribute to rising expectations in this field of public policy. First, it has been argued that there has been a 'decline in deference' towards, or an 'erosion of trust' in, medical professional judgment.[145] This may be seen as symptomatic of a greater public willingness to challenge authority, and to exercise a 'voice' (both by means of participation in decisions which affect individuals and by complaining when poor service is received or exercising the option to 'exit' where a choice of service is available): developments which clearly flow from the rise in consumerist attitudes to healthcare. The effect of this has been to call the traditional paternalistic model of medical practice into question, with patients playing a more active part in the diagnosis, treatment and management of their condition, and a growing role for patient groups (such as Women Fighting for Herceptin, noted in Chapter 1) as mechanisms through which service users can seek to influence the standard and range of treatments which are offered.

The tendency for patients to become more actively involved in diagnosis, treatment and management of conditions is fuelled by a second significant trend: the increasing availability of information technology and its use for health-related matters. Here, the impact upon expectations – and hence upon expenditure – arises from the existence of websites and other information sources which enable comparison of procedures and,

---

[142] This has been defined as 'providing a framework through which NHS organisations are accountable for continually improving the quality of their services and safeguarding high standards of care by creating an environment in which excellence in clinical care will flourish': G. Scally and L. Donaldson, 'Clinical Governance and the Drive for Quality Improvement in the New NHS in England' (1998) 317 *British Medical Journal*, 61 at 62.

[143] The programme of National Service Frameworks was introduced to the NHS in 1998: see Department of Health, *National Service Frameworks* (London: The Stationery Office, 1998 (HSC 1998/074)). The Frameworks establish a minimum set of standards for clinical care and identify key interventions for a defined service or disease group (such as cancer, coronary heart disease and mental health). The objective is to improve performance and to reduce variations in standards of service across the NHS.

[144] See Wanless, *Securing Our Future Health: Interim Report* at paras. 5.25–26.

[145] See *ibid.* at para. 7.24; and further, D. Mechanic, 'Changing Medical Organisation and the Erosion of Trust' (1996) *Milbank Quarterly*, 171; H. Davies, 'Falling Public Trust in Health Services: Implications for Accountability' (1999) 4 *Journal of Health Services Research and Policy*, 193. For a more general discussion, see O. O'Neil, *A Question of Trust* (Cambridge: Cambridge University Press, 2002).

perhaps most significantly, which provide information on new technologies to treat particular conditions.[146] As seen in the case of Herceptin, availability of information on medical advances can generate significant patient and public pressure to expand the scope of treatments and services offered by a health system, with a consequent impact upon expenditure. However, even in the absence of an innovatory treatment or technique, patients are likely to be better informed about their health as a consequence of developments in information technology, with the consequence that they will tend to demand services of higher quality, thus placing further upward pressure on health expenditure.[147]

While it is clearly more difficult to quantify the impact of rising expectations upon health expenditure than some of the other drivers discussed here,[148] the impact of this determinant should not be underestimated. Its importance can be demonstrated by the UK's experience in the early decades of existence of the NHS. Health expenditure in the UK as a proportion of GDP actually *declined* in the first half of the 1950s and did not regain the level attained in 1950–1 until 1966–7.[149] Despite this, Klein, Day and Redmayne note that 'there was little – if any – public discussion of rationing in the early years when the NHS budget was most hard-pressed'.[150] This apparent paradox may be explained by low levels of public expectations of what the NHS was able to achieve, with long waiting lists and limited availability of treatments seemingly regarded as facts of life. It might therefore be concluded that 'political and public expectations about rationing are not necessarily a function of the balance between supply and demand but rather reflect the balance between supply and expectations'.[151] Explanations of the need for the rationing of healthcare resources which are rooted solely in economic analysis may, for this reason, therefore be incomplete.

---

[146] The Wanless Report estimates that there were around 10,000 health information websites and that the number of health websites in the EU was increasing by 300 per month in 2001. It also estimates that over 60 per cent of UK internet users have used the web to obtain information on health-related issues: Wanless, *Securing Our Future Health: Interim Report* at para. 7.29.

[147] For a general discussion of this and the other social trends connecting to rising expectations, see J. Neuberger, 'The Educated Patient: New Challenges for the Medical Profession' (2000) 247 *Journal of Internal Medicine*, 6.

[148] But note the estimates arrived at by the Wanless Report, above n. 144 and accompanying text.

[149] See C. Emmerson, C. Frayne and A. Goodman, *Pressures in UK Healthcare: Challenges for the NHS* (London: Institute for Fiscal Studies, 2000) at 57.

[150] Klein, Day and Redmayne, *Managing Scarcity* at 40. [151] *Ibid.*

Conclusion

While acknowledging the import of Mullen's view that an unquestioning acceptance of the need to 'ration' healthcare resources in circumstances where supply is limited but demand is unconstrained by price may result in a failure to accord genuine consideration to alternative strategies such as the reduction of waste and the elimination of ineffective treatments, this chapter has nonetheless sought to demonstrate that demand, coupled with expectations as to what can and should be delivered, continues to outstrip supply in this field of public policy. This renders some form of limitation of the availability of potentially beneficial healthcare services and treatments a necessity, at least given existing and all reasonably foreseeable public and political preferences for the levels of funding and expenditure in this sector. Moreover, the factors outlined in the preceding section, while of varying weight, point clearly to the existence of continued upward pressure on healthcare costs, making measures of containment increasingly imperative. It follows that the key topics for debate which arise from the allocation of healthcare resources are 'not *whether* healthcare is rationed but ... *how* it is rationed'[152] and, in respect of the latter, *how healthcare can be rationed in a manner which is publicly acceptable*. These two questions will be explored in depth in the next two chapters of this book.

---

[152] Locock, 'The Changing Nature of Rationing' at 92. Emphasis in original. See also Hunter, 'Rationing Health Care' at 877; A. Maynard, K. Bloor and N. Freemantle, 'Challenges for the National Institute for Clinical Excellence' (2004) 329 *British Medical Journal*, 229 at 229.

3   How Rationing Takes Place

The argument advanced in the preceding chapter was that the focus of debate for those working within the health policy community upon matters of the distribution of resources should be upon the problem of *how* to ration healthcare, and the related issue of *who* should do so. Yet, while these questions can be posed in a straightforward manner such as this, they are much less easily answered.

This chapter seeks to examine the mechanisms through which rationing of healthcare may occur, offering, first of all, a typology of the *forms of rationing* which might exist within a health system. This is an exercise of particular value in the context of the subject-matter of this book, in that the various rationing strategies which are employed tend to generate differing levels of patient and public opposition. They thus present contrasting challenges to the legitimacy of the body which is charged with undertaking the allocative decision, an issue which will be explored at greater length in the next chapter. Secondly, the issue of *who* should make the rationing decision will be canvassed, with consideration being given to the practicability and the perceived advantages and disadvantages of entrusting distributive choices to (amongst others) doctors, managers, politicians and the public. This leads to a related issue, which is fundamental to the argument presented in this text, namely that of the *relative visibility* of the rationing decision. The advantages and disadvantages inherent in more or less visible forms of rationing will be explored. It will be seen that there has been a recent – albeit not total – shift from 'implicit' modes, in which the resource basis of the decision is not communicated to the individual who is being denied access to beneficial treatment, to 'explicit' forms where those resource considerations are transparent both to the disappointed patient and the wider public.

Types of rationing

One possible strategy for managing the mismatch between demand for and supply of healthcare resources is, of course, to ration by price, restricting medical services to those with the ability to pay for them. As discussed in Chapter 2, there is debate among health policy theorists as to whether this may be said to constitute 'rationing' at all, given that the market functions as a mechanism through which demand and supply may be equalised without the necessity for state intervention. However, in view of this text's focus upon publicly funded healthcare, the types of rationing which will be outlined here, following the useful typology advanced by Klein, Day and Redmayne,[1] are those of a non-price variety.

The rationing technique which is most publicly visible, and which therefore tends to generate the greatest degree of public controversy – as exemplified by the Herceptin case discussed in Chapter 1 – is rationing by denial. Straightforwardly, this consists of a decision not to provide a particular beneficial medical treatment either to an individual (such as the experimental cancer treatment sought by the father of Jaymee Bowen, who suffered from acute myeloid leukaemia),[2] or to a group of patients with common disease patterns (for example, in the Herceptin case, denial of the drug to all women with HER2-positive early stage breast cancer within a particular geographical area).[3]

Closely related to this strategy is rationing by selection. As with rationing by denial, this amounts to an outright exclusion of access to a particular treatment, but in this instance the decision to exclude rests not upon the nature of the treatment which is demanded, but rather upon the characteristics of the potential beneficiaries. For example, a decision may be taken to restrict IVF treatment to women under a certain age, or to provide free prostate cancer screening only to men over 65. Again, such decisions may be justified by reference to the 'need' criterion (defined in terms of capacity to benefit) – in the two examples cited, denial of access to older women or younger men may be seen to reflect a clinical judgment that these groups will not receive significant health gains from provision of the service in question. However, rationing by selection according to clinical need can shade easily into selection according to desert or merit, especially when the latter criterion is understood to refer to an individual's stewardship of his/her own health.[4] Thus, a refusal to provide hip and knee replacements to those over a certain body mass

[1] R. Klein, P. Day and S. Redmayne, *Managing Scarcity* (Buckingham: Open University Press, 2000) at 11–12.
[2] See *R* v. *Cambridge Health Authority, ex parte B* [1995] 1 WLR 898, discussed at length in Chapter 6 below.
[3] See the discussion of *R (on the application of Rogers)* v. *Swindon NHS Primary Care Trust and Secretary of State for Health* [2006] 1 WLR 2649 ('*Rogers*') in Chapter 6 below.
[4] 'Merit' can also be evaluated with reference to an individual's contribution to society: for example, their role as a carer of others, especially dependent children. For discussion, see A. Culyer, 'Equity – Some Theory and its Policy Implications' (2001) 27 *Journal of Medical Ethics*, 275 at 278.

index, or guidelines which may function to restrict the availability of certain treatments to smokers and drinkers, *may* be clinically justifiable on the basis that the such patients have lower potential health gains from treatment than others, but they are likely to be perceived by the disappointed patient (and possibly by the wider public) as a 'penalty' for a self-inflicted illness. Consequently, selection according to desert is a matter of significant ethical controversy, notwithstanding that there is some (albeit limited) evidence of public support for distribution along such lines.[5]

A third method of rationing is rationing by delay. This technique finds expression in one of the most common features of publicly funded health systems, the waiting list, which applies particularly, though not exclusively, to cases of elective surgery. However, there are a number of related but less obvious forms of delay, including waits in a doctor's surgery, fixing appointments for a date well in the future, or lengthy exchanges of letters.[6] These mechanisms ostensibly serve to dampen demand, in part by deterring individuals from seeking medical treatment at all (thus linking to the strategy of rationing by deterrence which is discussed below), in part by encouraging those with sufficient disposable income to seek more rapid treatment in the private healthcare sector, and in part through 'decay', as individuals upon a waiting list no longer require medical treatment, either because the condition has ameliorated or because this or another condition has caused their death.

Despite their prevalence, waiting lists seem, at least until recent times, to have generated less controversy and hence lower levels of public opposition, than strategies of rationing by denial or selection. Two possible, and related, explanations for this seemingly surprising state of affairs may be posited. First, the public may find this strategy tolerable simply because they are accustomed to waiting for certain services. As New and LeGrand comment:

the existence of waiting lists and the reality of delays at the doctor's surgery were, it could be argued, perceived more as 'taking one's turn in the queue' than evidence that choices were being made between those making claims on public resources. After all, queuing is something we do when wait for a bus, or when we wait at a supermarket checkout, and so would not suggest that there was any fundamental mismatch between demand and supply.[7]

---

[5] See R. Cookson and P. Dolan, 'Public Views on Health Care Rationing: a Group Discussion Study' (1999) 49 *Health Policy*, 63 at 70–71.

[6] Klein, Day and Redmayne, *Managing Scarcity* at 12.

[7] B. New and J. LeGrand, *Rationing in the NHS: Principles and Pragmatism* (London: King's Fund, 1996) at 23.

This factor appears likely to account for broad acceptance of waiting times for surgery among the British public in the early years of the NHS, shortly after the Second World War. By contrast, recent societal developments, such as the rise of consumerism and a faster pace of life, have contributed to growing public pressure for more rapid access to healthcare, reflected in a number of the legal challenges discussed in Chapters 6 to 8. Such an analysis therefore serves to reinforce the significance of expectations as a factor determining the acceptability of allocative decision-making in the healthcare context, an issue raised in the previous chapter.[8]

Secondly, while the *existence* of waiting lists may be relatively apparent to the public, their *role* as a rationing strategy may not. That is, the reason why the provision of medical treatment is delayed may not be perceived as being connected to scarcity of resources. Waiting lists are therefore more acceptable than overt decisions to deny or select particular patients for treatment because they are less likely to be regarded as amounting to 'rationing',[9] that is 'they permit a blurring of the ... capacity for or commitment to certain sorts of treatment. Waiting lists veil the discrepancies which exist between what is offered and what can be done. To be on a waiting list is to be betwixt and between; to be accepted as a suitable case for treatment, even if the prospect of that treatment being delivered may be distant or absent.'[10] In this sense, waiting lists may therefore be viewed as akin to forms of implicit rationing,[11] the meaning and significance of which term will be explored below.

Other mechanisms which may be pursued in an effort to balance demand and supply in healthcare are less visible and are correspondingly less likely to be recognised by the wider public as amounting to strategies for rationing. Thus, there is rationing by deterrence, in which obstacles are placed in the path of those seeking to access healthcare services, thereby increasing the costs of entry into the system: examples might include unhelpful administrative staff (such as doctors' receptionists) or failure to provide information. Rationing by deflection consists of channelling prospective patients to alternative services, programmes or organisations – an instructive illustration of this strategy is afforded by the

---

[8] Above Chapter 2, n. 138 and accompanying text.

[9] See D. Mechanic, 'Dilemmas in Rationing Health Care Services: the Case for Implicit Rationing' (1995) 310 *British Medical Journal*, 1655 at 1658.

[10] S. Frankel and R. West, 'What Is to Be Done?' in S. Frankel and R. West, *Rationing and Rationality in the National Health Service: the Persistence of Waiting Lists* (Basingstoke: Macmillan, 1993) at 125.

[11] See L. Locock, 'The Changing Nature of Rationing in the National Health Service' (2000) 78 *Public Administration*, 90 at 93.

Auton case (discussed at length in Chapter 7),[12] in which the refusal of the government of British Columbia to offer funding for Lovaas Applied Behavioural Therapy for autistic children between the ages of three and six was justified, in part, by the transfer of responsibility for matters relating to child and youth mental health from the Ministry of Health to the Ministry of Children and Families. A further option is rationing by dilution, which consists of a reduction in the quantity and/or quality of services provided, albeit that no one individual or treatment is excluded from coverage. This occurs, for example, when medical professionals spend less time with patients and when less intensive care is offered. An obvious example of this phenomenon is a reduction in the numbers of available hospital beds, with the consequence that lengths of stay in hospital are necessarily shortened and it becomes more difficult to gain initial admission.[13] Similarly, a concentration of specialist treatment facilities in a particular geographical location, requiring patients to travel long distances for care, amounts to a strategy of dilution (coupled with one of deterrence), even though the justification may be advanced that such a focus will enhance the quality of services which are available.[14] Finally, there is rationing by termination, which refers simply to the premature withdrawal of treatment, for example by discharge from hospital earlier than might be thought to be medically advisable.

While the above represents a useful taxonomy to assist in building understanding of rationing strategies, it should be noted that rationing in any given healthcare episode is likely to involve a complex interaction between, and combination of, these techniques, and that these will be deployed at various points by a number of health professionals. This is vividly captured in the following passage:

Everyone in any healthcare system is (to exaggerate only a little) taking decisions about how best to prioritise resources all the time. The process starts from the moment I enter my general practitioner's surgery. The receptionist takes a decision, when I ask for an appointment, about how urgent my case is (rationing by deterrence or delay). When I eventually get to see my doctor, he or she will decide whether to give me five minutes or ten (dilution). Next will come a decision about whether or not to refer me to hospital (selection/denial), unless I short-circuit the whole process by having a heart attack. Then I may or may not be put on a waiting list (selection/denial), and eventually – if I survive and depending on the priority

---

[12] *Auton* v. *British Columbia (Attorney General)* [2004] 3 SCR 657.

[13] See Canadian Nurses Association, *Ethics in Practice* (C.N.A.: Ottawa, 2000 (September)) at 2.

[14] For an example, see 'Cancer patient, 87, forced to travel 500 miles a week', *The Guardian*, 4 April 2006. The UK Government's policy on the provision of specialised cancer centres is set out in Department of Health, *The NHS Cancer Plan: a Plan for Investment, a Plan for Reform* (London: Department of Health, 2000).

rating I get (delay) – I may get treated in hospital. While I am there, doctors will take decisions about just what resources to throw at me (dilution), and just how many tests and investigations to order. Finally, there will be decisions about how long to keep me in hospital (termination).[15]

Who should ration?

It is apparent, therefore, that even the 'micro' level of resource allocation, entailing prioritisation of access to treatment between different patients and judgments as to the intensity of treatment which should be offered, will engage a variety of individuals in the decision-making process. If the scope of analysis is expanded to include consideration of the 'meso' and 'macro' levels of rationing, the range of stakeholders who may be involved expands still further. Is it possible to establish which of these groups ought to have *primary* responsibility for making rationing decisions?

New has identified six candidates for this role: namely, the public, health-care professionals, managers, central and/or local government, 'experts' (such as health economists and epidemiologists) and/or 'groups with moral author-ity' (such as the clergy), and the judiciary.[16] Of these, healthcare professionals are consistently regarded as the preferred agents to undertake rationing.[17] (Interestingly, this is the case not only amongst members of the public surveyed, but also within the medical profession itself,[18] suggesting that the latter is willing to accept the burden of rationing healthcare, notwithstanding the distress which such decisions may cause and the recent impact of man-agerialist techniques upon the provision of healthcare.)[19] By contrast, govern-ment is viewed as the least acceptable decision-maker on rationing questions, with managers and experts also gaining minimal levels of support.[20]

---

[15] R. Klein, 'Dimensions of Rationing: Who Should Do What?' (1993) 307 *British Medical Journal*, 309 at 309.

[16] B. New, 'The Rationing Agenda in the NHS' in B. New (ed.), *Rationing – Talk and Action in Health Care* (London: BMJ, 1997) at 19–20.

[17] See A. Bowling, 'Health Care Rationing: the Public's Debate' (1996) 312 *British Medical Journal*, 670 at 673; J. Kneeshaw, 'What does the Public think about Rationing? A review of the evidence', in New (ed.), *ibid.* at 72; C. Bryson and B. New, 'Health Care Rationing: A Cut Too Far?' in R. Jowell, J. Curtice, A. Park *et al.*, *British Social Attitudes: the Seventeenth Report* (London: Sage, 2000) at 42.

[18] See C. Heginbotham, 'Health Care Priority-Setting: a Survey of Doctors, Managers and the General Public', in R. Smith (ed.), *Rationing in Action* (London: BMJ, 1993) at 147; D. Hunter, *Desperately Seeking Solutions* (London: Longman, 1997) at 27.

[19] For discussion of these issues, see below.

[20] See Kneeshaw, 'What Does the Public Think About Rationing?' at 72; Bryson and New 'Health Care Rationing: a Cut Too Far?' at 42. There appears to have been no survey which examines the attitude of the public towards the involvement of the judiciary in rationing questions, but for views expressed by academic commentators, the media and judges themselves, see Chapter 5 below.

An interesting question arises in this context as to the appropriate role for the public in rationing decisions. Opinion surveys suggest that support for greater public involvement is, at best, mixed. One study showed that 88% of the British public favoured the use of surveys of public opinion in the planning of health services, but also that only 17% of those questioned thought that the public should be responsible for rationing.[21] Another survey reported that only 7% and 35% of respondents believed that the public should have respectively 'all or most of the say' and 'some of the say' on health rationing decisions, with 44% believing that the public should have 'none of the say'.[22] Comparable figures have been obtained from research conducted in Canada.[23] These results are consistent with the view, advanced by Lomas, that the public are 'reluctant rationers', that is that 'the willingness and self-perceived ability of average citizens to contribute to resource allocation decisions is quite limited.'[24] Possible reasons for this attitude are examined further below.

How should the results summarised here be interpreted? While it is trite to observe that decisions upon the structure of, and allocation of responsibilities within, a health system should not be dictated by surveys of public opinion, it is submitted that these are nonetheless of significance. They would seem to indicate that the public prefers resource allocation decisions to be driven primarily by clinical considerations, rather than the political, financial or economic factors with which the other actors are likely to be principally concerned. Moreover, they may also suggest a preference for a flexible, discretionary form of decision-making which responds to individual clinical circumstances, as distinct from a centralised and predetermined framework of rules and principles to guide rationing decisions. There is, indeed, survey evidence to support such a conclusion.[25] Hence, in terms of the discussion which follows, an 'implicit' mode of rationing appears to possess greater legitimacy – due to the trust shown by the public in the medical profession's suitability for making distributive choices on clinical grounds – than an 'explicit'

---

[21] See Bowling, 'Health Care Rationing: the Public's Debate' at 673.

[22] See Bryson and New, 'Health Care Rationing: a Cut Too Far?' at 42.

[23] See J. Abelson, J. Lomas, J. Eyles et al., 'Does the Community Want Devolved Authority? Results of Deliberative Polling in Ontario' (1995) 153 Canadian Medical Association Journal, 403, reporting that two-thirds of citizens did not want to take responsibility for rationing.

[24] J. Lomas, 'Reluctant Rationers: Public Input into Health Care Priorities' (1997) 2 Journal of Health Services Research and Policy, 103 at 107.

[25] See Bryson and New, 'Health Care Rationing: a Cut Too Far?' at 43, reporting that 25% of those surveyed were of the opinion that 'there should be publicly available guidelines about who should receive priority for healthcare', as distinct from 60% who felt that 'medical experts should be allowed to make these sorts of decisions as they see best.'

approach in which politicians, experts and managers visibly prioritise treatment on a resource-driven basis on the basis of predetermined rules or guidelines. This conclusion has important implications for public policy, as will be discussed in Chapter 4.

Implicit and explicit rationing defined

It was noted above that certain techniques of rationing tend to be more publicly visible than others. The denial of a specific treatment or service which the patient has requested, or which has been recommended for them by a clinician, is likely to be more readily perceived as an instance of the deprivation of care which is beneficial and desired by the patient,[26] than is a rude and unhelpful attitude on the part of a receptionist in a doctor's surgery. Nevertheless, even those strategies which appear, at first glance, to be overtly concerned with bringing about an equalisation between the demand and supply of healthcare resources may be disguised. Thus, denial of a particular treatment may be presented to the patient as a matter of clinical judgment and will very probably be mediated by the principle of 'need'. Hence, a patient may ostensibly be refused medical treatment because their needs are not considered to be sufficiently urgent or because they cannot be said to 'need' a particular form of treatment in that they cannot benefit from it,[27] even though resource considerations may, in reality, be the primary motivation underpinning the decision. In other cases, the decision may be more clearly presented as an issue of the availability of resources. Thus, a body responsible for commissioning provision of health services for its local population may choose to exclude certain services from coverage on grounds of cost (and may publicise this fact in its purchasing plan), although even in such cases additional considerations, such as the lack of efficacy of the treatment, will frequently be advanced as justification for the decision.[28]

This brings us to the heart of a key debate within the health policy community,[29] which bears significant implications for the thesis pursued

---

[26] See Maynard's definition, above Chapter 2, n. 23 and accompanying text.

[27] On the Maynard definition, this form of denial does not constitute rationing, since the latter only refers to healthcare from which the patient may benefit.

[28] For an example, see the discussion of *R* v. *North West Lancashire Health Authority, ex parte A, D and G* [2000] 1 WLR 977 ('*A, D and G*'), in Chapter 6 below.

[29] Perhaps the most useful exposition of this debate is that provided by Hunter, *Desperately Seeking Solutions*. Other valuable contributions include D. Mechanic, *Future Issues in Health Care: Social Policy and the Rationing of Medical Services* (New York: Free Press, 1979), especially Chapter 8; R. Maxwell, *Rationing Health Care* (London: Churchill Livingstone), 1995; New (ed.), *Rationing – Talk and Action in Health Care*, especially Chapters 1 to 3; Mechanic, 'Dilemmas in Rationing Health Care Services'; A. Coulter

subsequently in this book. That is, once it is accepted that the rationing of healthcare resources is inevitable, should this task be carried out *implicitly* or *explicitly*? In order to comprehend the arguments which have been advanced in support of the opposing positions on this question, it is necessary first to offer a more precise explanation of these two terms.

Implicit rationing of healthcare resources has been defined by Coast as 'the unacknowledged limitation of care', that is, it occurs 'when care is limited and when neither decisions about which forms of care are provided or the bases for those decisions are clearly expressed'.[30] Locock offers a similar definition, arguing that 'in implicit rationing the reasoning involved is not clearly stated to anyone except (or possibly including) the person making the decisions, or active decision-making is avoided altogether.'[31] Implicit rationing, therefore, eschews the transparent deployment of rules or principles which define the basis upon which distribution takes place, with the consequence that those using healthcare services are unaware of the existence of rationing, or – perhaps more accurately – do not perceive that the decision is resource-based in nature.[32]

As Locock observes, implicit rationing is frequently taken to mean that which is carried out by clinicians.[33] This understanding reflects the fact that, in the implicit mode, the allocative character of the decision is generally camouflaged beneath clinical judgment – that is, doctors 'offer medical reasons to justify decisions which are in fact motivated by economic considerations or constraints'.[34] In turn, the clinician may be more or less conscious that the decision rests upon such factors. In a classic study of allocative decision-making in the NHS, Aaron and Schwartz argued that, in seeking medical justifications for decisions which are dictated by resource considerations, doctors 'internalised' resource limits and presented the decision as the optimal or routine one in the clinical circumstances of the patient's case.[35] Thus, a patient may be informed that there are no (further) effective treatments for his/her condition, or that a specific treatment carries undesirable side effects: the extent to which the clinician may be aware that the rationale

and C. Ham (eds.), *The Global Challenge of Health Care Rationing* (Buckingham: Open University Press, 2000); and C. Ham and A. Coulter, 'Explicit and Implicit Rationing: Taking Responsibility and Avoiding Blame for Health Care Choices' (2001) 6 *Journal of Health Services Research and Policy*, 163.

[30] J. Coast, 'The Rationing Debate: Rationing Within the NHS Should Be Explicit: The Case Against' (1997) 314 *British Medical Journal*, 1118 at 1118.

[31] Locock, 'The Changing Nature of Rationing' at 93.

[32] See E. Tragakes and M. Vienonen, *Key Issues in Rationing and Priority-setting for Health Care Services* (Copenhagen: WHO, 1998) at 4.

[33] See Locock, 'The Changing Nature of Rationing' at 93.

[34] V. Schmidt, 'Models of Health Care Rationing' (2004) 52 *Current Sociology*, 969 at 972.

[35] H. Aaron and B. Schwartz, *The Painful Prescription: Rationing Hospital Care* (Washington DC: Brookings Institution, 1984) at 100–102.

for the withholding of treatment relates to scarcity of resources is likely to vary between individuals. However, as Locock also notes, if implicit rationing centres upon the failure to provide accurate (i.e. resource-based) reasons for decisions which limit the availability of beneficial care, it need not be restricted to those which entail the exercise of clinical judgment.[36] Strategies of rationing by deterrence, such as the unhelpful receptionist, may therefore fall within this definition, as may the waiting list (which may be regarded as a managerial, rather than clinical tool). And while implicit rationing tends to take place primarily at the 'micro' level,[37] it is not implausible for decisions at the 'meso' or 'macro' levels to contain elements of camouflage which serve to obscure the financial dimension of the decision. Thus, a decision not to provide Herceptin may be explained as based upon the absence of regulatory approval.[38] Similarly, at a systemic level, the gradual erosion of NHS adult dental services may be regarded as an example of implicit rationing of this form of healthcare,[39] as new dental contracts which have been rejected by a number of dentists are justified by government as a means of modernising the system of payment for dental services, and guidelines which extend the interval between 'check-ups' are explained as a means to 'free up time that dentists can use to see a greater range of patients and improve access to NHS services'.[40]

Explicit forms of rationing, by contrast, render decisions as to the provision of care visible both to patients and to the wider public, and make transparent the fact that such decisions rest upon resource constraints. No attempt, therefore, is made to conceal the fact that an individual is being deprived of care from which (s)he could benefit. This mode of rationing entails 'trying to establish all the rules beforehand':[41] that is, formulating principles which may guide the distribution of resources with a view to making 'a clear attempt to distinguish who will receive what'.[42] It therefore focuses upon the development of normative and/or technical criteria to underpin allocative decision-making and the establishment of procedures and institutions through which such decisions can be made: these techniques will be analysed in greater depth below. Consequently, explicit rationing results in a shift of responsibility for allocative decision-making away from clinicians at the 'micro' level. As Locock states, 'the decisions are agreed and understood by a group of

---

[36] Locock, 'The Changing Nature of Rationing' at 93.
[37] See Tragakes and Vienonen, *Key Issues in Rationing* at 10.
[38] This was the position of Swindon NHS Trust in *Rogers*, as discussed in Chapter 6 below.
[39] See Locock, 'The Changing Nature of Rationing' at 93.
[40] Department of Health Press Release 2006/0138 (7 April 2006). See further 'Almost 1 m lose NHS dental care', *The Guardian*, 7 April 2006.
[41] Mechanic, 'Dilemmas in Rationing Health Care Services' at 1659.
[42] Locock, 'The Changing Nature of Rationing' at 93.

people, not just the individual clinician. (This does not necessarily include the patient or the public, however).'[43] Instead, decisions upon the distribution of scarce healthcare resources are increasingly likely to be taken at the 'meso' and 'macro' levels, for example by health authority managers or by government agencies or ministers, prompting one commentator to categorise explicit rationing as an 'administrative' mechanism.[44] However, it should be noted that, even when steps have been taken to make rationing of health resources explicit, clinicians may still play a significant role in distributive decision-making, for example through the application of criteria of exceptionality which permit clinical judgment as to the appropriateness and effectiveness of treatment in the particular circumstances of an individual case to override managerial or political guidelines on allocation.[45] It is therefore preferable to regard implicit and explicit forms of rationing as 'points on a continuum',[46] with the consequence that the strategies may be used in combination rather than constituting mutually exclusive alternatives.[47]

Why ration implicitly?

Those who favour the implicit rationing of healthcare resources seek to marshal a number of related arguments in favour of their position.

First, and most obvious, is the 'deprivation disutility' suffered by the individual who is denied access to care. This is associated with 'knowing that something could have been done, but was not'.[48] It may be argued that a patient who is informed that her personal prospects are poor or that no suitable donor can be found, is treated more humanely than one who is told that alternative treatments are available, but that these are too expensive. That is, the former patient is spared the anguish, resentment and despair which the latter patient is likely to experience. Mechanisms of implicit rationing therefore function as 'merciful lies',[49] and in circumstances of scarcity which necessitate the making of 'tragic choices',[50] they 'serve to conceal these choices. They make invisible their contingency by couching them in the language of necessity. The defenders of this policy argue that it permits affected patients to make peace with their fate.'[51]

---

[43] *Ibid.*   [44] Mechanic, *Future Issues in Health Care* at 96.
[45] See the discussions of *A, D and G* and *Rogers*, Chapter 6 below.
[46] Locock, 'The Changing Nature of Rationing' at 93.
[47] See Ham and Coulter, 'Explicit and Implicit Rationing' at 166.
[48] Coast, 'The Rationing Debate' at 1119.
[49] Schmidt, 'Models of Health Care Rationing' at 976.
[50] See the discussion in Chapter 4 below.
[51] Schmidt, 'Models of Health Care Rationing' at 976.

Moreover, as noted by Coast, this form of disutility may extend beyond those directly affected, to embrace not only immediate family and friends but also the public in general, especially in instances where the rationing decision attracts extensive media coverage, as in the cases of 'Child B' and Ann-Marie Rogers which are discussed in Chapter 6.

Secondly, implicit forms of rationing may be preferable to those which are explicit because they minimise the 'denial disutility' experienced by those who are involved in making the decision to restrict access to beneficial care. At the 'micro' level, this has traditionally been the responsibility of medical professionals, but in such cases, the denial disutility is 'minimised by the doctor's ability to justify, both personally and to the patient, the absence of treatment on medical grounds'.[52] The 'internalisation' of resource constraints therefore in effect serves to disguise the nature of the decision not only to the patient, but also to the clinician, as captured in Aaron and Schwartz's observation that 'doctors gradually redefine standards of care so that they can escape the constant recognition that financial limits compel them to do less than their best.'[53] Conversely, if clinicians were obliged to explain that a denial or delay of care was motivated by financial considerations, any utility derived from greater honesty is likely to be more than offset by anguish and despair at the inability to carry out the fundamental role of the doctor – reflected in the Hippocratic Oath – to act for the benefit of patients according to his/her judgment,[54] given that (s)he will be aware that less than optimal treatment is being provided for reasons of resource constraint.

Again, denial disutility may extend beyond the medical professional who is directly responsible for decisions on treatment, to others who may become involved in undertaking allocative choices in a system where rationing is explicit. Especially pertinent here is the impact upon the public, from whom some input in establishing the rules or principles to guide allocative decisions will frequently be sought by governments seeking to implement explicit forms of rationing.[55] As noted above,[56]

---

[52] Coast, 'The Rationing Debate' at 1118.

[53] Aaron and Schwartz, *The Painful Prescription* at 101.

[54] See A. Campbell, G. Gillett and G. Jones, *Medical Ethics* (Melbourne: Oxford University Press, 4th edn, 2005) at 277.

[55] For a discussion of the participatory strategies implemented in various health systems, see Ham and Coulter, 'Explicit and Implicit Rationing' at 165. There is likely to be a lesser role for public participation in systems where explicit rationing is undertaken primarily upon the basis of technical criteria (such as clinical and cost-effectiveness), but even in such cases the public may contribute to the 'social value' dimension of the technocratic judgment. For discussion, see Chapter 4, nn. 198–9 and accompanying text.

[56] See Lomas, 'Reluctant Rationers'.

members of the public are 'reluctant rationers'. This is in part because they find it difficult to comprehend the technical language of epidemiology and health economics in which issues of healthcare rationing tend to be expressed, but also because they too are likely to suffer anguish, dissatisfaction and resentment at being held (at least partially) responsible for denial of treatment, especially in instances where visible victims are affected and accountability cannot be evaded.[57]

These arguments focus upon the effect which explicit forms of rationing may have upon individuals, whether those seeking treatment, or those involved in decisions to withhold it. However, another powerful rationale for preferring implicit to explicit rationing focuses upon the *systemic* consequences of adopting the latter mode. Here, the case is put most strongly by Mechanic:

An important weakness of explicit rationing is that it inevitably gives preference to some who care less about treatment than others who are excluded. Thus it results in many disaffected people who are a continuing force challenging either the rules of allocation or decisions to withhold greater investment in the area. Implicit rationing, despite its imperfections, is more conducive to stable social relations and a lower level of conflict. . .Explicit rationing is also likely to confront government and the political process with unrelenting agitation for budget increases. . .explicit rationing is inevitably unstable because of the ability of small groups to evoke public sympathy and support in contesting government decision-making. Those who care deeply but are denied access will inevitably challenge the explicit judgment through the mass media and other ways, undermining support for purchasing decisions and pushing the health system towards more flexible implicit approaches.[58]

The claim that implicit rationing is more socially stable than explicit approaches clearly connects to the 'disutility' arguments canvassed above. That is, the anguish and resentment which is likely to be felt by patients, doctors and the public in circumstances where decisions are explicitly based upon resource considerations may well translate into broader, systemic challenges articulated via the media, political and legal arenas. This follows from the character of healthcare rationing as 'inescapably a political process',[59] in which decisions on resource allocation are susceptible to contestation, interest group lobbying, strategising and manipulation. In short, the greater visibility of decision-making inherent in explicit rationing is likely to engender conflict which is

---

[57] See D. Callahan, 'Ethics and Priority Setting in Oregon' (1991) 10 *Health Affairs*, 78 at 85.
[58] Mechanic, 'Dilemmas in Rationing Health Care Services' at 1658.
[59] Klein, 'Puzzling Out Priorities' at 959.

unlikely to occur if the nature of those decisions is disguised, for example behind a veil of clinical judgment.

A further argument posited in favour of implicit rationing is one which will resonate particularly with public lawyers familiar with the arguments as to the relative virtues of rule-based and discretionary decision-making. Explicit mechanisms of rationing, based as they are upon published rules, principles or guidelines, are criticised for their failure to respond to the 'uncertainty inherent in clinical practice',[60] and are therefore 'likely to fall short relative to the complexity of circumstances surrounding serious illness and comorbidities or to be so complex and detailed that they are impracticable'.[61] Similarly, it is argued that they fail to take account of the preferences, tastes and demands of the patient – such as the determination to overcome illness – which might be thought relevant to the resource allocation decision.[62] By contrast, mechanisms of implicit rationing are more responsive to the individual clinical and personal circumstances of each patient's case, as this mode of allocation vests discretion ('judgment') in the clinician, rather than being based upon predetermined criteria.

Last, but certainly not least, proponents of implicit rationing contend that it is, in practice, impossible to establish rules, principles or technical criteria which might guide explicit rationing decisions and which will achieve widespread social acceptability. Thus, Klein argues that 'it is positively undesirable (as well as foolish) to search for a set of principles or techniques that will make our decisions for us'.[63] This view, which rests upon the ethically plural nature of society, coupled with an awareness that decisions on allocation of resources for healthcare necessarily raise social and moral issues which cannot be resolved by the application of technical expertise, will be examined in greater depth in the following chapter, as it is fundamental to the 'legitimacy problem' which is said to attend explicit processes of rationing healthcare.

Why ration explicitly?

In view of the significant deficiencies of explicit rationing which have been identified here, can any case be made for decision-making in which the

---

[60] M. McKee and A. Clarke, 'Guidelines, Enthusiasms, Uncertainty and the Limits to Purchasing' (1995) 310 *British Medical Journal*, 101 at 101.

[61] Mechanic, 'Dilemmas in Rationing Health Care Services' at 1657.

[62] See *ibid.* at 1658. It may be countered that consideration of such factors is ethically questionable, shading into allocation according to desert.

[63] Klein, 'Dimensions of Rationing' at 310.

resource-based rationale for withholding of treatment is visibly communicated to patient, physician and public?

From the perspective of those whose treatment is being denied or delayed, the claim that an explanation which conceals the genuine, financial reasons for the rationing decision respects the humanity of the patient can be countered by other arguments from individual autonomy. Specifically, patients may be said to have a right to be told the truth – even if this is distressing – because 'a person's freedom to make informed choices should be respected. As a general rule, by explaining the truth about diagnosis, prognosis and treatment options, we generate the basis for that freedom and expect patients to make appropriate decisions about their treatment.'[64] Possession of such information will therefore enable one to take steps to plan one's life, in accordance with principles of liberal individualism. As Schmidt observes:

precisely because they do not know about the rationing which takes place (or where it is most prevalent and which categories of patients it affects most), people are kept from taking other possible precautions. Were one (made) aware of the often rather idiosyncratic (if not to say, arbitrary) rationing decisions which doctors daily make without admitting them, then one might consider purchasing additional coverage on the private insurance market. But one cannot make a rational choice about the appropriate amount of additional coverage if one does not know what is included in the basic package, what one is and is not entitled to in the public sector. In effect this amounts to depriving people of life chances. They may virtually die although they could have lived had they been properly informed about their condition and the extra payment it requires for treating it with state of the art medical procedures.[65]

Viewed in this light, the 'merciful lies' rationale for implicit rationing smacks of unacceptable paternalism,[66] premised on the view that the public is unable to understand and cope with the difficult choices inherent in healthcare rationing and that it is therefore better to pretend that these do not exist at all. Furthermore, the contention that anguish, resentment and despair is diminished by concealing the true nature of a rationing decision beneath a clinical cloak holds true only as long as the resource-based rationale remains hidden from public view. The disutility generated by the feelings of betrayal which are experienced if and when patients (and the wider public) become aware that they have been misled

---

[64] M. Gold, 'Is Honesty Always the Best Policy? Ethical Aspects of Truth Telling' (2004) 34 *Internal Medicine Journal*, 578 at 578.

[65] Schmidt, 'Models of Health Care Rationing' at 977–8.

[66] See L. Doyal, 'The Rationing Debate: Rationing Within the NHS Should Be Explicit: The Case For' (1997) 314 *British Medical Journal* 1114 at 1118; Hunter, *Desperately Seeking Solutions* at 135.

as to the nature of decisions to withhold treatment may well exceed the disutility arising from the distress of telling the truth about rationing.[67] In such circumstances, implicit rationing is unlikely to be the most socially stable option, contrary to the views of commentators such as Mechanic.

The claim that medical professionals will be more comfortable with implicit forms of rationing because these minimise the distress and anguish which is caused by communicating the truth about scarcity of resources to patients may also be called into question. Here too, there may be greater disutility associated with dishonesty than with revealing the truth that resources are finite: this is especially the case the longer that the pretence continues. As Doyal notes, 'sustaining deception over time can itself be distressing, especially if patients begin to ask more direct questions about why they are not receiving care which they have heard is available to others.'[68]

Moreover, from a systemic perspective, it has been argued that the medical community is 'becoming increasingly restive about having to carry responsibility for scarcities beyond its control and which it would much rather ameliorate through more resources devoted to healthcare'.[69] Shifting attitudes are evident here. Doctors may be said to have 'colluded' in a system of implicit rationing as a quid pro quo for retention of autonomy from over-rigid state regulation; however, once that autonomy began to be eroded as a concomitant of the growing influence of managerialism and the marketplace, they became increasingly reluctant to accept responsibility for decisions which might be seen to rest more properly with accountable politicians. On this analysis, 'instead of being respected professionals who have been granted important freedoms and discretionary powers, doctors feel dumped on and the 'fall-guys' (and gals) required to enact the government's dirty business'.[70]

Relatedly, the restrictions on clinical freedom and shifts in responsibility toward political or administrative mechanisms which characterise explicit rationing may reflect concerns as to the legitimate moral authority of medical professionals to undertake rationing decisions. This is the case notwithstanding the high levels of public support which exist for doctors to play the primary role as agents for the rationing of healthcare resources.[71] As Schmidt observes, 'rationing is not about the proper application

---

[67] See Doyal, *ibid.* at 1117; Schmidt, 'Models of Health Care Rationing' at 977.
[68] *Ibid.*
[69] Schmidt, 'Models of Health Care Rationing' at 977. See further Klein, Day and Redmayne, *Managing Scarcity* at 121.
[70] Hunter, *Desperately Seeking Solutions* at 56.
[71] See above n. 17 and accompanying text.

of medical knowledge but rather the distribution of scarce societal resources, and for this task physicians possess neither any special expertise nor prerogative.'[72] That is, the inherently political nature of the choices which are involved – most obviously at the 'macro' and 'meso' levels, but also where judgments are made on withholding or delaying treatment for a particular patient for reasons of finite resources – necessitates that the locus of accountability should lie elsewhere, for:

there is nothing in medicine that tells one who ought to receive better or worse forms of treatment *if* not all can be treated equally well. When such questions arise, they must be dealt with in their *own* terms, in terms of public policy and of ethical rightness. They concern competing interests and conflicting values, and hence must be taken out of the doctors' office and into the public arena where they truly belong.[73]

This leads to a much broader argument in favour of explicit rationing mechanisms, which will resonate powerfully with public lawyers and which is fundamental to the theme of this book.[74] Here, the emphasis is upon the contribution which transparency can make to good administrative decision-making and the realisation of democratic principles within society. This occurs in a number of ways.

First, explicitness 'satisfies the requirement that, in a democratic society, all decisions must be capable of passing the test of public scrutiny'.[75] In particular, accountability for the stewardship of resources within a publicly funded system will be illusory in the absence of information as to the true nature of the decisions taken. If the fact of scarcity is concealed, the public will not be in a position to challenge the choices which have been made or to demand explanation and justification for them. The significance of this has been stressed by Longley:

The central prerequisite for genuine accountability is clearly openness, a transparency which needs to embrace all decision-making from policy setting, through implementation to monitoring. A commitment to openness is of prime importance in order to counteract any tendency to control or distort information which might in turn prevent issues being the subject of proper debate and reduce capacity for reasoned choices to be made about priorities and resource distribution ... The same commitment also implies an obligation on the part of decision-makers to give explanations and justifications for their activities. The articulation of reasons for action or inaction is beneficial to accountability in several ways. It not only assists the development of standards and principles, but encourages more

---

[72] Schmidt, 'Models of Health Care Rationing' at 977.
[73] *Ibid.* Emphasis in original.
[74] See especially the discussion of the relevance of theories of deliberative democracy to rationing, below Chapter 4.
[75] Klein, Day and Redmayne, *Managing Scarcity* at 112.

care and deliberation on the purposes of action by decision-makers and also provides a basis for criticism and facilitates challenge to decisions which appear arbitrary.[76]

Secondly, as this passage also makes clear, explicitness will contribute to consistency of decision-making. Decision-makers who are placed under an explanatory obligation must ensure that the choices which are made can be justified by reference to past practice, as well as to the predetermined rules, principles and/or technical criteria which form the basis of explicit mechanisms of rationing. This provides the counterbalance to the argument from clinical discretion advanced above. Implicit forms of rationing have been criticised for a tendency to give rise to incoherent, inefficient, idiosyncratic, and even arbitrary decisions as to who receives treatment and who does not.[77] Explicit mechanisms should minimise this prospect, not least because the visible nature of any persisting divergences (such as geographical variations in access to particular forms of care) will generate public and political pressure for uniformity,[78] thus enabling a progression towards equity in access to efficient healthcare.

Furthermore, it may be seen as especially important to ensure accountability for the rationing of healthcare resources because of the propensity for shifting responsibility and avoiding blame in this context. Decisions to limit access to medical treatments and services are inevitably unpopular, and political leaders therefore 'seek to avoid blame either by ducking tough choices or by devolving responsibility to others'.[79] For this reason, implicit modes of rationing are often favoured by politicians. By contrast, transparency as to the existence of rationing and the ethical and scientific criteria upon which allocative choices are based reduces the opportunity for diffusion and avoidance of blame, enabling the public to hold those who are charged with making such choices properly to account through political, media and/or legal mechanisms. Additionally, as suggested by Longley and as will be analysed in greater depth in the next chapter, explicitness provides the precondition for a genuine debate upon the rationing of healthcare within civil and political society, which is

[76] D. Longley, *Public Law and Health Service Accountability* (Buckingham: Open University Press, 1993) at 7–8. See further New, *Rationing – Talk and Action in Health Care* at 22; Doyal, 'The Rationing Debate' at 1117.

[77] See Schmidt, 'Models of Health Care Rationing' at 979; Locock, 'The Changing Nature of Rationing' at 103; A. Maynard, 'Rationing Health Care' (1996) 313 *British Medical Journal*, 1499.

[78] In this context, note the Blair Government's attempts to address the problem of 'postcode prescribing' in the NHS, for which see below.

[79] Ham and Coulter, 'Explicit and Implicit Rationing' at 165. See further above Chapter 2, n. 46 and accompanying text.

impossible to bring about as long as the fact of scarcity remains largely concealed from public view.

However, if opportunities for 'blame avoidance' provide a strategic reason for governments to preserve implicit forms of rationing, there are significantly more powerful counter-currents. Undoubtedly the major impetus for the adoption of explicit modes by policy-makers arises from the growing need, for the reasons identified in Chapter 2, to contain the spiralling costs of healthcare.[80] In this regard, implicit rationing is problematic because resource allocation decisions usually rest with individual clinicians, albeit within the broad parameters of the 'macro' and 'meso' levels of allocation. This affords negligible opportunity for governments to exercise systematic, centralised control over 'what were often perceived to be the idiosyncratic and often extravagant practices of doctors'.[81] Policy-makers seeking to restrict expenditure on healthcare will therefore look to establish explicit mechanisms, institutions and processes which serve to limit clinical autonomy and which minimise the capacity to make subjective allocative decisions. These approaches will now be outlined.

Strategies of explicit rationing

From the arguments presented above, it may be surmised that the debate on implicit versus explicit modes of rationing is finely balanced, which may explain the intensity of recent academic interest in rationing as the theoretical issues are gradually worked through.[82] Nonetheless, from the perspective of public policy, it seems clear that there has been a trend in the direction of explicitness, with governments adopting a 'more systematic approach to the determination of service coverage than has usually been the case in the past'.[83] As suggested, this is in large part driven by a need to respond to increasing pressures on expenditure within publicly funded healthcare. However, the impact of public expectations (which, as discussed in Chapter 2, are a key determinant of these rising costs of

---

[80] See *ibid.* at 163; Tragakes and Vienonen, *Key Issues in Rationing* at 4.

[81] Klein, Day and Redmayne, *Managing Scarcity* at 104.

[82] See K. Obermann and D. Buck, 'The Health Care Rationing Debate: More Clarity by Separating the Issues?' (2001) 2 *Health Economics in Prevention and Care*, 113 at 115, noting that the number of journal articles referencing rationing which are indexed in Medline increased more than tenfold between 1987 and 1997. The authors also detect a decline in academic interest from the late 1990s onward, which they attribute to the fact that 'the coverage of the theoretical issues involved in rationing has been fairly extensive and is coming to an end whilst empirical studies have not yet had time to report': *ibid.* at 114.

[83] Ham and Coulter, 'Explicit and Implicit Rationing' at 163.

healthcare) should not be overlooked. Notwithstanding the claim that implicit forms of rationing are politically and socially more stable than their explicit counterparts, it would appear that a more rights-conscious and consumerist public is beginning to become more conscious of, and unhappy with, the 'benign deceit' of implicit rationing.[84] In the words of Tragakes and Vienonen:

rapidly growing public expectations of what the healthcare system can or should provide increase public awareness of the system's deficiencies. In so doing, they also translate into dissatisfaction with the system's lack of transparency and implicit forms of rationing and priority-setting, which tend to become increasingly visible as users of health services come to perceive them for what they are.[85]

If this argument is accepted, a move towards explicit mechanisms might in fact be seen as an attempt by government to *minimise* public discontent and attendant electoral unpopularity.[86]

Endorsement by policy-makers of the general theoretical arguments in favour of a more explicit approach to the rationing of healthcare resources does not, of course, represent the end of the story. Explicitness has still to be operationalised: that is, the rules, principles and/or criteria upon which allocative decisions are to be based need to be established. Strategies to achieve this goal have diverged across health systems worldwide and it is beyond the scope of the present text to discuss these in depth.[87] However, certain significant features may be outlined.

A useful typology is offered by Ham, who identifies two main approaches to explicit rationing, rationing by exclusion[88] and rationing by guideline.[89] In the former case, the coverage of the health system is limited through specification of a 'menu' of core treatments and services which are to be made publicly available and, as a concomitant, stipulation of those which fall outside the scope of universal provision. Consequently, certain treatments will be unavailable to *all* patients. The most stark example of this strategy was the attempt made in Oregon to establish a

---

[84] A phrase coined in New and LeGrand, *Rationing in the NHS* at 24.

[85] Tragakes and Vienonen, *Key Issues in Rationing* at 4.

[86] See further below Chapter 4, for analysis in terms of 'legitimacy'.

[87] For discussion, see Hunter, *Desperately Seeking Solutions*, Chapter 5; C. Ham, 'Priority-Setting in Healthcare: Learning from International Experience' (1997) 42 *Health Policy*, 49; Tragakes and Vienonen, *Key Issues in Rationing*; Coulter and Ham (eds.), *The Global Challenge of Health Care Rationing*; C. Ham and G. Robert (eds.), *Reasonable Rationing* (Buckingham: Open University Press, 2003) and articles in (1999) 50 *Health Policy*, issues 1–2.

[88] 'Rationing by exclusion' could be viewed as synonymous with 'rationing by denial', but it is submitted that it is better used to refer to the decision, taken at the 'macro' or 'meso' levels, to withhold access to a *range* of treatments or services.

[89] C. Ham, 'Health Care Rationing' (1995) 310 *British Medical Journal*, 1483.

(publicly funded) Medicaid package by ranking different conditions and treatments in order of priority,[90] following which the state legislature was expected to determine how many of the condition/treatment 'pairs' it could afford to fund. Significant difficulties emerged during the course of this experiment. An exclusive reliance on the use of 'Quality-Adjusted Life Years' as a metric for determining priorities produced anomalous results,[91] with the consequence that an approach based upon cost-effectiveness had to be abandoned in favour of a more participatory strategy. This itself could not be regarded as representative given the high proportion of healthcare employees found to have attended public meetings.[92] Nonetheless, the Oregon model has provoked much comment, especially as regards the visibility of the process and the effort which was made to legitimate rationing decisions through the involvement of the public and the institutions of representative democracy.[93] However, the example has proved difficult to follow. For example, in both New Zealand and the Netherlands, committees were established to define a core of universally available services,[94] but in neither case was this goal achieved. In the former case, the 'restricted menu' approach was explicitly rejected as being inappropriate, it being acknowledged that even low-priority treatments and services might be appropriate and effective in particular clinical circumstances.[95] And in the Netherlands, a framework was drawn up to assist in decision-making by policy-makers as to which services should be covered, but a basic package of services was not defined. Rather, it was proposed that insurers should be free to make variations in the services offered, within the limits prescribed by law as to the nature, content and extent of rights to healthcare.[96]

---

[90] Oregon Health Services Commission, *The 1991 Prioritization of Health Services* (Salem: Oregon Health Services Commission, 1991, No. 8746).

[91] See further below Chapter 4, nn. 55–58 and accompanying text. For discussion of their use in the Oregon context, see P. Ubel, *Pricing Life: Why It's Time for Health Care Rationing* (Cambridge, Mass.: MIT Press, 2000) 1 at 8–9; F. Honigsbaum, J. Calltorp, C. Ham *et al.*, *Priority-Setting Processes for Healthcare* (Oxford: Radcliffe Medical Press, 1995); J. Blumstein, 'The Oregon Experiment: the Role of Cost-Benefit Analysis in the Allocation of Medicaid Funds' (1997) 45 *Social Science and Medicine*, 545.

[92] See J. Dixon and H. Welch, 'Priority-Setting: lessons from Oregon' (1991) 337 *Lancet*, 891 at 892.

[93] See Klein, Day and Redmayne, *Managing Scarcity* at 113–14; Hunter, *Desperately Seeking Solutions* at 103.

[94] National Advisory Committee on Core Health and Disability Services, *Third Report: Core Services for 1995/96* (Wellington: Core Services Committee, 1994); Ministry of Welfare, Health and Cultural Affairs, *Choices in Health Care. A Report by the Government Committee on Choices in Health Care, The Netherlands* (Rijswijk: Ministry of Welfare, Health and Cultural Affairs, 1992).

[95] See J. Cumming, 'Defining Core Services: New Zealand Experiences' (1997) 2 *Journal of Health Services Research and Policy*, 31 at 32.

[96] See Tragakes and Vienonen, *Key Issues in Rationing* at 27.

For their part, clinical guidelines have been defined as 'systematically developed statements *to assist practitioner and patient decisions* about appropriate healthcare for specific clinical circumstances'.[97] For example, 'they may offer concise instructions on which diagnostic or screening tests to order, how to provide medical or surgical services, how long patients should stay in hospital, or other details of clinical practice.'[98] They function primarily as mechanisms for quality improvement and assist in achieving consistency of care by identifying effective treatments and setting out 'best practice' on the management of particular conditions. Yet they may also act as rationing tools by indicating which treatments are ineffective and by describing the content, quality and terms of access for the management of a condition. In this manner, guidelines 'advise on the appropriate selection criteria for identifying those patients that can benefit most from an intervention, whether it is a diagnostic procedure or some form of treatment. The flip side of the coin is that they can also be used to exclude individual patients[99] for which only a small benefit can be expected.'[100] A key distinction from the first strategy, however, is that – as the definition offered by the Institute of Medicine makes apparent – guidelines function as recommendations: they are non-binding. As Eddy notes, the purpose of guidelines 'is to modify the behaviour of practitioners to steer their decisions toward actions that the policy-makers consider desirable'.[101] Consequently, it is open to a physician to depart from a guideline if (s)he considers it appropriate to do so on the basis of the individual clinical circumstances of the patient's case. Guidelines do not, therefore, operate as blanket exclusions: rather, they specify conditions of eligibility for access to care (which may, of course, be relatively restrictive), but ultimately leave the decision as to whether the patient meets the specified conditions to the medical professional.

The less prescriptive character of guidelines may make this strategy preferable to the 'limited menu' approach in the eyes of policy-makers.

---

[97] M. Field and K. Lohr (eds.), *Clinical Practice Guidelines: from Development to Use* (Institute of Medicine, Washington, DC: National Academy Press, 1992) at 2. Emphasis added.

[98] S. Woolf, R. Grol, A. Hutchinson *et al.*, 'Potential Benefits, Limitations and Harms of Clinical Guidelines' (1999) 318 *British Medical Journal*, 527 at 527.

[99] And, it might be added, particular treatments whose beneficial effect is minimal.

[100] O. Norheim, 'Clinical Guidelines: Healthcare Rationing and Accountability for Reasonableness', in J. Tingle and C. Foster (eds.), *Clinical Guidelines: Law, Policy and Practice* (London: Cavendish, 2002) at 162. See further J. Grimshaw and A. Hutchinson, 'Clinical Practice Guidelines – Do They Enhance Value for Money in Healthcare?' (1995) 51 *British Medical Bulletin*, 927.

[101] D. Eddy, 'Clinical Decision-making: from Theory to Practice. Guidelines for Policy Statements: the Explicit Approach' (1990) 263 *Journal of the American Medical Association*, 2239 at 2243.

Thus, in New Zealand, the abandonment of the attempt to define a core package of services reflected the political controversy to which such a strategy gave rise,[102] coupled with acknowledgement that patient heterogeneity made outright exclusion unfair and impracticable. It was replaced by an attempt to build consensus with the medical profession through the development of guidelines and clinical priority assessment criteria which might assist in decision-making on when services should receive public funding.[103] In effect, such an approach preserves key benefits of implicit rationing by maintaining some autonomy for clinicians and, for governments, enabling diffusion of blame for rationing choices as 'it leaves ultimate responsibility for deciding who should get access to healthcare resources to agencies such as sickness funds and health authorities at the meso level and to physicians at the micro level'.[104] However, rationing by guideline also renders decisions as to allocation of healthcare resources and the rationale for these decisions more transparent and publicly accessible, since they may be regarded as a 'tool to communicate with the public how much of a beneficial procedure can be provided for a certain amount of money'.[105] Moreover, guidelines enhance consistency of decision-making, and should function to contain costs by restraining idiosyncratic and outdated practices by individual clinicians.

Whichever of the two strategies outlined above is adopted, it will be necessary to make judgments as to the appropriate function and characteristics of publicly funded healthcare, so that the 'rules' can be established. For example, it may be decided to offer, or to recommend that clinicians provide, only those services and treatments which are of proven clinical effectiveness, or only those services and treatments which are of proven cost-effectiveness, or only those services and treatments which are relevant to, or appropriate within, a health system.[106] In practice, a combination of these approaches is likely.[107] Axiomatically, therefore, data on technical issues such as the clinical and cost-effectiveness of medical treatments will be required. Here, there is a key

---

[102] See Hunter, *Desperately Seeking Solutions* at 106.

[103] Edgar defines this as meaning 'under what circumstances services would be beneficial, who should receive the services first, and how long they should have to wait': Edgar, 'Rationing in Health Care – a New Zealand Perspective on an International Dilemma' (2001) 81 *Schweizerische Arztezeitung*, 190 at 191. See also C. Feek, W. McKean, L. Henneveld *et al.*, 'Experience with Rationing Health Care in New Zealand' (1999) 318 *British Medical Journal*, 1346.

[104] Ham and Coulter, 'Explicit and Implicit Rationing' at 165.

[105] Feek, McKean, Henneveld *et al.*, 'Experience with Rationing Health Care in New Zealand' at 1348.

[106] See New and LeGrand, *Rationing in the NHS* at 32.

[107] For example, see the framework produced in the Netherlands: Ministry of Welfare, Health and Cultural Affairs, *Choices in Health Care*.

role for the techniques of 'evidence-based medicine'. This is a 'scientific-bureaucratic' model of medical practice which 'asserts that valid and reliable knowledge is mainly to be obtained from the accumulation of research conducted by experts according to strict scientific criteria',[108] (particularly the systematic review of the results of randomised controlled trials). Health economics, which assesses all relevant costs, benefits, and outcomes related to a medical intervention, will also be crucial.[109] There may, accordingly, be a need to establish new institutions and processes with responsibility for gathering of the required information: thus, agencies may be created and charged with the task of appraisal of the evidence on the clinical and cost-effectiveness of medical treatments and services. Additionally, any framework for explicit rationing of healthcare resources should be informed by the social and ethical principles which are considered to underpin a particular health system and the allocative choices which must be made within it. In this regard, and notwithstanding the deficiencies which were outlined above,[110] there may be a place for participation by the public, notably in articulating the community's vision of a health system and the values which it holds in respect of the appropriate distribution of resources between competing uses.[111] It is therefore to be expected that mechanisms to enable such participation will be devised.

Explicit rationing in practice? The UK experience

An instructive illustration of the manner in which strategies of explicit rationing may evolve is provided by events in the NHS following the creation of the 'internal market' in healthcare in the early 1990s. A brief survey of these will accordingly be offered.

Prior to the enactment of the Health and Community Care Act 1990, which gave legislative effect to the Conservative Government's market-oriented reforms of the NHS, rationing of healthcare in the UK was predominantly implicit in nature.[112] As noted above, physicians within

---

[108] S. Harrison, 'New Labour, Modernisation and the Medical Labour Process' (2002) 31 *Journal of Social Policy*, 465, 469; see also D. Sackett, 'Evidence-Based Medicine: What It Is and What It Isn't' (1996) 312 *British Medical Journal*, 71.

[109] See J. Schwartz, G. Vanscoy and T. Lee, *Healthcare Economics: The New Tool for Clinical Decision Making* (Center for Continuing Education in Health Sciences: University of Pittsburgh, 1995).

[110] See above n. 24 and accompanying text.

[111] For discussion of participatory strategies in various health systems worldwide, see Coulter and Ham (eds.), *The Global Challenge of Health Care Rationing*.

[112] See New and LeGrand, *Rationing in the NHS* at 7; S. Harrison and G. Wistow, 'The Purchaser/Provider Split in English Health Care: Towards Explicit Rationing?' (1992)

the NHS tended to 'internalise' resource limitations and present decisions to withhold treatment as governed by clinical, rather than financial
considerations. Waiting lists were more publicly visible – and generated
some controversy – but, as argued previously, were not widely regarded as
a form of rationing.

The establishment of the 'internal market' was not ostensibly designed
to effect a shift from these implicit strategies to explicit forms of rationing.[113] Rather, its objective was to enhance 'supply side' efficiency, by
separating the roles of purchasers and providers of healthcare. Purchasers
(such as district health authorities and 'fundholding' general practitioners) were responsible for identification of healthcare needs and priorities within a defined population and for the consequent distribution of
resources: they have been described as acting as 'the citizen's agent in a
quasi-market';[114] while providers (such as hospitals, community health
services, ambulance services, etc.) would compete for 'contracts' with
purchasers for the provision of healthcare services.[115] However, the
identification of the health needs of the population and prioritisation
between these 'seem to represent a decisive step in the direction of explicit
rationing'.[116] In particular, the obligation imposed upon purchasers to
publish plans and to enter into contracts specifying which services and
treatments would be made available to a resident population rendered
significantly more visible to the public the fact that access to certain forms
of healthcare which might prove beneficial to particular individuals was
being denied.

In these circumstances, some attempts were made by purchasers to
ration by exclusion, that is, to specify a menu of available services. Studies
of health authority purchasing plans show that, in the early years of the
'internal market', a small number of health authorities stated explicitly
that specific forms of treatment – mainly those at the 'margins' of the
NHS, such as tattoo removal, reversal of sterilisation or vasectomy, and
breast augmentation – would not be made available.[117] However, as the
'marketplace' evolved, such strategies were modified in response to opposition both from the medical profession (which perceived a challenge to
its clinical autonomy and asserted the need to respond to the particular

---

Policy and Politics, 123 at 123; N. Freemantle, I. Watt and J. Mason, 'Developments in
the Purchasing Process in the NHS: towards an Explicit Politics of Rationing? (1993) 71
Public Administration, 535 at 536.

[113] See New and LeGrand, *ibid.* at 10.

[114] Harrison and Wistow, 'The Purchaser/Provider Split in English Health Care' at 124.

[115] For discussion of the precise legal nature of the 'NHS contract', see K. Barker, 'NHS
Contracts, Restitution and the Internal Market' (1993) 56 *Modern Law Review*, 832.

[116] Harrison and Wistow, 'The Purchaser/Provider Split in English Health Care' at 124.

[117] See Klein, Day and Redmayne, *Managing Scarcity* at 68–70.

circumstances of individual patients)[118] and from the wider public (which perceived a 'weakening of the NHS' commitment to a comprehensive service').[119] Instead, the focus shifted to negotiation with local clinicians of protocols and guidelines which would specify the conditions for eligibility for treatment. Hence, as Klein, Day and Redmayne observe, the criteria for access to treatment were 're-medicalized', reflecting a more traditional division of responsibility between clinicians and purchasers, albeit within a more explicit framework in which collective, rather than individual, judgments were made on effectiveness and appropriateness.[120]

Although the incoming Labour Government of 1997 maintained that it was 'abolishing' the 'internal market',[121] its reforms to the NHS preserved many of its key structural elements.[122] Thus, the Government committed itself to retaining the separation between the planning of hospital care and its provision,[123] albeit that the language of 'purchasing' was replaced by that of 'commissioning', and contracts were replaced by longer-term service agreements.[124] In such an environment, the explicit mode of resource allocation which had developed by the mid-1990s remained largely dominant, albeit that increased funding for the NHS in the early years of the Labour Government may have somewhat reduced the necessity for explicit rationing decisions.[125] However, two key objectives of the reform programme, directed at quality enhancement, had an impact upon the way in which rationing was carried out. First, the Government sought to minimise 'unacceptable variations in performance and practice' which it considered were adversely affecting public confidence in the NHS.[126] A prominent goal in this regard was to end the practice of 'postcode prescribing', in which the availability of specific treatments depended upon the geographical 'accident' of residence, with certain health authorities refusing to provide treatments which were available elsewhere, sometimes in neighbouring districts. Secondly, and consistently with developments in other fields of public policy,[127] the

---

[118] See *ibid.* at 71.   [119] New and LeGrand, *Rationing in the NHS* at 16.
[120] Klein, Day and Redmayne, *Managing Scarcity* at 71–2.
[121] See Department of Health, *The New NHS: Modern, Dependable* (London: HMSO, 1997, Cm 3807) at para. 2.9.
[122] See H. Davies, 'Understanding Organizational Culture in Reforming the National Health Service' (2002) 95 *Journal of the Royal Society of Medicine*, 140 at 140.
[123] See Department of Health, *The New NHS: Modern, Dependable* at para. 2.6.
[124] *Ibid.* at para. 9.14.   [125] See Locock, 'The Changing Nature of Rationing' at 106.
[126] Department of Health, *A First-Class Service: Quality in the New NHS* (London: HMSO, 1998) at para.1.6.
[127] See especially Cabinet Office, *Modernising Government*, (London: HMSO, 1999, Cm 4310), Chapter 2.

Government emphasised the need for allocative decisions in healthcare to be based upon evidence of effectiveness, with a view to eliminating those services which had been shown to be ineffective, thereby achieving savings and promoting consistent 'best practice' across the NHS.

The key mechanism to achieve these goals has been NICE, an agency operating independently of government, which was established in 1999. This body is responsible for the production of guidance to the NHS in England and Wales in two areas which have significant implications for resource allocation: appraisals of new and existing medical technologies, and clinical practice guidelines on the appropriate care and treatment of specific diseases and conditions.[128] The Institute evaluates evidence on clinical and cost-effectiveness and involves a variety of stakeholders in its work, with a view to achieving consistent clinical standards across the NHS and reaching national-level decisions on access to treatments, especially those which are newly-developed. It describes the legal status of its guidance as follows:

Once NICE guidance is published, health professionals are expected to take it fully into account when exercising their clinical judgment. However, NICE guidance does not override the individual responsibility of health professionals to make appropriate decisions according to the circumstances of the individual patient in consultation with the patient and/or their guardian/carer.

In particular, guidance that does not recommend a treatment or procedure, or that recommends its use only in defined circumstances, is not the same as a ban on that treatment or procedure being provided by the NHS. If, having considered the guidance, a health professional considers that the treatment or procedure would be the appropriate option in a given case, there is no legal bar on the professional recommending the treatment or on the NHS funding it.[129]

However, it is important to note that the recommendations which NICE issues on the use of medical technologies (but not its clinical practice guidelines) carry a mandatory funding requirement.[130] This means that

---

[128] See NICE, *A Guide to NICE* (London: NICE, 2005) at 6 for full description of its functions and its geographical coverage. Other agencies perform similar functions in respect of the NHS in Scotland, while the Northern Ireland Executive has a 'formalised relationship' with the Institute: see NICE, Press Release 2006/030 (28 June 2006).

[129] NICE, *Legal Context of NICE Guidance* (London: NICE, 2004) at 3. Note that the courts may regard NICE guidance as establishing the standard of care for the purposes of claims in medical negligence, with the consequence that departure from it may be acceptable but will require demonstrable justification relating to individual clinical circumstances. See *ibid.* at 4; I. Kennedy and A. Grubb, *Medical Law* (London: Butterworths, 3rd edn, 2000) at 125.

[130] See Department of Health, *Directions to Primary Care Trusts and NHS Trusts in England concerning Arrangements for the Funding of Technology Appraisal Guidance from the National Institute for Clinical Excellence* (1 July 2003) and Welsh Assembly, *Directions to Local Health Boards and NHS Trusts in Wales* (23 October 2003).

NICE's decisions will, in practice, frequently pre-empt local choices on priorities. Most controversially, where NICE refuses to recommend a treatment or proposes that its use be restricted to certain classes of patient, access will almost certainly be withheld as financially hard-pressed commissioners of healthcare cite the lack of evidence of clinical and cost-effectiveness as a justification for diverting limited resources elsewhere.

To an extent, therefore, the form of rationing which has emerged in the NHS in recent years may be described as a 'mixed model, . . . which places trust in clinical judgment to interpret priority criteria established explicitly at a national level'.[131] There remains a significant role for implicit mechanisms, notably in the context of the decisions which medical professionals take as to whether to apply NICE guidance (with its implications for the use of resources) to the particular clinical circumstances of the patient's case.[132] However, such decisions take place within an increasingly explicit overall framework. In this respect, the establishment of NICE represents an attempt to render more transparent – at a national level – the rationales for and process by which key allocative choices within the NHS are made, especially those which relate to the introduction of those new medical technologies which frequently carry the potential to save lives, but whose high development costs make them expensive. Moreover, it illustrates the current prevalence of evidence-based approaches to the resolution of allocative problems in healthcare and demonstrates the utility of guidelines as a rationing strategy. The latter point is perhaps especially pertinent in view of the fact that the single instance in which the Labour Government engaged in rationing by denial – the announcement, aptly described by Klein as 'perhaps the first explicit, national rationing decision in the history of the NHS',[133] that Viagra would not be made available on the NHS – proved to be highly controversial. It generated significant opposition both from clinical professionals who considered their autonomy to be prejudiced and from the drug manufacturer, which challenged the initial decision and its subsequent confirmation in 2001, in judicial review proceedings.[134]

---

[131] Locock, 'The Changing Nature of Rationing' at 108.

[132] See Ham and Coulter, 'Explicit and Implicit Rationing' at 167.

[133] R. Klein, 'Setting Priorities: What is Holding Us Back – Inadequate Information or Inadequate Institutions?' in Coulter and Ham (eds.), *The Global Challenge of Health Care Rationing* at 25.

[134] For discussion of these cases, see below, Chapter 6.

Conclusion

The developments outlined above, while particular to the NHS, are nonetheless broadly illustrative of global trends in health policy since the 1990s. Confronted by growing demands upon limited healthcare resources, and unwilling or unable to raise levels of general taxation to cope with such pressures, governments worldwide have sought to adopt strategies which function to limit the scope of coverage of health systems. This is manifested in a shift away from a reliance upon medical professionals to carry out resource allocation under a 'cloak' of clinical judgment, towards more explicit forms of rationing which enable more comprehensive centralised control to be exerted over health expenditure. In the NHS, this initially took the form of limiting the availability of certain treatments and services, although the rationale for such exclusions was not always readily apparent.[135] In other systems, such as New Zealand and the Netherlands, attempts were made to construct comprehensive, principled, rational frameworks for rationing of resources.

However, with the partial exception of Oregon,[136] implementation of such strategies has proved problematic, as the drawbacks of explicit rationing, notably its greater instability, the reduced scope for 'blame avoidance' and the difficulty in achieving consensus upon underlying substantive principles to guide allocation decisions, have become apparent. The consequence has been a 'partial retreat from explicitness',[137] reflected in the growing role for evidence-based guidelines produced through agencies such as NICE. These preserve a level of clinical autonomy as regards their implementation in the particular circumstances of the patient's case – a key characteristic of implicit forms of rationing – but also provide a systematic framework for decision-making, with visible justifications for restrictions upon access based upon criteria of clinical and cost-effectiveness. At the same time, some treatments or services continue to be explicitly excluded, often on a one-off basis, as in the case of Viagra on the NHS.

---

[135] See New and LeGrand, *Rationing in the NHS* at 16.

[136] It has been powerfully argued that the Oregon Health Plan did not, in practice, function as a cost-containment device, given that the scope of services offered actually *increased* and that the package was funded through the 'familiar' mechanisms of raising revenue through taxation and increasing reliance upon privately-funded managed care plans. On this analysis, 'systematic rationing simply has not arrived in Oregon': see L. Jacobs, T. Marmor and J. Oberlander, 'The Oregon Health Plan and the Political Paradox of Rationing; what advocates and critics have claimed and what Oregon did' (1999) 24 *Journal of Health Politics, Policy and Law*, 161 at 177.

[137] Ham and Coulter, 'Explicit and Implicit Rationing' at 168.

A useful summary of these trends is provided by Ham and Coulter, who have drawn attention to a 'new synthesis' in which 'in practice, rationing is likely to combine explicit and implicit decision-making and to result in the exclusion of services at the margins and the development of guidelines in the mainstream.'[138] These authors suggest that 'the recent interest in explicit rationing may be a temporary aberration in a much longer history of muddling through and evading responsibility. In other words, the political costs of explicitness may outweigh the benefits and this could result in a return to previous decision-making processes.'[139] However, it is submitted that the better view is captured in their observation, and that of Hunter, that recent events have resulted in a 'release of the rationing genie from the bottle'.[140] That is, now that the existence of healthcare rationing has been exposed to public view, as has been the effect of the strategies described here, there is no prospect of a wholesale return to the relative stability of the status quo ante of 'concealed' rationing choices, even on the assumption that the medical profession would be prepared to reassume the burden of primary responsibility of allocation of scarce resources.

While it would therefore be misleading to describe recent health policy as having ushered in an era of 'pure' explicit rationing, there is no doubt that allocation of resources in many health systems worldwide in the early twenty-first century is undertaken in a considerably more visible fashion than was previously the case. Although this development promises to yield significant benefits for governments in that it will significantly enhance their capability to keep a lid upon expenditure, it also carries significant 'political costs', as Ham and Coulter note. In particular, a health system characterised by explicit strategies of resource allocation may tend to suffer from repeated episodes of social and political instability. The next chapter seeks to identify the precise nature and causes of this problem in more detail and to analyse the proposals which have been made to address it.

---

[138] *Ibid.* at 166, 163.   [139] *Ibid.* at 168.

[140] *Ibid.*; Hunter, *Desperately Seeking Solutions* at 126 ('with the genie well and truly out of the bottle'). *Cf.* Harrison and Wistow, 'The Purchaser/Provider Split in English Health Care' at 124, arguing that 'a step [in the direction of explicit rationing] ... is probably irreversible'. See further the discussion in Chapter 4 below.

4   Rationing and the Problem of Legitimacy

The instability of explicit forms of rationing: tragic choices

In their well-known work on 'tragic choices', Guido Calabresi and Philip Bobbit provide a means by which we may better understand the instability which is generated by strategies of explicit rationing of the type outlined in the preceding chapter. While the authors of this text eschew simple distinctions between those choices which are 'tragic' and those which are merely 'difficult',[1] it is notable that they consider the provision of haemodialysis machines to represent the 'paradigmatic' example of the tragic choice,[2] and that the book makes frequent reference elsewhere to scarce medical resources. It therefore seems justifiable to regard the rationing of healthcare as a form of tragic choice, and it is certainly the case that works in this field make liberal use both of Calabresi and Bobbit's terminology and of their analysis.[3]

Calabresi and Bobbit are concerned with those scarce goods whose distribution 'entails great suffering or death'. It has been argued that their scope of enquiry may best be defined as 'life and death cases',[4] but as this statement makes apparent, it is more accurate to view the authors' focus as being upon those choices where no outcome is without significant human cost in terms of suffering, albeit that life itself may not necessarily

---

[1] G. Calabresi and P. Bobbit, *Tragic Choices: the Conflicts Society Confronts in the Allocation of Tragically Scarce Resources* (New York: W. W. Norton & Co, 1978) at 17. For criticism of this approach, see the review by B. Chapman (1979) 29 *University of Toronto Law Journal*, 182.

[2] *Ibid.* at 177.

[3] See e.g. B. Bloom, 'Rationing Health Care: Tragic Choices' (1986) 8 *Transactions and Studies of the College of Physicians of Philadelphia*, 27; D. Weigert, 'Tragic Choices: State Discretion over Organ Transplant Funding for Medicaid Recipients' (1994) 89 *Northwestern University Law Review*, 268; R. James and D. Longley, 'Judicial Review and Tragic Choices: *ex parte B*' [1995] *Public Law*, 367; C. Ham and S. Pickard, *Tragic Choices in Health Care: the case of Child B* (London: King's Fund, 1998); G. Rutecki and S. Kilner, 'Dialysis as a Resource Allocation Paradigm: Confronting Tragic Choices Once Again?' (1999) 12 *Seminars in Dialysis*, 43.

[4] B. Barry, 'Tragic Choices' (1984) 94 *Ethics*, 303 at 304.

be at stake. What is key, however, is not the subject-matter of the choice (thus, in addition to examples drawn from healthcare, Calabresi and Bobbit discuss, inter alia, conscription and the right to have children), but rather the fact that the choice in question gives rise to irreconcilable conflicts of values. This is explained as follows:

when attention is riveted on such distributions they arouse emotions of compassion, outrage and terror. It is then that conflicts are laid bare between on the one hand, those values by which society determined the beneficiaries of the distributions, and (with nature) the perimeters of scarcity, and on the other hand, those humanistic moral values which prize life and well-being. In such conflicts, at such junctures, societies confront the tragic choice. They must attempt to make allocations in ways that preserve the moral foundations of social collaboration. If this is successfully done, the tragic choice is transformed into an allocation which does not appear to implicate moral contradictions. Morally debasing outcomes are averted. But unless the values held in tension have changed, the illusion that denies their conflict gives way and the transformation will have only been a postponement. When emotions are again focused on the tragic choice, action will again be required. 'We have a prospect of insuperable moral difficulty, a nightmare of justice in which the assertion of any right involves a further wrong, in which fate is set against fate in an intolerable necessary sequence of violence'. Thus the detail of the pattern of tragic choices is movement. In them society confronts the grave and constant in human suffering. Action in the context of necessary scarcity brings ultimate values, the values by which a society defines itself, into conflict. We ask, 'What course without evils?' but we know that no true answer will give us comfort.[5]

Calabresi and Bobbit's thesis is therefore that it is in the context of 'particularly painful choices' that the values by which a society defines itself come into conflict.[6] In order to preserve the moral cohesiveness of society by minimising such conflict, it is necessary to devise a form of allocation for those scarce goods the distribution of which causes suffering. The book discusses four such mechanisms for allocation: the market, accountable political processes, lotteries and custom, and also considers 'modified' versions of the first two which purport to minimise inherent defects – these include decision-making through decentralised, unaccountable agencies and non-money markets (e.g. those in which payment is made by way of time rather than money).

It is crucial to the authors' argument that the adoption of any one of these methods is likely only to forestall conflict temporarily: the means of allocation which is selected is unlikely to satisfy all fundamental values (simply because they are, ultimately, irreconcilable) and 'emotions of

---

[5] Calabresi and Bobbit, *Tragic Choices* at 18–19.   [6] *Ibid.* at 17.

compassion, outrage and terror' will therefore resurface. At this point, the 'movement' which characterises tragic choices becomes apparent as 'society evades, confronts and remakes the tragic choice',[7] by adopting another mechanism of allocation which better meets the neglected moral value than the first method chosen. In turn, this method will be replaced in due course, as it will not satisfy all of the values which society holds to be important. The existence of a state of flux such as this might be thought to be uncomfortably volatile. Yet Calabresi and Bobbit argue that this 'cycle strategy'[8] in fact offers the best prospect of preserving 'the moral foundations of social collaboration' since it does not necessitate a once and for all rejection of a given fundamental value, but rather allows for all values to receive support, albeit on a sporadic basis:

we have come to think that a society may limit the destructive impact of tragic choices by choosing to mix approaches over time. Endangered values are reaffirmed. The ultimate cost to other values is not immediately borne ... Since the values endangered by any given approach vary, a society which wishes to reject none of them can, by moving, with desperate grace, from one approach to another, reaffirm the most threatened basic value and thereby seek to assure that its function as an underpinning of the society is not permanently lost.[9]

The authors acknowledge that this pattern of movement is less easily discernible in situations where 'the focus of attention has narrowed to the precise technological good at stake' – by which it would appear that they allude to the 'meso' level of allocative decision-making, at which it is determined which treatments and services are to be given precedence within an overall budget allocated towards a programme such as the provision of healthcare – than at a 'macro' level where choices are made between differing policy goals. However, even at this level, oscillation between different forms of distribution will occur 'as such attention changes its focus'. Thus, in the illustration given by the authors, the diversion of scarce resources towards the provision of iron lungs is likely to prove temporary as the values and concerns of society evolve, resulting in an (equally temporary) preference for funding cardiac surgery or bone marrow transplants.[10]

As this instance demonstrates, even though some of the mechanisms for allocation which are discussed in the book may be regarded as unsuitable for the purpose, there is much in Calabresi and Bobbit's thesis which is of pertinence to the rationing of healthcare resources. For example, they offer an important insight in the context of an account of the 'customary approach' to resource allocation, which is defined as 'an

---

[7] *Ibid.* at 19.   [8] *Ibid.* at 195.   [9] *Ibid.* at 196, 198.   [10] *Ibid.* at 195.

attitude which may be given effect by any of the other methods, or their combinations. The attitude consists of the avoidance of self-conscious choice: the method of choosing is not explicitly chosen and may not even be known by the mass of the people. The actual allocations evolve in the society without any explicit selection'.[11] Clearly, this description is apposite to the implicit forms of healthcare rationing described in the previous chapter, and in this regard it is interesting to note that the authors consider the customary approach to be 'precarious' in that:

Any loss of innocence not only destroys the value of the approach, but also suggests that we were kept innocent ... At this point a choice not to choose, a choice to remain as we are, becomes itself a clear decision and as such is subject to the same costs as chosen allocations. It was only our ignorance of the costly choices imbedded in the unchosen status quo that had materially reduced the price in ideals ... This is not to say that we should not have emerged from naïveté to sophistication. Whether the Tree of Knowledge is the Tree of Life depends on whether, now that we are aware of what we are doing, we can do sufficiently better to make up for the costs of clearly choosing. But whether we can or not, we cannot turn back: we now know that either way, we are choosing to take some people's lives. We have moved beyond the customary situation.[12]

This serves to reinforce the point made at the conclusion of the preceding chapter, that a shift from implicit towards explicit strategies of rationing is an irreversible step.

The primary value of the 'tragic choices' analysis for the argument presented in this book derives, however, from its capacity to explain the nature of the instability which tends to accompany explicit allocative decision-making. It was noted above that, in its explicit form, healthcare rationing becomes an area of acute conflict of a political (and, as will shortly be seen, legal) character: such an observation may, indeed, be regarded as somewhat self-evident given that politics is – at least on one definition – centrally concerned with the allocative questions of 'who gets what, when and how'.[13] However, Calabresi and Bobbit's account takes us a step further than this by pointing out that where a decision to allocate scarce resources carries significant human cost, more than 'mere' political disagreement is entailed. Rather, such choices expose conflicts between certain deeply held and seemingly incommensurable ethical positions which are the keystones of a society's moral architecture and which, if removed, render social collaboration unworkable. An allocative decision of the type outlined in *Tragic Choices* is, therefore, not simply open to contention on the grounds that it is based upon inadequate evidence or

---

[11] *Ibid.* at 44–45.   [12] *Ibid.* at 46–47.
[13] H. Lasswell, *Politics: Who Gets What, When and How* (New York: McGraw-Hill, 1936).

that it reflects a (possibly transient) governmental preference for providing assistance to a particular group of 'sufferers' at the expense of another – though it may indeed be contested on such grounds. Instead, it will be viewed, both by those who are directly affected by it and by others who share a similar ethical perspective, as *immoral*. It is therefore liable to generate especially profound unease and dissatisfaction. As will be seen presently, these sentiments may well manifest themselves in challenges to the decision-maker's moral authority, with significantly deleterious consequences for the latter's attainment of legitimacy.

Since a reversion to the status quo ante of implicit (or 'customary') allocative decision-making is impossible for the reasons previously outlined, the conflict which is engendered as tragic choices are made can only be managed, on the Calabresi and Bobbit thesis, by means of 'movement' from one allocative mechanism to another. Yet, while this approach provides continued reassurance that no moral values have been permanently excluded, it inevitably tends to exacerbate an already high level of systemic instability. Accordingly, it may be considered advantageous to investigate other strategies which might offer a more durable means of managing conflict. The process-based mechanisms which are discussed below may be seen as an attempt to achieve this goal.

Of the criticisms which have been expressed of Calabresi and Bobbit's work, perhaps the most straightforward is that the discussion of the process of decision-making is too abstract and that the fact of scarcity is too readily treated as a given.[14] At a more theoretical level, Barry questions the assumption which underlies the book, that situations exist in which any choice which is made is morally wrong, observing that 'as is well known, some philosophers hold that in any situation, however sticky, there is always a (relatively) best thing to do. There cannot be a situation in which all alternatives are wrong'.[15] In particular, he takes issue with the claim that society values human life in such a way that 'no outcome can be justified if it causes some to live and some to die because one value is that life has "infinite value"'.[16] For Barry, even if such values exist, they may not be immutable. Thus, he argues that 'it may be possible to convince them [i.e. 'people'] not to hold a value such as that of the infinite value of life, but to accept that trade-offs are unavoidable and should be faced rationally ... I see no reason for accepting our

---

[14] For a critique along such lines, see the review by C. Gwin (1978) 93 *Political Science Quarterly*, 506.
[15] Barry, 'Tragic Choices' at 306–7.
[16] *Ibid.* at 308. It should be recalled that Barry defines tragic choices only as those involving 'life or death' decisions: see above n.4 and accompanying text.

unreflective judgments as the last word. Surely it ought to be possible by thinking systematically about things to refine our ideas',[17] albeit that he acknowledges that institutional changes may be necessary to bring about such a state of affairs.

It is submitted that, in this regard, Barry offers a crucial corrective to the Calabresi and Bobbit thesis. As these authors explain, tragic choices generate instability because they reveal the existence of profound moral conflicts within society. Nevertheless, it is surely important that attempts should be made to discuss, defend and reflect upon the conflicting beliefs which are held in an effort to build a more stable and lasting societal consensus. In this respect, the assumption that moral preferences are fixed and must simply be 'managed' in their present form should be rejected. Of course, it may transpire that the moral values which exist within society are, ultimately, irreconcilable and that no such consensus can be achieved. However, if that is the case, the *process of reasoned reflection, presentation of evidence and argumentation* which has taken place may nonetheless assist in building stability, as participants in such a process develop an understanding of the conflicting moral standpoint and an appreciation of its basis in rationality, even if they remain unwilling to jettison their own beliefs. As will be seen subsequently in this chapter, this is precisely the approach which has been championed in recent theoretical work which seeks to address the problem of legitimacy to which explicit forms of rationing tend to give rise.

The 'special moral importance' of healthcare

'Tragic choices', including those relating to the allocation of scarce healthcare resources, may therefore be said to be possessed of a type of moral 'rawness': that is, they are particularly prone to laying bare the incommensurability of competing values of distributive justice which are widely held throughout society. In due course, these principles will warrant examination. However, before embarking upon such an analysis, a further issue needs to be addressed: namely, the reason for the morally painful nature of such decisions. That is, *why* does the rationing of healthcare tend to give rise to ethical conflict of the profundity claimed by Calabresi and Bobbitt?

An answer to this question can be derived from the work of Norman Daniels, who has argued that healthcare has 'special moral importance'. Daniels seeks to apply Rawls' concept of the 'fair equality of opportunity'

---

[17] *Ibid.* at 307–8.

to the healthcare context. In his earlier work, Rawls himself had not extended his theory of justice to health, seeking simplification by considering only those individuals who were 'normal, active and fully co-operating members of society over the course of a complete life'.[18] Health was not, therefore, considered to be one of the primary social goods (rights, liberties, opportunities, powers, income, wealth, and a sense of one's own worth), which are the 'things that every rational man is presumed to want' because of their value as means towards realising a particular plan of life irrespective of what this might turn out to be.[19] Rather, it was to be regarded (alongside 'goods' such as intelligence and imagination) as a 'natural' good, to which Rawls argued that his 'difference principle' – that distribution of goods should be carried out in a manner which is to the advantage of the least well-off in society so that inequalities in opportunity might be minimised – did not apply. Such a position could be justified on the basis that application of the difference principle in the context of health may necessitate distribution of excessive resources to those with extreme health needs, possibly to the detriment of society as a whole; and that measuring health may entail investigation of subjective utility values (such as quality of life) which cannot easily be compared in a pluralist society in which differing views are held about what constitutes a good life.[20] However, the consequence, as Daniels notes, is that 'in effect, *there is no distributive theory for healthcare because no one is sick!*'.[21]

While concurring with Rawls that *health* may not be an appropriate focal variable for assessing social justice, Daniels seeks to establish what is special about *healthcare*.[22] He rejects the notion that healthcare is of importance only because it reduces pain and suffering, and thus tends to increase utility, observing both that other goods which are not regarded as comparable in importance may also do this and that pursuit of life goals which are valuable to a particular individual (and which therefore give rise to happiness and satisfaction) may not necessarily be undermined by ill health or disability. He argues instead that the special importance of healthcare derives from its impact upon *opportunity*. Disease and disability operate to impair normal species functioning and, as a consequence,

---

[18] J. Rawls, 'Social Unity and the Primary Goods' in A. Sen and B. Williams (eds.), *Utilitarianism and Beyond* (Cambridge: Cambridge University Press, 1982) at 168.

[19] J. Rawls, *A Theory of Justice* (Oxford: Oxford University Press, revised edn, 1999) at 54.

[20] See K. Arrow, 'Some Ordinalist-Utilitarian Notes on Rawls' Theory of Justice' (1973) 20 *Journal of Philosophy*, 251 at 251, 254.

[21] N. Daniels, *Just Health Care* (Cambridge: Cambridge University Press, 1985) at 43. Emphasis in original.

[22] For an argument in favour of recognising the special moral importance of health, based upon the Aristotelean conception of 'human flourishing', see J. Ruger, 'Health and Social Justice' (2004) 364 *Lancet*, 1075.

reduce the 'range of opportunity open to the individual in which (s)he may construct his/her "plan of life" or "conception of the good"'.[23] The primary function of healthcare – which Daniels construes broadly to include public health measures in addition to forms of preventative, acute and chronic care for the individual[24] – is to correct such impairments and to restore the individual to normal functioning. Accordingly, those who wish to preserve opportunities to form, pursue and revise their life-plans and to participate as fully in the political, social and economic life of a society as they could have done had they not been ill or disabled, will seek to establish institutions which deliver healthcare. On such an analysis, the appropriate principle of distributive justice for the regulation of a healthcare system is the principle of fair equality of opportunity. This has implications for system design, in particular that there should be universal access to care (either through public funding or mixed public and private insurance schemes) and that healthcare should not be distributed according to ability to pay.[25]

Significantly, Daniels also notes that healthcare is not the only important good, and that other social institutions which affect opportunity should be weighed against those which deliver healthcare. This allows him to concede the need for 'reasonable resource constraints' and for 'judgments about which medical needs are more important than others'.[26] For Daniels, therefore, the equality of opportunity account does not directly posit a right to healthcare:

rather, the particular rights and entitlements of individuals to have certain needs met are specified only *indirectly*, as a result of the basic healthcare institutions acting in accord with the general principle governing opportunity. Deciding which needs are to be met and what resources are to be devoted to doing so requires careful moral judgement and a wealth of empirical knowledge about the effects of alternative allocations.[27]

The consequence of this is that 'priority-setting and rationing is thus a requirement of justice, since meeting healthcare needs should not and need not be a bottomless pit'.[28]

However, it is important to recognise that Daniels sets himself limited objectives. He seeks to delineate principles of justice to govern the design of basic healthcare institutions and to define what the moral function of a health system should be.[29] He therefore acknowledges that specific

---

[23] Daniels, *Just Health Care* at 27, 49.
[24] N. Daniels, 'Justice, Health and Healthcare' (2001) 1 *American Journal of Bioethics*, 2 at 2.
[25] See *ibid*. at 4.   [26] *Ibid*.   [27] *Just Health Care* at 53–4. Emphasis in original.
[28] Daniels, 'Justice, Health and Healthcare' at 4.
[29] See Daniels, *Just Health Care* at 2, 9, 41.

allocative decisions taken within the broad moral framework of fair equality of opportunity may draw upon other principles of justice, such as utilitarianism, which will be analysed in the next section.[30] To this extent, his theory of just healthcare does not offer precise guidance as to how to carry out a rationing choice in a manner which may publicly be regarded as fair, and does not attempt to resolve the conflict between differing ethical perspectives as to the appropriate basis for the allocation of healthcare resources. Nonetheless, these issues have received attention elsewhere in his work and the proposed means of addressing them will be examined in detail below.

As a number of commentators have argued, Daniels' thesis is not unproblematic. One difficulty lies in establishing the meaning of a deviation from normal species functioning. Woolfolk and Doris observe that a condition such as extreme shyness could be regarded as such a deviation, particularly as it might reduce the prospects of successful reproduction.[31] However, Daniels' adoption of a biomedical model of health and disease – which he considers, 'for the general run of cases', to draw a 'fairly sharp line between uses of healthcare services to prevent and treat diseases and uses which meet other social goals'[32] – leads him to deny that such a condition is within the proper ambit of healthcare institutions. It may plausibly be argued that the definition which is adopted is too narrow, centring as it does upon health as the absence of disease. Certainly, the World Health Organization has adopted a much more expansive approach, defining health as 'a state of complete physical, mental, and social wellbeing, and not merely the absence of disease or infirmity',[33] a description which Daniels perhaps too readily dismisses by stating that 'health is not happiness, and confusing the two over-medicalises social philosophy'.[34]

Another issue which arises out of Daniels' theory relates to its treatment of the elderly. If healthcare is special because of its impact upon equality of opportunity, is there justification in restricting access to services for those whose opportunities (for example, pursuit of a career as a brain surgeon) seem to lie in the past? That is, does this analysis lead to an endorsement of 'age rationing'? Daniels has attempted to deal with this issue by arguing that fair equality of opportunity should be measured relative to the age of the individual, thus permitting distribution of

---

[30] *Ibid.* at 4, 42. Note, however, that Daniels considers Rawlsian theory to be the most compatible with his account, and libertarianism the least: *ibid.* at 42.

[31] R. Woolfolk and J. Doris, 'Rationing Mental Health Care: Parity, Disparity and Justice' (2002) 16 *Bioethics*, 469 at 471–2.

[32] Daniels, *Just Health Care* at 30–31.

[33] Preamble to the Constitution of the World Health Organization.

[34] Daniels, *Just Health Care* at 29.

resources to those whose opportunities are more limited by disease and ill-health than their peers.[35] Nonetheless, he concedes that a model of prudent allocation of resources over a life span, which he regards as being fair, may render age rationing permissible.[36] Yet, as noted in Chapter 2, society tends to allocate a large proportion of its healthcare resources to the elderly, and it is not clear that rationing by age is supported by the public.[37] There is therefore a mismatch between these results and the theoretical position which is developed by Daniels.

Furthermore, critics have argued that there may be effects of healthcare other than that upon equality of opportunity which render it of special moral significance. This view is well expressed by Buchanan, who opines that 'even if one reason why healthcare is important is that it contributes significantly to attainment of the normal opportunity range, this is surely not the only reason, or in many cases not the most basic one. After all, healthcare often relieves suffering, prevents unwanted death, or enhances one's capacity for enjoying what everyone is able to do, even when it does not extend one's range of opportunities'.[38] Significantly, Daniels himself concedes that healthcare is 'non-homogenous' in function and that, in this respect, his 'account of what makes healthcare special is not intended to be exhaustive or exclusive'.[39]

The potency of the various critiques of Daniels' thesis suggest that work remains to be done upon specification of the *precise characteristics* of healthcare which endow it with special nature as a social good. However, from the perspective of the argument advanced in this book this is, in fact, of relatively little import. Rather, the value of Daniels' analysis lies in the implications to which it gives rise. If, as is widely accepted, healthcare may be regarded as possessing an elevated moral status of the sort which Daniels has identified, allocation of this good will tend to generate problems of distributive justice which are both of

[35] See N. Daniels, *Am I My Parent's Keeper? An Essay on Justice Between the Old and the Young* (New York: Oxford University Press, 1988), especially Chapters 3, 4.

[36] Daniels, 'Justice, Health and Healthcare' at 5.

[37] See C. Bryson and B. New, 'Health Care Rationing: a Cut Too Far?' in R. Jowell, J. Curtice, A. Park *et al.*, *British Social Attitudes: the Seventeenth Report* (London: Sage, 2000) at 27, 34; but *cf.* J. Kneeshaw, 'What Does the Public Think About Rationing? A Review of the Evidence' in B. New (ed.), *Rationing – Talk and Action in Health Care* (London: BMJ, 1997) at 69.

[38] A. Buchanan, 'The Right to a Decent Minimum of Health Care' (1984) 13 *Philosophy and Public Affairs*, 55 at 63. Other criticisms which Buchanan makes of Daniels' approach are rebutted in N. Daniels, 'Fair Equality of Opportunity and Decent Minimums: a Reply to Buchanan' (1985) 14 *Philosophy and Public Affairs*, 106.

[39] Daniels, *Just Health Care* at 49, 81–2.

profound societal significance and which are not susceptible to simple resolution.[40] In such circumstances, attempts to allocate resources may engender widespread social instability.

Conflicting principles of distributive justice?

Healthcare, then, appears to have special significance – which, at least arguably, derives from its impact upon equality of opportunity – with the consequence that measures which restrict its availability, although permissible on the basis that scarce resources may on occasion need to be devoted to the provision of other social goods, are likely to generate considerable moral unease. The 'tragic choices' thesis builds upon this account by stressing the apparent incommensurability of the moral positions which are exposed when such measures are adopted, and the consequent systemic instability which arises.

The ethical perspectives which are inherent in the allocation of healthcare resources now require fleshing out in more detail. However, the objective here is a limited one. While 'justice' as a moral principle is acknowledged to be a fundamental constituent of bioethics,[41] the goal of this book is not to conduct a detailed exposition and evaluation of those principles of moral philosophy which are most pertinent to questions of the distribution of scarce healthcare resources. Readers seeking such an

---

[40] The view that healthcare possesses special moral significance is further supported by the weight of literature on the topic of equity in health, which demonstrates the importance attached to the establishment of principles for the fair distribution of healthcare as a social good. See inter alia, A. Culyer and A. Wagstaff, 'Equity in Health and Healthcare' (1993) 12 *Journal of Health Economics*, 431; E. van Doorslaer, A. Wagstaff and F. Rutten, *Equity in the Finance and Delivery of Health Care: an International Perspective* (Oxford: Oxford University Press, 1993); A. Culyer, 'Equity – Some Theory and its Policy Implications' (2001) *Journal of Medical Ethics*, 275 at 278; A. Sen, 'Why Health Equity?' (2002) 11 *Health Economics*, 659.

[41] See especially T. Beauchamp and J. Childress, *Principles of Biomedical Ethics* (Oxford: Oxford University Press, 3rd edn, 2001), Chapter 6. The authors have developed a framework of four principles by reference to which rules can be developed for healthcare ethics: namely, beneficence, non-maleficence, respect for autonomy and justice. The latter term is defined as meaning 'obligations of fairness in the distribution of benefits and risks' and has been further subdivided by Gillon into 'justice as fair distribution of scarce resources (distributive justice), justice as respect for people's rights (rights-based justice) and justice as respect for morally acceptable laws (legal justice)': R. Gillon, 'Preface: Medical Ethics and the Four Principles' in Gillon (ed.), *Principles of Health Care Ethics* (Chichester: John Wiley & Sons, 1994) at xxv. Each of these is relevant to the discussion in this book. Note that NICE has endorsed the 'four principles' approach in respect of the 'social values' dimension of its work: see National Institute for Health and Clinical Excellence, *Social Value Judgements: Principles for the Development of NICE Guidance* (London: NICE, 2005) at para. 2.1.

analysis are directed elsewhere.[42] Rather, the aim is offer an outline of the key elements of the dominant ethical approaches to healthcare allocation, with a view to establishing the extent to which there may be conflict between these and, in consequence, the extent to which there is potential for the establishment of a societal consensus on the appropriate moral principles which should guide decision-making in this context.

Butler has contended that rationing of healthcare is not per se unethical. The basis of this argument is the need for management of the inevitable mismatch between the demand for and supply of healthcare resources, which, in the absence of strategies of rationing, necessitates 'the allocation of such a large proportion of the national income to healthcare that any government which tried to do so would rightly stand accused of dereliction of duty'.[43] He concludes from this, contentiously, that governments cannot be held morally culpable for failing to remove the need for rationing, and that consequently 'rationing itself cannot give rise to legitimate moral concern'.[44] This constitutes an endorsement of the view of Daniels, noted above, that rationing is, in fact, a *requirement* of justice, not a violation of it.[45] However, Butler observes that questions as to justice and fairness do clearly arise in respect of the manner in which health services are structured, the process by which allocative decisions are made, and the *outcomes* of care, that is the results and effects which are produced by the provision of healthcare services.[46] It is within the latter context – with its attendant implications for ascertainment of the morally proper objectives of healthcare – that the distinctive ethical approaches to healthcare rationing can perhaps most easily be articulated, albeit that (as will be analysed subsequently in this chapter), the difficulty in resolving the conflicts which exist between these perspectives has led to a shift of attention towards the establishment of morally acceptable *procedures* for decision-making.

The ensuing discussion adopts a tripartite classification of relevant substantive principles of rationing. It should be noted that other philosophical theories may be pertinent: for example, in addition to those outlined below, Beauchamp and Childress consider communitarian and libertarian approaches to justice in healthcare.[47] However, Cookson and

---

[42] See e.g. Beauchamp and Childress, *Principles of Biomedical Ethics*; Gillon (ed.), *Principles of Health Care Ethics*; J. Butler, *The Ethics of Health Care Rationing* (London: Cassell, 1999); R. Cookson and P. Dolan, 'Principles of Justice in Health Care Rationing' (2000) 26 *Journal of Medical Ethics*, 323.

[43] Butler, *ibid.* at 38. *Cf.* Mullen's arguments, above Chapter 2, n. 86 and accompanying text.

[44] *Ibid.* at 39.   [45] Above n. 28 and accompanying text.

[46] See Butler, *The Ethics of Health Care Rationing* at 124.

[47] See Beauchamp and Childress, *Principles of Biomedical Ethics*, Chapter 6.

Dolan distinguish three dominant principles from the literature on rationing,[48] and a similar typology is presented elsewhere.[49] Since, as previously discussed, the objective here is not to present an exhaustive analysis of all approaches which are potentially applicable but rather to illuminate the nature of ethical conflict, the account will focus upon these three main principles.

An individualistic approach: meeting health needs

Healthcare services may be oriented towards the improvement of the health of the individual by providing resources to address the 'need' which that individual has. The meaning – and elasticity – of this concept was examined in Chapter 2,[50] where it was observed that it functioned as a criterion enabling priorities to be established between individuals in situations where insufficient resources are available to provide optimum treatment to all who might require it. It should also be noted that defining 'need' as 'clinical' (or medical) in nature, which represents the dominant manner in which the concept is commonly understood, necessarily vests the key role in decision-making on allocation of healthcare resources in physicians. That said, if 'need' is extended to embrace capacity to benefit, information on the clinical effectiveness of treatments and services becomes relevant to allocative decision-making, creating space for the techniques of 'evidence-based medicine' and privileging the work of scientific researchers such as epidemiologists.

The centrality of 'need' to an understanding of justice in the allocation of scarce healthcare resources is easy to discern. As Butler states, 'as a generality, the culture of healthcare systems (particularly those which are centrally funded and politically driven) does reflect, to a greater or lesser degree, the importance of relative need in the way resources are rationed. No system openly dismisses the relevance of need in the ordering of people's claims'.[51] Furthermore, 'need' appears to be viewed as a more morally acceptable principle for distribution of scarce resources between patients than alternative ethical principles such as desert, although the boundary between these concepts becomes elusive once 'need' is

---

[48] See Cookson and Dolan, 'Principles of Justice' at 323.
[49] See Butler, *The Ethics of Health Care Rationing*, Chapter 5; NICE, *Social Value Judgements* at para. 2.1.4. Note, however, that the Institute downplays the significance of the 'need principle' as distinct from the other two approaches, arguing that it 'takes no account of other issues and provides no solution to problems relating to a healthcare system as a whole': *ibid*.
[50] See Chapter 2, nn. 58–63 and accompanying text.
[51] Butler, *The Ethics of Health Care Rationing* at 88.

considered in relative, rather than personal terms. However, 'need' (in whatever manner this is defined) appears to possess most value as a principle of justice at the 'micro' level, at which decisions are made as to the distribution of resources between individual patients. It is less clear that it can offer a basis for ethically appropriate allocative decision-making of a more systemic character – such as whether to allocate greater resources to treatment of cancer than to coronary disease or mental health – or that it can offer specific guidance on how best to divide resources between alternative uses (such as the purchase of differing pharmaceutical interventions of equal clinical efficacy) once programmatic priorities (say, for the treatment of cancer) have been established.

A utilitarian approach: maximising health gain

Alternatively, healthcare may be distributed in such a manner as to bring about the best possible consequences, consonant with utilitarian models.[52] Given constraints upon resources, the objective of the provision of healthcare services will not be maximisation of the health of each individual patient irrespective of cost, but rather the maximisation of the health of the group or population as a whole.[53] Thus, the most common approach in this context is the maximisation of aggregate population health.[54] This entails provision of treatment to those who stand to gain the largest amount of health over their remaining lifespan, and thus necessitates some form of evaluation of the gains in health which may derive from particular forms of treatment.

Such measurement normally occurs through cost-effectiveness analysis, which is a means of presenting trade-offs in explicit, quantified terms,[55] and which, in principle, enables comparison of the benefits derived from ostensibly incomparable programmes.[56] The unit of measurement commonly utilised in the healthcare context is the 'Quality-Adjusted Life Year' (QALY). This entails an estimation of the additional

---

[52] Though note that there is a distinction from the focus of 'classical' utilitarianism upon the maximisation of happiness or utility, in that the approach outlined here seeks to maximise welfare, understood primarily in terms of measurable health outcomes. See Butler, *The Ethics of Health Care Rationing* at 135; Cookson and Dolan, 'Principles of Justice' at 326; P. Ubel, *Pricing Life: Why It's Time for Health Care Rationing* (Cambridge, Mass: MIT Press, 2000) at 68.

[53] See Butler, *The Ethics of Health Care Rationing* at 134.

[54] See Cookson and Dolan, 'Principles of Justice' at 326.

[55] See Beauchamp and Childress, *Principles of Biomedical Ethics* at 196; and, generally, M. Gold, J. Siegel, L. Russell, M. Weinstein (eds.), *Cost-Effectiveness in Health and Medicine* (New York: Oxford University Press, 1996).

[56] See Ubel, *Pricing Life* at 5.

quantity (that is, numbers of years) of life which should result from a particular form of treatment, multiplied by *quality* of life measured on a scale such that zero denotes death, one denotes a total absence of disability and distress, and other states of disability and illness receive a value of between zero and one.[57] Employment of this tool therefore has the potential to permit policy-makers and allocative decision-makers to evaluate the relative cost-effectiveness of a range of treatments, perhaps even to the extent of producing a 'league table' ordered in ascending cost per QALY, as occurred in Oregon.[58]

In contrast to the 'need' principle, the QALY is more relevant to decision-making on the distribution of resources between services (treatment for cancer versus treatment for coronary heart disease), or the comparative evaluation of interventions for a particular disease (as in the work of NICE), than to the establishment of priorities for treatment between individual patients.[59] Furthermore, the utilitarian assumptions upon which it is based generate significant moral difficulties and conflicts with the other principles outlined here. Perhaps the starkest of these is that, as Beauchamp and Childress observe, utilitarian approaches epitomised by the use of the QALY prioritise life-years over individual lives.[60] This can produce some anomalous – and ethically unacceptable – outcomes, as seen in the Oregon case, where certain routine treatments were ranked more highly than some life-saving treatments, on the basis that they were more cost-effective. This was morally problematic because of the potency of the 'rule of rescue', which accords priority in the allocation of healthcare resources to the severely ill, notwithstanding that this use of resources may not deliver the greatest benefit.[61] Opinion surveys consistently demonstrate that the public favours some degree of diversion of resources to those in immediate need.[62]

---

[57] For a fuller discussion, see Gold *et al*, *Cost-Effectiveness*; E. Nord, *Cost-Value Analysis in Health Care: Making Sense out of QALYs* (Cambridge: Cambridge University Press, 1999).

[58] See above Chapter 3, nn. 90–92 and accompanying text.

[59] See Butler, *The Ethics of Health Care Rationing* at 137.

[60] See Beauchamp and Childress, *Principles of Biomedical Ethics* at 211; and see further J. Harris, 'QALYfying the Value of Life' (1987) 13 *Journal of Medical Ethics*, 117.

[61] For discussion in the Oregon context, see D. Hadorn, 'Setting Health Care Priorities in Oregon: Cost-Effectiveness meets the Rule of Rescue' (1991) 265 *Journal of the American Medical Association*, 2218.

[62] See e.g. E. Nord, 'The Trade-Off Between Severity of Illness and Treatment Effect in Cost-value Analysis of Health Care' (1993) 24 *Health Policy*, 45; Ubel, *Pricing Life* at 69–76; R. Cookson and P. Dolan, 'Public Views on Health Care Rationing: a Group Discussion Study' (1999) 49 *Health Policy*, 63 at 71.

Other morally contentious implications may flow from adoption of a utilitarian approach to healthcare resource allocation. For example, it may conflict with egalitarian principles that all human beings are of equal worth,[63] in that, while a healthy life-year is, in principle, of equal value to every person, cost-effectiveness analysis on the basis of QALYs appears discriminatory against the elderly. This follows from the fact that treatment of the young will inevitably produce more QALYs than treatment of the old, especially given that the quality of life of the latter is likely to be lower. This has led some commentators to describe QALY-based cost-effectiveness analysis as 'ageist'.[64] Moreover – and somewhat paradoxically in view of the 'shorthand' conception of utilitarianism as 'the greatest good for the greatest number'[65] – employment of this technique may result in priority being given to the saving of one life rather than several. This will occur if the QALY score assigned to the former is greater than the total QALYs generated from treatment of all the other individuals.[66]

An egalitarian approach: reducing inequalities in health

It is also possible for healthcare to be distributed in such a way that individuals receive, as far as possible, equal shares of this social good. This egalitarian approach has a number of variants in the healthcare context. It is reflected, for example, in the 'fair innings' argument for intergenerational equity, which holds that the young should have priority over the old in access to life-extending medical treatment, since this will equalise the opportunity for individuals to flourish across a 'normal life-span'.[67] It finds further expression in the 'fair opportunity' account offered by Daniels, which was outlined above. In this regard, 'forms of healthcare that have a significant effect on preventing, limiting, or compensating for reductions in normal species functioning should receive priority in designing healthcare institutions and allocating healthcare'.[68] And, as a goal of public policy, egalitarianism is manifested in attempts to

---

[63] Although the implications would be acceptable for those subscribing to the 'fair innings' argument, for which see below and – possibly – also for followers of Daniels' 'fair opportunity' rule: see above.

[64] A. Campbell, G. Gillett and G. Jones, *Medical Ethics* (Melbourne: Oxford University Press, 4th edn, 2005) at 260. See further Beauchamp and Childress, *Principles of Biomedical Ethics* at 211.

[65] See NICE, *Social Value Judgements* at para. 2.1.4.

[66] See Beauchamp and Childress, *Principles of Biomedical Ethics* at 211.

[67] For discussion, see J. Harris, *The Value of Life* (London: Routledge and Kegan Paul, 1985) at 91–4; A. Williams, 'Intergenerational Equity: an Exploration of the "Fair Innings" Argument' (1997) 6 *Health Economics*, 117.

[68] Beauchamp and Childress, *Principles of Biomedical Ethics* at 234.

narrow the so-called 'health gap': that is, inequalities in the distribution of disease, disability and mortality between the socially advantaged and disadvantaged.

Laudable as such objectives may appear to be, they are not uncontentious when set against the other principles outlined here. In particular, the 'fair innings' approach – although consonant with deployment of QALYs to achieve utilitarian goals – conflicts with the moral imperative to provide healthcare to those with the greatest and most immediate needs. Further, by stereotyping the elderly as uniform members of a class, it violates notions of individual autonomy.[69] Problems with the 'fair opportunity' model have been outlined above, but it should also be noted that questions arise as to the acceptability of limiting access to healthcare services for those individuals who may be said to have chosen not to exercise their opportunity for health, for example by incurring diseases as a result of an unhealthy lifestyle, which may be one implication of application of the 'fair opportunity' rule.[70] Surveys of the public suggest that there is disagreement as to the justifiability of such a stance, indicating that altruism and the principle of need continue to play a part;[71] moreover, there is an internal contradiction within the egalitarian approach in so far as the socially disadvantaged appear more likely to engage in unhealthy behaviour such as drug abuse and smoking. Finally, a policy to reduce health inequalities by diverting resources towards geographical areas of social deprivation is problematic from an egalitarian perspective if it entails a reduction of the resources available for those in more advantaged regions and communities, for it discriminates against the latter and to that extent, violates the principle that all individuals are of equal worth.[72]

The impossibility of consensus on substantive principles?

The above outline suggests that, although there may on occasion be points at which the key principles of distributive justice converge to produce an ethically 'right answer' to problems of allocation of scarce healthcare resources, there will nonetheless be numerous (and far more frequent) instances in which application of one of these principles in a particular allocative scenario will conflict with the deeply held moral beliefs of individuals, especially – though not exclusively – those which

---

[69] See e.g. J. Grimley Evans, 'Rationing Health Care by Age – the Case Against' in New (ed.), *Rationing – Talk and Action in Health Care* at 116.

[70] See Cookson and Dolan, 'Principles of Justice' at 327.

[71] See e.g. Cookson and Dolan, 'Public Views on Health Care Rationing' at 71.

[72] See Butler, *The Ethics of Health Care Rationing* at 144–5.

are possessed by patients who are denied access to treatments and services as a result of the rationing choice. The difficulties have been well captured by Gillon:

> In the context of resource allocation, there are conflicts between the following common moral concerns: to provide sufficient healthcare to meet the needs of all who need it; when this is impossible, to distribute healthcare resources in proportion to the extent of people's healthcare needs; to allow healthcare workers to give priority to the needs of *their* patients; to allow people as much choice as possible in the selection of their healthcare; to maximise the benefit produced by the available resources; to limit the demands on the purses of those who provide the resources, whether as taxpayers or as subscribers to health insurance schemes. All these criteria for just allocation of healthcare resources have moral justifications (and there are other candidates too), and not all can simultaneously be met.[73]

As Calabresi and Bobbit have taught us, this is a highly unstable situation and it is therefore important to find some means to manage the ensuing moral conflict if the cohesiveness of society is to be preserved.

In such circumstances, it might be thought that the appropriate task of the moral philosopher or health ethicist is to engage in inquiry in an attempt to develop a coherent theory on the fair distribution of healthcare resources which may command widespread consensus and which, doubtlessly drawing upon the general theories of justice articulated above, might provide guidance upon specific allocation questions. However, as Cookson and Dolan have noted,[74] there has been considerable reluctance to undertake such an exercise, suggesting an undue readiness to 'throw up our hands because quite general principles fail us'.[75] Drawing upon empirical research which indicates that the public supports a combination of substantive ethical principles on distributive justice, the authors argue that there is scope for further philosophical work to be undertaken to develop a theoretical position which reflects the pluralistic approach favoured by the public and which might therefore form the basis of an acceptable consensus.

However, it remains unclear whether it would, in fact, be possible to expound an acceptable theory of this type, especially given the significant points of divergence between the general principles enumerated above. Certainly, no such theory exists at present. Moreover, were such a theory to be constructed, it is likely that, in common with the general ethical

---

[73] Gillon (ed.), *Principles of Health Care Ethics* at xxv. Emphasis in original.
[74] See Cookson and Dolan, 'Principles of Justice' at 328.
[75] N. Daniels and J. Sabin, *Setting Limits Fairly* (New York: Oxford University Press, 2002) at 33.

principles outlined in the preceding section,[76] it would be insufficiently determinate to resolve conflicts as to the appropriate allocation of resources in a particular treatment context.

In consequence, and notwithstanding the instructive observations of Cookson and Dolan on the point, it is submitted that the better view is that which is widely acknowledged within the health policy community, namely that since 'distributive issues remain highly contested',[77] consensus upon the appropriate substantive principles to achieve a fair allocation of resources to meet reasonable healthcare needs in conditions of scarcity is likely to be impossible to secure. Support for such a conclusion can be derived from a number of sources. First and most straightforward, as highlighted both by Daniels and by Williams and Yeo,[78] modern society is politically, socially and ethically pluralist, and agreement upon substantive principles in such circumstances will accordingly remain elusive, in any field of public policy. More specific to the healthcare context – and relating to the discussion in the preceding section – Holm contends that:

the purpose of a public healthcare system is unclear. It is not there simply to maximise the amount of health in a society (however we choose to measure health). It is not there merely to treat diseases (however we choose to define disease). It is not there solely to meet healthcare needs (however we choose to define healthcare needs). And it is not there to ensure equality in health status (however we choose to conceptualise equality). The goal of a public healthcare system is a composite of many goals, including fuzzy goals such as maintaining a sense of security in the population. There is no natural way to balance these goals against each other. We can state that one goal is more important than another in specific situations, but an attempt to raise one goal as the most important in all situations is implausible.[79]

Of course, attempts have been made – notably by Daniels – to specify what the goals of a healthcare system should be, but, as previously discussed, these have not commanded universal acceptance. If uncertainty persists as to the proper function of healthcare, it cannot be expected that agreement can be reached on how it should be distributed.

Additionally, a useful illustration of the difficulties inherent in establishing consensus upon appropriate substantive principles of distributive

---

[76] On this issue, see especially Daniels and Sabin, *ibid.* at 32; G. van der Wilt, 'Cost-Effectiveness Analysis of Health Care Services and Concepts of Distributive Justice' (1994) 2 *Health Care Analysis*, 296 at 301.

[77] Daniels, 'Justice, Health and Healthcare' at 2.

[78] J. Williams and M. Yeo, 'The Ethics of Decentralising Health Care Priority-Setting in Canada' in A. Coulter and C. Ham (eds.), *The Global Challenge of Health Care Rationing* (Buckingham: Open University Press, 2000) at 126.

[79] S. Holm, 'Goodbye to the Simple Solutions' (1998) 317 *British Medical Journal*, 1000 at 1001.

justice in healthcare rationing is afforded by experience in Sweden. The Swedish approach differs from those systems outlined in Chapter 3 in that no attempt was made to specify a 'package' of core services to be covered by the publicly funded health system: instead, specification of an 'ethical platform' for rationing was considered to be fundamental. To this end, the Swedish Priorities Commission established three key ethical principles in rank order: the principle of human dignity, the principle of need and solidarity and the principle of cost-efficiency.[80] These are now reflected in legislation governing the organisation and administration of healthcare in Sweden.[81] However, the apparent agreement upon the relevance and ordering of these principles is less complete than might appear to be the case at first glance. First, although the report produced by the Commission reflected consensus across the spectrum of Swedish party politics and no major political disagreements arose during its preparation, this was in part due to deliberate avoidance of contentious issues in the interests of achieving a united front.[82] Relatedly, the report provided very little detail on how the ethical principles should be applied to real-life situations of resource allocation, further reducing the scope for disagreement.[83] This tends to reinforce the point made above, that any ethical approach which commands consensus is likely to be insufficiently precise to provide guidance in specific allocative episodes. Third, the Commission's decision to rank the three ethical principles has been criticised (significantly, perhaps, by a health economist who might be expected to be primarily concerned with the lowest-ranked value, cost-efficiency) for lack of flexibility, the claim being that it may not always be appropriate to meet the greatest need first, irrespective of cost or alternative uses for the resources.[84] Finally, (and consistently with the view expressed by Holm) Liss has argued that the three principles offer no clear statement as to the central goal of the healthcare system – indeed, he sees the principle of need and solidarity and the principle of cost-effectiveness as presupposing the existence of unstated goals – and therefore cannot provide specific guidance as to which are the relevant facts

[80] Swedish Parliamentary Priorities Commission, *Priorities in Health Care: Ethics, Economy, Implementation* (Stockholm: Ministry of Health and Social Affairs, 1995) at 5. For discussion of the meaning of these principles, see J. Calltorp, 'Priority-Setting in Health Policy in Sweden and a Comparison with Norway' (1999) 50 *Health Policy*, 1.

[81] Law No. 142 of 17 April 1997 amending the Health and Medical Care Law (No. 763) of 1982, ss 2 and 2A.

[82] See Calltorp, 'Priority-Setting in Health Policy' at 5.   [83] *Ibid.* at 5–8.

[84] See A. Williams, 'Tydligare Definitioner Och Bättre Fakta Krävs' ('Clearer Definitions and Better Facts are Required') (1996) 93 *Läkartidningen*, 3376, cited in P-E. Liss, 'Hard Choices in Public Health: the Allocation of Scarce Resources' (2003) 31 *Scandinavian Journal of Public Health*, 30 at 30.

(individual clinical need, cost-effectiveness of interventions, etc.) to be considered in reaching a rationing decision.[85]

Ultimately, the elusiveness of consensus on substantive principles which would determine how scarce healthcare resources can fairly be allocated may be said merely to follow from certain characteristics of general theories of distributive justice such as those analysed in the preceding section. First, the generality of ethical principles of this type means that they cannot, in themselves, afford solutions to particular problems of allocation which may arise at the 'micro' or even 'meso' levels of healthcare rationing, even if one *were* to command widespread acceptance. Secondly, in any event, such acceptance appears implausible in view of the fact that these theories, reflecting the moral pluralism of society, offer 'a philosophical reconstruction of a valid perspective on the moral life, but one that only partially captures the range and diversity of that life', and in consequence 'different conceptions of the just society underlie them, and pursuing one goal is likely to undercut another'.[86] Reasonable people may therefore disagree about the appropriate ethical principle(s) which is/are to be applied in questions of healthcare rationing, and, given a state of ethical pluralism, such views should be accorded proper respect.

The 'legitimacy problem'

Thus far, Calabresi and Bobbit's 'tragic choices' thesis has done the bulk of the work of explaining the instability to which explicit rationing choices give rise. Where a decision-maker publicly makes a choice in a situation of scarcity which carries significant cost in terms of human suffering, the conflict between competing ethical principles for the distribution of healthcare resources will be visibly exposed, generating profound moral outrage (given the special moral importance of healthcare) which jeopardises the cohesiveness of society.

This account of instability may be further developed, however, with reference to the work of Norman Daniels and James Sabin on the problem of *legitimacy* which arises in situations where limits must be set upon access to healthcare resources. As noted above, Daniels' theory of just healthcare allows for the existence of 'reasonable resource constraints', signalling recognition of the importance of allocating resources for the provision of social goods other than healthcare. However, Daniels

---

[85] P-E. Liss, 'The Significance of the Goal of Health Care for the Setting of Priorities' (2003) 11 *Health Care Analysis*, 161.

[86] Beauchamp and Childress, *Principles of Biomedical Ethics* at 272, 231.

acknowledges that the existence of such limits creates difficulties. He argues that, if consensus existed as to substantive principles of justice which would determine how limits to healthcare might fairly be set, there would be less scope for systemic instability, and existing institutional mechanisms and decisional processes would be capable of responding to any conflicts which arose:

If societies agreed on such [i.e. ethical] principles, people could simply check social decisions and practices against the principles to see if they conformed with them. Where decisions, practices, and institutions failed to conform, they would be unjust and people should then change them. Disagreements about the fairness of actual distributions would then be either disagreements about the interpretation of the principles or about the facts of the situation. Many societies have well-established and reliable, if imperfect, legal procedures for resolving such disputes about facts and interpretations.[87]

By contrast, in the absence of substantive agreement, deep moral controversy is inevitable, and in such circumstances suspicion, distrust and resistance are liable to arise.[88] Daniels and Sabin characterise this as a challenge to the legitimate moral authority of those responsible for undertaking rationing decisions, and their proposals – which are discussed in detail in the next section of this chapter – seek to provide a response to the question: 'under what conditions should we view such decisions as a legitimate exercise of moral authority?'.[89]

How far may the 'legitimacy problem' analysis be regarded as relevant to the strategies of explicit rationing in healthcare of a publicly funded type, which forms the subject-matter of this book? First, it should be noted that Daniels and Sabin argue that the model which they develop to address the problem of legitimacy represents a '"middle-way" position that seeks to incorporate the strengths and insights of both the explicit and implicit approaches to limit setting'.[90] Nonetheless, it is submitted that both the problem which they identify and the solution which they propose are much more applicable to an environment of explicit rationing. This follows from the argument posited in the previous chapter, that implicit forms of rationing tend to be more socially stable and generate lower levels of denial and deprivation disutility: consequently, they are much less likely to give rise to a challenge to the moral authority of the

---

[87] Daniels, *Just Health Care* at 9.
[88] See N. Daniels, 'Accountability for Reasonableness in Private and Public Health Insurance' in Coulter and Ham (eds.) *The Global Challenge of Health Care Rationing* at 89.
[89] Daniels, *Just Health Care* at 9.
[90] Daniels and Sabin, *Setting Limits Fairly* at 5–6; see also N. Daniels, 'Accountability for Reasonableness' (2000) 321 *British Medical Journal*, 1300 at 1301.

rationing decision-maker than explicit choices, which visibly expose conflicting ethical positions. Similarly, the emphasis of Daniels and Sabin's 'accountability for reasonableness' model upon transparency (to be noted below) also appears considerably more consonant with explicit strategies rather than implicit decision-making in which the true rationales are concealed from patients and the wider public.

Secondly, it is important to recognise that Daniels and Sabin's initial formulation of the problem of legitimacy arose in the context of privately funded healthcare, specifically that of insurers operating managed care plans (frequently, on behalf of employers) in the United States. Measures of cost containment adopted within such a system tend to generate especially profound levels of public unease because they are perceived as motivated by a desire to boost profit levels. Such an attitude may be explained by a lack of public awareness of the need for the rationing of healthcare, with the insured population accustomed to the 'experience of medical benefits flowing without constraint and costs rising without visible consequence'.[91] In the absence of knowledge of scarcity, the assumption is drawn that limit-setting is a mere exercise in self-interest on the part of insurers. By contrast, in a publicly funded system, where awareness of limitations on available resources is greater, such measures can be more easily justified as decisions based upon a utilitarian calculus and taken in the wider public interest.

Nevertheless, it does not follow that publicly funded healthcare is exempt from problems of legitimacy. Daniels and Sabin argue that the 'legitimacy problem' is 'fundamental, regardless of the details of the financing and delivery systems that differentiate healthcare systems in different countries ... every health system must address the problem of legitimacy'.[92] This view has been endorsed by other analysts, who have sought to adapt the Daniels and Sabin thesis to a number of primarily publicly funded systems, particularly the UK.[93] However, as noted by Daniels and Sabin themselves, the nature of the legitimacy problem in such a system is likely to differ from that which occurs under private funding.[94] The authors characterise the key distinction as lying in the fact

---

[91] Daniels and Sabin, *ibid.* at 6.
[92] *Ibid.* at 4. See also *ibid.*, Chapter 10, which examines international approaches to the 'legitimacy problem'.
[93] See Ham and Pickard, *Tragic Choices in Health Care*; C. Ham, 'Tragic Choices in Health Care: Lessons from the Child B case' (1999) 319 *British Medical Journal*, 1258; K. Syrett, 'A Technocratic Fix to the "Legitimacy Problem"? The Blair Government and Health Care Rationing in the United Kingdom' (2003) 28 *Journal of Health Politics, Policy and Law*, 439.
[94] Daniels and Sabin, *Setting Limits Fairly* at 7.

that, in the case of publicly funded care, the problem of legitimacy resides not in *who* sets limits on access to healthcare (since in a publicly funded system this will normally be an agency which is, to a greater or lesser extent, democratically accountable), nor in *whether limits on access to healthcare resources are necessary at all* (since there is likely to be broad public awareness and acceptance of the need for rationing) but rather in *how the decision to limit access has been arrived at in the particular case.*[95] In consequence, the patient is likely to challenge the authority of the decision-maker on the basis of the evidence and ethical criteria which form the basis of the decision to refuse treatment and (relatedly) the reasons which are (or are not) given, the overall rationality and transparency of the decision-making process, the failure to take proper account of the individual's particular need for treatment (perhaps relating to the existence of exceptional circumstances) and the absence of any possibility for appeal and reconsideration.

The view that problems of legitimacy subsist within publicly funded, as well as privately funded healthcare clearly has considerable validity. As argued above, rationing decisions will tend to expose deeply held moral perspectives and, in such circumstances, distrust of and disagreement with the decision-making process – well captured in the oft-repeated refrain that those responsible for the allocation of healthcare resources are 'putting a price on life' – will frequently be manifested in political pressure, media outcry and litigation (as discussed in Chapter 1 and further developed in Chapters 6 to 8). In such circumstances, the authority of the decision-maker to make particular moral judgments is placed under serious challenge. It may be argued that this is illustrative of Habermas' 'legitimation crisis' thesis, which posits a disjuncture between public expectations and the capacity of the modern welfare state, given available resources, to meet those expectations.[96]

Nonetheless, even if the existence of a problem of legitimacy within publicly funded healthcare is acknowledged, it does not necessarily follow that Daniels and Sabin have correctly identified the nature of that problem. In dismissing the relevance of the 'whether' and 'who' questions in such systems, the authors argue that 'there is widespread understanding and acceptance of the need to share limited resources under politically negotiated budget constraints. Similarly, there is familiarity with the need for appropriate institutional authorities, empowered by the political

---

[95] *Ibid.* at 5. *Cf.* above n. 46 and accompanying text.

[96] See J. Habermas (trans. T. McCarthy), *Legitimation Crisis* (Boston: Beacon Press, 1975). For application in the context of the rationing of healthcare, see B. New and J. LeGrand, *Rationing in the NHS: Principles and Pragmatism* (London: King's Fund, 1996) at 8–9.

process, to make decisions that affect access to medical services'.[97] However, it is submitted that this assessment fails to differentiate, as Lomas has sought to do in a related context,[98] between the various roles played by individuals within a health system and the impact which these have upon the 'legitimacy problem'. As *taxpayers*, people are likely to be willing to accept limits on access to treatments and services with a view to minimising the financial burden which they face, and no problem of legitimacy will arise. But as *patients*, personal imperatives of survival and the reduction of pain and suffering will almost certainly lead to the espousal of a differing moral perspective from that adopted by the rationing body. Here, it is far from clear that the individual is concerned by legitimacy in the sense of *how* rationing choices are made: it appears more likely that, absent an improbably altruistic outlook, that person will regard rationing as unacceptable *per se, in view of its probable impact in the particular circumstances of her/his case* – moreover, (s)he may question whether the body making the rationing decision is the appropriate authority, preferring (for example) to trust the judgment of medical professionals. If this analysis is correct, the 'legitimacy problem' as it applies to *patients* in publicly funded systems or sectors does, in fact, relate to whether rationing should take place at all and, if so, who should undertake it – questions which, for Daniels and Sabin, characterise the 'legitimacy problem' in market-based systems. And while the distrust experienced by such patients will not extend to suspicion that rationing choices are motivated by profit considerations, it is clear that such decisions attract resistance because they are viewed as prioritising *cost* over individual clinical need.

However, it is preferable to regard this reasoning as constituting a refinement to the Daniels and Sabin thesis, rather than a refutation of it. This is because a further role for individuals within a health system is as *citizens*. In this capacity, some may already recognise the need for limitations on access to treatments and services to allow for the sharing of resources, but it follows from the very fact of ethical pluralism within society – from which the problem of legitimacy arises – that this view will not command universal understanding or acceptance. It appears more plausible that this group, as distinct from patients, will be responsive to the process of 'social learning' which can be brought about by means of imposition of the conditions of 'accountability for reasonableness', the goal of which is to develop appreciation 'of the need for limits and the

---

[97] Daniels and Sabin, *Setting Limits Fairly* at 5
[98] J. Lomas, 'Reluctant Rationers': Public Input into Health Care Priorities' (1997) 2 *Journal of Health Services Research and Policy*, 103.

appropriate grounds and conditions for making decisions about them'.[99] Here, the 'how' question is crucial, for fair procedure – in the form of consistency, transparency, relevance and opportunities for review and appeal – will enable the attainment and enrichment of such an understanding. On this analysis, therefore, the problem of legitimacy is best regarded as flowing from the failure of the public to comprehend the necessity of rationing healthcare resources, and, in consequence, the preferred response (discussed below) is to educate citizens with a view to their engagement in a process of public deliberation from which legitimacy will ultimately derive. In addition, it is to be hoped that those patients who personally suffer as a consequence of limit-setting decisions will, through such a process, also come to accept the rationing choice, but the primary focus is upon the *systemic* stability to be engendered by public understanding and deliberation.

Responding to the 'legitimacy problem': towards procedural justice?

Notwithstanding the need for clarification in certain regards, it is submitted that Daniels and Sabin's analysis offers a valuable and compelling account of the nature of the instability to which the rationing of healthcare gives rise. It suggests, moreover, that a significant problem of public policy has emerged as a result of the attempts, analysed in Chapter 3, to develop a more systematic approach to the allocation of healthcare resources in view of the continuing political imperative to control expenditure in this field. Public challenges to the authority of bodies making allocative choices – whether framed in terms of the 'who', 'whether' or 'how' questions outlined in the preceding section – are troublesome because legitimacy may be regarded as fundamental to institutional effectiveness, as argued by Freedman:

Institutional legitimacy is an indispensable condition for institutional effectiveness. By endowing institutional decisions with an inherent capacity to attract obedience and respect, legitimacy permits an institution to achieve its goals without the regular necessity of threatening the use of force and creating renewed episodes of public resentment ... substantial, persisting challenges to the legitimacy of governmental institutions must be regarded with concern, for such challenges threaten to impair the capacity of government to meet its administrative responsibilities effectively.[100]

---

[99] Daniels and Sabin, *Setting Limits Fairly* at 170–71.

[100] J. Freedman, *Crisis and Legitimacy: the Administrative Process and American Government* (Cambridge: Cambridge University Press, 1978) at 10. See also M. Weber, *The Theory of Social and Economic Organisation* (New York: Free Press, 1964) at 130–32.

Accordingly, it is important to formulate some means of addressing the 'legitimacy problem' in order to ensure that the institutional framework through which the allocation of healthcare resources takes place continues to function in an effective manner.

To this end, the strategy which has attracted widespread support from academic commentators and policy-makers alike has been to place increasing emphasis upon the *process* by which rationing decisions are reached, so as to assure those affected by them and the wider public that they have been fairly based upon relevant criteria, even if the substantive outcome is one which may be subject to contestation on moral grounds. This approach may be seen as illustrative of an increasing interest in application of procedural forms of justice to problems of the exercise of public power.[101] Drawing most conspicuously upon the Rawlsian notion that distribution should be treated as a matter of 'pure procedural justice [which] obtains when there is no independent criterion for the right result: instead there is a correct or fair procedure such that the outcome is likewise correct or fair, whatever it is, provided that the procedure has been properly followed',[102] the basic elements of this strategy may be clearly discerned from the following three passages:

When we lack consensus on principles that tell us what is fair, or even when we have general principles but are burdened by reasonable disagreements about how they apply, we may nevertheless find a process or procedure that most can accept as fair to those who are affected by such decisions. The fair process then determines for us what counts as a fair outcome.[103]

Given conflicting values, the process of setting priorities for healthcare must inevitably be a process of debate. It is a debate, moreover, which cannot be resolved by an appeal to science and where the search for some formula or set of principles designed to provide decision-making rules will always prove elusive. Hence the crucial importance of getting the institutional setting of the debate right: of ensuring that the debate will not be dominated by one particular interest . . . and that all voices can make themselves heard. I am not arguing that getting the process right will necessarily produce the 'right' answers. I do not think that in the context of setting healthcare priorities there is necessarily a 'right' answer, independent of an ever-shifting context. My contention is less ambitious: it is that the right process will produce socially acceptable answers – and that this is the best we can hope for.[104]

---

[101] For discussion, see especially J. Black, 'Proceduralizing Regulation Part I' (2000) 20 *Oxford Journal of Legal Studies*, 597 and 'Part II' (2001) 21 *Oxford Journal of Legal Studies*, 33.

[102] Rawls, *A Theory of Justice* at 75; see especially Daniels, 'Justice, Health and Healthcare' at 10.

[103] Daniels and Sabin, *Setting Limits Fairly* at 4.

[104] R. Klein 'Setting Priorities: What is Holding Us Back – Inadequate Information or Inadequate Institutions?' in Coulter and Ham (eds.), *The Global Challenge of Health Care Rationing* at 21.

Even if there is no 'right' answer, this does not mean that all answers are equally valid. Particularly in cases where consensus does not exist, decision-makers should strive for 'morally defensible' decisions, that is, decisions for which all relevant considerations have been duly entertained and the justificatory reasons have been clearly laid out. If others do not accept the answer, they should at least understand and appreciate the reasons that led to it and be able to challenge it on grounds of principle.[105]

Consequently, on this analysis, legitimacy does not arise from the achievement of a particular substantive outcome, but rather is a function of the fairness of the procedure which has been followed in reaching the rationing decision. This hypothesis corresponds both with empirical studies which suggest that institutional arrangements are publicly perceived as legitimate if they employ fair decision-making procedures,[106] and with philosophical arguments, notably again those advanced by Rawls, that a belief in the justice or fairness of government institutions is central to public allegiance.[107]

The most comprehensive procedural model which has been developed in this context is that of 'accountability for reasonableness', which has been put forward by Daniels and Sabin. The authors argue that fair process in the rationing of healthcare resources will be characterised by a number of key features, and that compliance with these will significantly facilitate resolution of the problem of legitimacy, in a manner which will be analysed in more detail below. Their 'central thesis' is that 'reasons or rationales for important limit-setting decisions should be publicly available. In addition, these reasons must be ones that "fair-minded" people can agree are relevant to pursuing appropriate patient care under necessary resource constraints'.[108] To this end, they posit four conditions: *publicity* (public accessibility of rationing decisions and their rationales), *relevance* (rationales for decisions should rest on evidence, reasons and principles 'that all fair-minded people can agree are relevant to deciding how to meet the diverse needs of a covered population under necessary resource constraints'),[109] *revision and appeals* (the existence of mechanisms for challenge and dispute resolution and opportunities for revision

[105] Williams and Yeo, 'Ethics of Decentralising' at 126.
[106] See e.g. J. Thibaut and L. Walker, *Procedural Justice* (Hillsdale, NJ: Erlbaum, 1975) (on the legal process); T. Tyler, 'Governing amid Diversity: the Effect of Fair Decision-Making Procedures on the Legitimacy of Government' (1994) 28 *Law and Society Review*, 809 (on the legislative process).
[107] See e.g. J. Rawls, 'The Idea of an Overlapping Consensus' (1987) 7 *Oxford Journal of Legal Studies*, 1, especially at 18–23.
[108] Daniels and Sabin, *Setting Limits Fairly* at 44.
[109] N. Daniels and J. Sabin, 'The Ethics of Accountability in Managed Care Reform' (1998) 17 *Health Affairs*, 50 at 57.

and improvement of policies in light of new evidence) and *enforcement* (voluntary or public regulation of the process to ensure that the other conditions are met).

Some critical observations may be made in respect of these conditions. First, as noted previously,[110] the model appears most consonant with explicit forms of rationing. In *Setting Limits Fairly*, the authors offer a specific critique of implicit rationing, arguing that 'nonpublicity is ... infeasible for a very basic reason: it does not work',[111] and that 'non-publicity risks undercutting the public sense that fairness obtains in the system'.[112] They also characterise the opinions of 'colleagues who support the implicit rationing position' that greater openness will exacerbate distrust and lead to litigation as being 'only speculation'.[113] These arguments seem to undercut the claim that the model combines the strengths of both implicit and explicit approaches. Daniels seeks to substantiate the latter assertion by contending that, 'like implicit rationing, it [the model] does not require that principles for rationing be made explicit ahead of time'.[114] Yet the weight of this distinction is weakened by the argument that one of the key benefits of the 'publicity' condition is that it enables the development of a body of 'case law', reflecting 'a *commitment* to continue to act on the cited reasons and rationales in future cases'.[115] While departure from such case law is considered permissible,[116] there nevertheless appears to be relatively little distinction between this approach and that of 'trying to establish all the rules beforehand' which characterises explicit rationing.[117] One might therefore query whether the 'publicity' condition – and perhaps, the 'accountability for reasonableness' model in general – amounts to much more than a plea for adoption of explicit strategies of rationing. If that is so, it is open to the charge that, far from resolving problems of legitimacy as it purports to do, such approaches tend particularly to generate such difficulties and thus to exacerbate instability, as argued previously both in this chapter and in Chapter 3.

While Daniels and Sabin appear conscious of the weakness of the model on this point, their somewhat unpersuasive response is that it is 'our belief that greater openness, at worst, is no more likely than our current approach to cause further erosion of trust and increased litigiousness'.[118] However, it is submitted that 'accountability for reasonableness'

---

[110] See above n.90 and accompanying text.
[111] Daniels and Sabin, *Setting Limits Fairly* at 40.   [112] *Ibid.*
[113] *Ibid.* at 50.   [114] Daniels, 'Accountability for Reasonableness' at 1301.
[115] Daniels and Sabin, *Setting Limits Fairly* at 48. Emphasis in original.
[116] *Ibid.*   [117] See above Chapter 3, n. 41 and accompanying text.
[118] Daniels and Sabin, *Setting Limits Fairly* at 51.

may be differentiated from strategies of explicit rationing in two respects. First, while visibility is central to both approaches, the inclusion in the model of three other conditions (relevance, revision and appeals and enforcement) which may not *necessarily* be present within the processes and institutions established by governments pursuing explicit strategies of rationing, serves to indicate that securing social acceptability through procedural justice is not a matter of transparency of decision-making alone. Secondly, as will be noted in the next section of this chapter, compliance with the conditions of 'accountability for reasonableness' does not, of itself, result in legitimacy. *Rather, the key to the attainment of legitimate moral authority lies in a process of public deliberation upon the need for rationing and the principles which should underpin allocative choices in healthcare, which process is facilitated by fulfilment of the four conditions.* Explicit decision-making of the type outlined in Chapter 3 is therefore likely to be a *necessary* precondition of the exercise of legitimate authority in the rationing of healthcare resources, notwithstanding the claim of Daniels and Sabin that their model draws upon the strengths of both implicit and explicit approaches. But, in so far as explicitness need not automatically lead to public deliberation (although, axiomatically, it is more likely to do so than implicit approaches), it is not in itself *sufficient* to generate such legitimacy.

A second difficulty lies with the 'relevance' condition. As the authors acknowledge, this places constraints upon the rationales which may acceptably be offered to justify a rationing decision.[119] In many instances, this will be unproblematic. 'Fair-minded people' (who are defined as those 'who in principle seek to cooperate with others on terms they can justify to each other ... [those who] accept the rules of the game')[120] would clearly not accept as relevant to decision-making on meeting the healthcare needs of the population in circumstances of limited resources, the fact that the individual denied care was from a minority ethnic group or was red-haired. However, the claim made by Daniels and Sabin is stronger than this. They argue that the reasons offered should aim to provide 'a reasonable construal of how the organisation (or public agency) seeks to provide "value for money" in meeting the varied needs of a defined population under reasonable resource constraints'.[121] The reference to 'value for money' appears to suggest that utilitarian rationales for rationing decisions are to be accorded precedence, a conclusion which draws support from Daniels' statement that 'people who share in the goal of meeting the varied medical needs of a population covered by limited resources would consider relevant the claim

---

[119] *Ibid.*   [120] *Ibid.* at 44.   [121] *Ibid.* at 51.

that a particular technology falls below some defensible threshold of cost-effectiveness or relative cost-worthiness'.[122] The difficulty here is that, while 'value for money' is clearly *one* relevant criterion in reaching decisions on the allocation of scarce healthcare resources, the existence of a state of ethical pluralism – upon which the 'legitimacy problem' thesis is itself premised – indicates that it cannot be the only one. Yet it is not clear how other moral principles which 'fair-minded people' might consider to be relevant to allocative decision-making within a particular historical, cultural, political or social context, such as solidarity[123] or the 'rule of rescue', are to be accommodated within this account, since organisations seeking to comply with such principles will not be 'seeking to provide "value for money"'.

One might conclude from this that the 'accountability for reasonableness' model is not, as its originators maintain, a matter of pure procedural justice, but rather that only certain substantive approaches to resource allocation are compatible with it. It is instructive that similar views, framed in the form of questions, have been expressed in other commentaries on the 'accountability for reasonableness' model, namely 'why presume that process can be so easily detached from content?',[124] and 'why should we think that there can be a reasoned assessment of the fairness of a process for rationing healthcare that does not incorporate a substantive preference about the scope of healthcare?'.[125] Concerns of this type have led Hasman and Holm to conclude that 'a central component in the accountability for reasonableness framework for priority-setting in healthcare, the distinction between reasonable and unreasonable decision-making, is significantly more complicated than is commonly appreciated. It is questionable whether there is a principled and non-contentious way of making this distinction, despite the claims of the originators of accountability for reasonableness'.[126]

Clearly, therefore, the 'accountability for reasonableness' model is far from unproblematic. Indeed, empirical research has yielded proposed refinements to the conditions set out by Daniels and Sabin.[127] These

---

[122] Daniels, 'Justice, Health and Healthcare' at 12.

[123] For discussion in the context of the Daniels and Sabin model, see A. Hasman and S. Holm, 'Accountability for Reasonableness: Opening the Black Box of Process' (2005) 13 *Health Care Analysis*, 261.

[124] M. Waymack, 'Daniels on Justice and Healthcare: Laudable Goals – Questionable Method' (2001) 1 *American Journal of Bioethics*, 28 at 28.

[125] S. Gorovitz, 'Justice in Healthcare and Dimpled Chads' (2001) 1 *American Journal of Bioethics*, 29 at 29–30.

[126] Hasman and Holm, 'Accountability for Reasonableness' at 272.

[127] See D. Martin, M. Giacomini and P. Singer, 'Fairness, Accountability for Reasonableness and the Views of Priority-Setting Decision-Makers' (2002) 61 *Health Policy*, 279.

are to be welcomed, since they address the criticisms previously outlined, while preserving the essential features of the model and, most importantly, its emphasis upon the importance of fair process. Thus, the 'publicity' condition may be viewed as possessing both external and internal aspects, the latter connoting understanding within the decision-making body of the nature of the decision being taken, the considerations under discussion and the process for reaching a conclusion. This more precise delineation makes apparent that 'publicity' amounts to more than a call for explicitness in rationing. Rather, it necessitates the development of particular institutional structures and processes to guarantee fair decision-making, both internally and externally. Similarly the 'relevance' condition may be recast to refer to the opportunity for inclusion of representatives from multiple perspectives to ensure that a range of values and principles are reflected in decision-making, with external consultation where particular viewpoints appear to be omitted. On this analysis, 'relevance' is to be judged not by appeal to (substantive) reasoning which 'fair-minded people' consider to be applicable to resolving the problem of meeting the community's health needs under resource constraints, but rather to the degree of inclusiveness which is afforded by the rationing body's procedural mechanisms.

The preferred reading of the work of Daniels and Sabin is, therefore, that it emphasises that attention to process, as distinct from the pursuit of an elusive substantive consensus, offers a means of achieving legitimation in the context of the rationing of scarce healthcare resources. In particular, it points to the central importance of commitment to values of transparency and accountability (in the form of the provision of reasons which can be seen to rest upon proper evaluation of a plurality of viewpoints and interests). However, the 'accountability for reasonableness' model itself provides little more than a framework – or the "'outer features'"[128] – of the procedural mechanisms which are required and the precise details of these will need to be worked out in more depth in each case.

There is no doubt that the process-oriented approach which is exemplified by the Daniels and Sabin thesis has been highly influential. The 'accountability for reasonableness model' has been applied in academic studies of, inter alia, priority-setting on new technologies,[129] 'last-chance'

---

[128] Hasman and Holm, 'Accountability for Reasonableness' at 268.
[129] P. Singer, D. Martin, M. Giacomini *et al.*, 'Priority-Setting for New Technologies in Medicine: a Qualitative Case Study' (2000) 321 *British Medical Journal*, 1316.

therapies,[130] hospital drug provision,[131] centralised processes for reviewing pharmaceuticals,[132] intensive care units,[133] and development of clinical guidelines.[134] In addition to its origins in managed care organisations in the US, institutions undertaking rationing decisions in the UK, Canada, the Netherlands, New Zealand, Norway[135] and Australia[136] have been evaluated for compliance with the model, and it has been proposed as a component of a framework for fair decision-making in health systems in developing nations.[137] Arguably of still more significance is the fact that NICE, regarded worldwide as a highly influential model for decision-making on the introduction of new and costly medical technologies,[138] has recognised the impossibility of substantive consensus in respect of the dimension of its work which has a bearing upon 'social values',[139] and has proclaimed its adherence to the 'accountability for reasonableness' approach as a form of procedural justice.[140] More broadly, policy-makers elsewhere[141] have shifted from earlier attempts to address problems of rationing through the application of technical criteria and have 'turned their attention to ways of strengthening decision-making processes to generate legitimacy for rationing as the limitations

---

[130] N. Daniels and J. Sabin, 'Last Chance Therapies and Managed Care: Pluralism, Fair Procedures and Legitimacy' (1998) 28 *Hastings Center Report*, 27.

[131] D. Martin, D. Hollenberg, S, MacRae *et al.*, 'Priority-setting in a Hospital Drug Formulary: a Qualitative Case Study and Evaluation' (2003) 66 *Health Policy*, 295.

[132] C. Mitton, M. McMahon, S. Morgan *et al.*, 'Centralized Drug Processes: Are They Fair?' (2006) 63 *Social Science and Medicine*, 200.

[133] D. Martin, P. Singer and M. Bernstein, 'Access to Intensive Care Unit Beds for Neurosurgery Patients: a Qualitative Case Study' (2003) 74 *Journal of Neurology, Neurosurgery and Psychiatry*, 1299.

[134] O. Norheim, 'Healthcare Rationing – Are Additional Criteria Needed for Assessing Evidence Based Clinical Practice Guidelines?' (1999) 319 *British Medical Journal*, 1426.

[135] C. Ham and G. Robert (eds.), *Reasonable Rationing* (Buckingham: Open University Press, 2003).

[136] Mitton, McMahon, Morgan *et al.*, 'Centralized Drug Processes'.

[137] N. Daniels, J. Bryant, R. Castano *et al.*, 'Benchmarks of Fairness for Health Care Reform: a Policy Tool for Developing Countries' (2000) 78 *Bulletin of the World Health Organization*, 740.

[138] See O. Wright, 'NICE Man with a Reason to Smile', *The Times*, 2 December 2003, reporting that sixty countries had, at that date, investigated the Institute with a view to adoption of the model.

[139] Defined as those 'which relate to society rather than to basic or clinical science: they take account of the ethical principles, preferences, culture and aspirations that should underpin the nature and extent of the care provided by the NHS': NICE, *Social Value Judgements* at para. 1.1.

[140] *Ibid.* at paras. 2.2.5., 3.3.8. For argument that the Institute has misapplied Daniels and Sabin's model, see J. McMillan, M. Sheehan, D. Austin *et al.*, 'Ethics and Opportunity Costs: Have NICE Grasped the Ethics of Priority-Setting?' (2006) 32 *Journal of Medical Ethics*, 126.

[141] Notably in Scandinavia: see Holm, 'Goodbye to the Simple Solutions'.

of technical approaches have been exposed'[142] – albeit that this has not necessarily taken the form of implementation of the 'accountability for reasonableness' framework.

Developing deliberation

Daniels and Sabin are at pains to point out that fulfilment of the conditions of 'accountability for reasonableness' should not be regarded as an end in itself. The authors argue that compliance with the model is not an alternative to a process of democratic debate upon the rationing of healthcare resources, but rather that it *facilitates* that process.[143] Crucially, they contend that it is this process which 'should be the ultimate authority for settling disputes about limit setting in healthcare'.[144] Thus, the source of legitimacy lies not in the fair procedure in which rationing bodies engage, but rather in a society's democratic arrangements, broadly understood to 'take place in various forms in an array of institutions, spilling over into legislative politics only under some circumstances'.[145] It is therefore of some importance to establish, first, how the conditions of 'accountability for reasonableness' are intended to connect to wider processes of democracy and, secondly, the understanding of 'democracy' which underpins the Daniels and Sabin approach. As will be seen, the account of democracy which is employed in this context is one which receives increasing support in the field of health policy.

The role of the four conditions of 'accountability for reasonableness' as 'connective tissue to . . . a broader democratic process'[146] comes about by way of the contribution which they can make to enhancing understanding (primarily among members of the public and, to a lesser extent, patients, but also among physicians where appropriate) of the need to set limits on access to medical services and treatments, and of the types of evidence, grounds and conditions which may appropriately play a part in rationing decisions. Compliance with the model consequently serves an 'educative function':[147] that is, it facilitates 'social learning about limits'.[148] Thus, provision of reasons for rationing choices is valuable not only because it promotes more careful reflection upon the part of the decision-maker and

---

[142] C. Ham and A. Coulter, 'Explicit and Implicit Rationing: Taking Responsibility and Avoiding Blame for Health Care Choices' (2001) 6 *Journal of Health Services Research and Policy*, 163 at 166; see also Coulter and Ham (eds.), *The Global Challenge of Health Care Rationing* at 1, 10.

[143] See Daniels and Sabin, *Setting Limits Fairly* at 63.   [144] *Ibid.* at 34.

[145] Daniels, 'Justice, Health and Healthcare' at 11.

[146] Daniels and Sabin, 'The Ethics of Accountability' at 61.

[147] Daniels, 'Justice, Health and Healthcare' at 11.

[148] Daniels, 'Accountability for Reasonableness' at 1301.

encourages consistent treatment of similar cases, but also because it familiarises the public with the body's process of reasoning such that 'over time, people will better understand the moral commitments of the institutions making them'.[149] The 'relevance' condition (whether understood in Daniels and Sabin's terms or in the modified form proposed by Martin *et al.*) serves as a form of 'dialogue'[150] with stakeholders and the wider public such that, even if they have no direct involvement in the decision-making process, they may recognise that relevant values (including those which they hold) have been taken into consideration. Similarly, the revision/appeals and enforcement conditions function in an educative manner by broadening the evidence and argumentation available to the decision-maker. By further elucidating the grounds for decision, they ensure particularly that those affected are better informed if seeking to continue dialogue with the decision-maker in other arenas such as the courts or the political process.

It is feasible that the comprehension of the need for healthcare rationing and awareness of the decision-making criteria underpinning limit-setting choices which occur as a result of compliance with the conditions of 'accountability for reasonableness' may themselves be sufficient to engender legitimacy. Thus, on occasion, the originators of the model appear to argue that 'education' of the public through fulfilment of the conditions will lead to acceptance. For example, claims are made that 'the social learning that this approach facilitates provides our best prospect of achieving agreement over sharing medical resources fairly',[151] and that 'only a public that has gone through a sustained educational process will be equipped to accept the fairness and legitimacy of limits'.[152] This reflects a widely held view that 'publicity' (which may be defined as 'the reasons that officials and citizens give to justify political actions, and the information necessary to assess those reasons')[153] connects to public confidence in decision-making and hence to legitimacy.[154] Thus, Galligan writes that 'the giving of reasons is a way of providing satisfaction to the parties ... one very particular form of satisfaction is that which comes from being able to see that one's case has been dealt with properly

---

[149] Daniels and Sabin, *Setting Limits Fairly* at 49.

[150] Daniels and Sabin, *ibid.* at 52, cite Schauer's statement that reason-giving serves to 'open a conversation': F. Schauer, 'Giving Reasons' (1995) 47 *Stanford Law Review*, 633 at 658.

[151] Daniels, 'Accountability for Reasonableness' at 1301.

[152] Daniels and Sabin, *Setting Limits Fairly* at 170.

[153] A. Gutmann and D. Thompson, *Democracy and Disagreement* (Cambridge, Mass: Belknap Press, 1996) at 94.

[154] See P. Craig, 'The Common Law, Reasons and Administrative Justice' (1994) 53 *Cambridge Law Journal*, 282 at 283.

according to authoritative standards'.[155] More strongly, Prosser considers accountability ('which is centred around the development of the means to ensure that justifications in the form of reasons must be given for action') to form a central component of the legitimate exercise of public power in the modern state,[156] while Gutmann and Thompson argue that 'only public justifications can secure the consent of citizens, whether it be tacit or explicit. Such justifications help sustain a sense of legitimacy that makes political cooperation possible in the face of continuing moral disagreements'.[157]

However, as previously outlined, and as befits an approach which sees fair process as instrumental rather than a goal in itself, the authors seek to take a further step beyond the 'educative' function. They argue that the value of the social learning which is fostered through compliance with the principles of accountability for reasonableness lies in its capacity to facilitate a process of *democratic deliberation* upon healthcare rationing, from which process legitimacy is ultimately derived. The thesis receives its fullest and most forceful exposition in the concluding chapter of *Setting Limits Fairly*:

accountability for reasonableness contributes in multiple, often indirect, ways to the deliberative quality of broader democratic processes that are ultimately responsible for regulating the fairness of the health system ... Imagine a system that fully implemented such accountability in the various institutions responsible for allocating and delivering healthcare. Learning about limits and how to establish them fairly would then take place where health plans and other provider organisations interact with various stakeholders – clinicians, employers, managers and patients. Through proper institutional support, learning would take place in the doctor-patient relationship ... Societal learning would take place as a result of these institutional interactions with specific stakeholders and more broadly in the aggregate. This learning would infuse in various ways into the process of deliberation that takes place in an array of democratic institutions: legislative and executive bodies, the courts, and private associations, including professional associations and private regulative bodies ... We assume the quality of deliberation in these bodies would improve, as would the outcomes of deliberation – legal supervision, government regulation, and self-regulation. Accountability for reasonableness is the mechanism through which this learning would be facilitated and improved deliberation made more feasible ... As the public understands more through these institutional policies and interaction with doctors in the system, public debate can be enriched ... Accountability for reasonableness

---

[155] D. Galligan, *Due Process and Fair Procedures* (Oxford: Clarendon Press, 1996) at 433.

[156] T. Prosser, 'Towards a Critical Public Law' (1982) 9 *Journal of Law and Society*, 1 at 11. See further below Chapter 5, nn. 107–9 and accompanying text.

[157] Gutmann and Thompson, *Democracy and Disagreement* at 100.

facilitates this democratic process by supporting the conditions under which it is possible and likely to be most effective.[158]

On this analysis, therefore, the social learning which occurs as institutions fulfil the conditions of accountability for reasonableness *empowers* the public (and other stakeholders) to deliberate in a more comprehensive, informed and focused manner upon the rationing of healthcare within a range of democratic institutions. Such deliberation will not necessarily produce consensus – indeed, given the profundity of moral disagreement previously outlined, such consensus is implausible. However, it should contribute to the attainment of legitimacy because the reasons, evidence and argumentation advanced in support of a particular position are those which all participants (even those who disagree with the decision which is ultimately reached) can accept as relevant and appropriate, given a commitment to seek mutually justifiable terms of cooperation.[159]

In this manner, the 'accountability for reasonableness' thesis connects to a much broader literature on deliberative forms of democracy within modern political theory.[160] Full discussion of deliberative democratic theory is well beyond the scope of the present text, not least because 'deliberative democracy means many things to different theorists'.[161] Nonetheless, in brief, its essential precondition has been identified as 'the requirement that communication induce reflection upon preferences in a non-coercive fashion'.[162] It therefore entails a collective process of public reasoning, as opposed to bargaining between competing interests. In contrast to 'classic' pluralist models of democracy, preferences are not regarded as exogenous and fixed: instead, the giving, weighing, acceptance and rejection of reasons encourages reflection upon, and possible transformation of, those preferences. In the words of Habermas, 'no force other than that of the better argument is exercised',[163] as distinct from aggregative forms of democracy, where preferences may be shaped by

---

[158] Daniels and Sabin, *Setting Limits Fairly* at 172, 174.   [159] See *ibid.* at 35–7.

[160] Among the more important contributions are: Gutmann and Thompson, *Democracy and Disagreement*; S. Benhabib (ed.), *Democracy and Difference: Contesting the Boundaries of the Political* (Princeton: Princeton University Press, 1996); J. Bohman, *Public Deliberation: Pluralism, Complexity and Democracy* (Cambridge, Mass.: MIT Press, 1996); J. Bohman and W. Rehg (eds.), *Deliberative Democracy: Essays on Reason and Politics* (1997); J. Elster (ed.), *Deliberative Democracy* (New York: Cambridge University Press, 1997) and J. Dryzek, *Deliberative Democracy and Beyond: Liberals, Critics, Contestations* (Oxford: OUP, 2000). See also the work of Habermas, especially *Between Facts and Norms: Contributions to a Discourse Theory of Law and Democracy* (Cambridge: Polity, 1996). For the work of Rawls, see further below Chapter 5.

[161] J. Parkinson, 'Why Deliberate? The Encounter between Deliberation and New Public Managers' (2004) 82 *Public Administration*, 377 at 379.

[162] Dryzek, *Deliberative Democracy* at 2.   [163] Habermas, *Legitimation Crisis* at 108.

coercion, manipulation, deception and interest group capture. Some deliberative theorists operate within a critical idiom which expresses dissatisfaction with standard representative forms of democracy,[164] while others emphasise the capacity of deliberation to generate improved decisional outcomes from existing institutions and processes.[165] Common to most deliberative theorists, however, is a concern with legitimacy, it being claimed that, at base, 'deliberative democracy refers to the idea that legitimate lawmaking issues from the public deliberation of citizens',[166] and that 'deliberative democracy is also an account of legitimacy'.[167]

Within the deliberative literature, the problems identified in this chapter have received greatest attention in Gutmann and Thompson's *Democracy and Disagreement*. Significantly, Daniels and Sabin acknowledge that the conditions which make up the 'accountability for reasonableness' framework, albeit developed independently of Gutmann and Thompson's work, 'fit reasonably well' with the principles put forward by the latter authors,[168] although they express some reservations as to their approach.[169]

Arguing that 'neither the theory nor the practice of democratic politics has so far found a way to cope with conflicts about fundamental values', Gutmann and Thompson seek to develop 'a conception of democracy that secures a central place for moral discussion in political life'.[170] This is centred upon 'reasoning reciprocally', which occurs when citizens 'seek fair terms of social cooperation for their own sake; they try to find mutually acceptable ways of resolving moral disagreements ... Citizens who reason reciprocally can recognise that a position is worthy of moral respect even when they think it morally wrong'.[171] In order to ensure that reasoning of this type occurs, conditions of publicity (which requires that

---

[164]   See e.g. Dryzek, *Deliberative Democracy* at 2–3, Chapter 1.
[165]   See e.g. J. Steele, 'Participation and Deliberation in Environmental Law: Exploring a Problem-solving Approach' (2001) 21 *Oxford Journal of Legal Studies*, 415.
[166]   Bohman and Rehg (eds.), *Deliberative Democracy* at ix. *Cf.* also Bohman, *Public Deliberation* at 184: 'a law is legitimate only if it is based upon the public reasons resulting from an inclusive and fair process of deliberation in which all citizens may participate and in which they may continue to cooperate freely'.
[167]   J. Parkinson, 'Legitimacy Problems in Deliberative Democracy' (2003) 51 *Political Studies*, 180 at 181.
[168]   Daniels and Sabin, *Setting Limits Fairly* at 66; Daniels, 'Justice, Health and Healthcare' at 11.
[169]   See N. Daniels, 'Enabling democratic deliberation: how managed care organisations ought to make decisions about coverage for new technologies', in S. Macedo (ed.), *Deliberative Politics: Essays on Democracy and Disagreement* (New York: Oxford University Press, 1999) at 198.
[170]   Gutmann and Thompson, *Democracy and Disagreement* at 1.   [171]   *Ibid.* at 2.

citizens and public officials publicly justify their actions) and accountability (which requires that policies be justifiable to a representative's
moral constituency) should also be present; and Gutmann and
Thompson also seek to advance substantive principles which they consider should govern the content of deliberation, namely basic liberty,
basic opportunity and fair opportunity. They envisage that the deliberative approach which they champion will have wide-ranging applicability,
extending throughout the political process and 'embrac[ing] virtually any
setting in which citizens come together on a regular basis to reach collective decisions about public issues', including 'not only legislative sessions,
court proceedings, and administrative hearings at all levels of government
but also meetings of grass roots organisations, professional associations,
shareholders' meetings and citizens' committees in hospitals and other
similar institutions'.[172] However, they do not presume that deliberation
will result in comprehensive moral consensus, given that 'moral disagreement is a permanent condition of democratic politics'.[173] Rather, decisions which emerge from a deliberative process should be regarded as
'provisional', always open to the force of better arguments and new
evidence. Nonetheless, even if the decisions which emerge from a deliberative process necessarily have a provisional status, as the products of
reciprocal reasoning they are likely to be more justifiable to those citizens
bound by them than decisions which are the outcomes of the existing
processes of representative democracy. As such 'citizens stand a better
chance of resolving some of their moral disagreements, and living with
those that will inevitably persist, on terms that all can accept'.[174]

The applicability of Gutmann and Thompson's account of deliberative
democracy to issues of healthcare rationing becomes apparent from the
authors' discussion of the sources of moral disagreement. The most
obviously relevant of these is that moral conflicts will occur when allocation of scarce resources becomes necessary, that is, problems of distributive justice will inevitably arise. However, the other three factors
identified by the authors – limited generosity (moral conflicts arise
because of constraints on mankind's capacity for altruism), limited
understanding (lack of knowledge of the costs and benefits of a particular
form of action) and incompatible values (pursuit of differing but worth-
while objectives in accordance with distinct moral perspectives) – also
characterise issues of healthcare rationing. Acknowledging this fact, the
authors explicitly cite denial of scarce life-saving medical treatment as
an instance of the type of moral disagreement for which deliberation is

---

[172] *Ibid.* at 12–13.   [173] *Ibid.* at 9.   [174] *Ibid.* at 51.

well-suited,[175] developing this analysis further in an extended discussion of a particular case of rationing, that of the decision of the Arizona legislature to withdraw public funding for liver and heart transplants.[176] The argument made is that deliberative democracy can respond to each of the various elements of moral conflict: to limited generosity through the development of participatory forums 'in which citizens are encouraged to take a broader perspective on questions of public policy than they might otherwise take';[177] to limited understanding by stimulating learning through reasoning, argumentation and the presentation of evidence; and to incompatible moral values by clarifying the nature of moral conflict, distinguishing claims rooted in self-interest from those which are public-spirited and identifying the moral claims which carry greatest weight. Again, however, it is in relation to scarcity of resources that Gutmann and Thompson's arguments are most readily seen as germane to the issues examined in this chapter:

Deliberation contributes to the legitimacy of decisions made under conditions of scarcity. Some citizens will not get what they want, or even what they need, and sometimes none will. The hard choices that democratic governments make in these circumstances should be more acceptable even to those who receive less than they deserve if everyone's claims have been considered on their merits rather than on the basis of wealth, status, or power. Even with regard to political decisions with which they disagree, citizens are likely to take a different attitude toward those that are adopted after careful consideration of the relevant conflicting moral claims than those that are adopted only after calculation of the relative strength of the competing political interests. Moral justifications do not of course make up for the material resources that citizens fail to receive. *But they help sustain the political legitimacy* that makes possible collective efforts to secure more of those resources in the future, and to live with one another civilly in the meantime.[178]

Gutmann and Thompson have offered a stimulating account of how society might democratically address the 'fact of reasonable pluralism'[179] which characterises fields of public policy such as the allocation of scarce healthcare resources and, in so doing, how problems of legitimacy which tend to arise in these areas might be tackled. Their thesis is, of course, not unproblematic. Critics have observed that the approach may too readily assume the eradicability of power relations and that the 'force of the better argument' which emerges from the deliberative process is itself a form of coercion of those who disagree with the decision reached.[180] Concern has also been expressed at the inclusion of substantive principles

---

[175] See *ibid.* at 12, 28–9.   [176] See *ibid.*, Chapter 6.
[177] *Ibid.* at 42.   [178] *Ibid.* at 41–2. Emphasis added.
[179] J. Rawls, *Political Liberalism* (New York: Columbia University Press, 1993) at xix.
[180] See E. Hauptmann, 'Deliberation = Legitimacy = Democracy' (1999) 27 *Political Theory*, 857.

within the theory. By so doing, Gutmann and Thompson seek to address the danger that the decision-making process will give rise to outcomes which are of profound moral injustice,[181] yet it is unclear how the substantive principles which are put forward can be justified save by means of the democratic process upon which they act as logically prior constraints.[182] A further objection – which is acknowledged as pertinent by the authors themselves – is that a shift towards deliberation 'has the risk of creating even greater conflict than it is intended to resolve. Once the moral sensibilities of citizens and officials are engaged, they may be less willing to compromise than before. More issues come to be seen by more citizens as matters of principle, creating occasions for high-minded statements, unyielding stands, and no-holds-barred opposition'.[183] The response to this criticism – which is not altogether convincing – is that 'no democratic political process can completely avoid the risks of intensifying moral conflict' and that 'other common ways of dealing with moral conflict [such as violence and manipulation] are clearly worse'.[184]

More generally, there are reasons to be sceptical as to the *feasibility* of realising a deliberative approach to democracy, whether based upon the analysis offered by Gutmann and Thompson or the work undertaken by other theorists. Various practical obstacles to the realisation of deliberation have been enumerated by critics, notably problems of motivation (persuading members of the public to participate in deliberation and ensuring that minority voices are properly heard), organisation (such as availability of time for meetings) and of scale (reconciling the conflict between the impracticability of involving everyone affected by a decision in deliberation and the principle that outcomes are only legitimate if all those subject to a decision assent to it through involvement in reflective deliberation).[185] There may also be a problem of 'difference', relating to distinctions in schemes of perception, cognition and discourse which lead to deficiencies in understanding which block communication between deliberants.[186]

---

[181] Beauchamp and Childress, *Principles of Biomedical Ethics* at 258 regard this as being a significant deficiency of procedural strategies (such as that of Daniels and Sabin) for setting priorities on the allocation of healthcare resources.

[182] See D. Weinstock (1997) 91 *American Political Science Review*, 724. For a spirited defence of their approach, which argues that a separation between procedural and substantive principles and theories is not sustainable, see A. Gutmann and D. Thompson, 'Deliberative Democracy Beyond Process' (2002) 10 *Journal of Political Philosophy*, 153.

[183] Gutmann and Thompson, *Democracy and Disagreement* at 44. See also Beauchamp and Childress, *Principles of Biomedical Ethics* at 258.

[184] Gutmann and Thompson, *ibid.*

[185] For discussion of the 'scale' problem, see Parkinson, 'Legitimacy Problems'.

[186] See Black, 'Proceduralizing Regulation Part II' at 38–45.

Of these, the issue of motivation is perhaps the most directly pertinent to the context of the rationing of healthcare resources. The reluctance of the public to become involved in allocative decision-making in this field has previously been noted.[187] It was observed that this attitude was underpinned by an unwillingness to be seen to be denying care to those enduring pain and suffering and a lack of comprehension of the technical discourse which tends to surround rationing questions. This clearly presents a problem for an approach, such as that of Daniels and Sabin, which seeks to ground legitimacy in a process of public deliberation. However, the 'educative' function performed by the conditions of 'accountability for reasonableness' should serve to diminish (albeit, perhaps not to eradicate) this difficulty. Explanation of limit-setting decisions will assist public understanding of the 'language' of healthcare rationing. Similarly, provision of reasons which rest upon principles and values articulated by stakeholders and which can be considered relevant by 'fair-minded' citizens, should serve to reduce 'denial disutility' as the latter develop an awareness of the significance of taking account of community values as well as those relating to individual clinical need. In short, fulfilment of the conditions of 'accountability for reasonableness' can (to adopt the terminology employed by Gutmann and Thompson) assist in addressing those issues of limited understanding and incompatible values which may serve as barriers to public involvement in rationing decisions, thus preparing the ground for deliberation.

Notwithstanding the concerns which surround them, deliberative approaches to decision-making are undoubtedly increasing in popularity in health systems worldwide. These may be seen as reflecting a broader trend within public policy in which the importance of 'active citizenship' is emphasised, in response to an apparent decline in interest in traditional forms of representative democracy and in an attempt to resolve complex social issues.[188] In the health field, various participatory mechanisms of a more or less deliberative nature have been employed. These include citizens' juries (where a small representative group of members of the public meet over several days to engage in a process of reflection, discussion and consideration of evidence upon a particular issue of policy or planning, culminating in a decision or set of recommendations in the form of a citizens' report), citizens' panels (groups of statistically representative citizens whose views are sought by public organisations on a regular basis), deliberation-oriented focus groups (one-off discussions of

---

[187] See above Chapter 3, n. 24 and accompanying text.
[188] For discussion, see e.g. J. Newman, M. Barnes, H. Sullivan *et al.*, 'Public Participation and Collaborative Governance' (2004) 33 *Journal of Social Policy*, 203.

a particular topic among individuals selected to represent a particular sector of society), and deliberative polling (which combines an opinion survey with opportunities for discussion and deliberation over a two to three day period).[189] The NHS in the UK has emerged as 'the principal laboratory for ... recent experiments with deliberative processes' in the healthcare context,[190] with citizens' juries proving especially popular as inputs to local decision-making on resource allocation.[191] However, similar deliberative techniques have been adopted elsewhere, including Canada,[192] New Zealand[193] and Australia.[194]

Two instances of deliberation upon the rationing of healthcare resources are particularly worthy of comment. First, as outlined in Chapter 3, during the early 1990s the Oregon Health Services Commission sought to involve the public in establishing a package of publicly-funded medical treatments and services. The objective was to elicit public opinion on priorities for certain categories of health (e.g. the relative priority accorded to treatment of life-threatening conditions as against preventive measures) and on the weightings attached to differing values (such as equity, ability to function, quality of life, length of life, personal choice). A number of mechanisms were utilised to achieve this goal, including community forums, a telephone survey and public hearings. However, the public was reluctant to participate: just over 1,000 citizens attended public meetings held to discuss priorities and almost 70 per cent of these worked in the health system.[195] One view of the process is therefore that the problem of motivation resulted in medical expertise playing the dominant role in the decision-making process, as distinct from the values of the public.[196] Others have been less negative, pointing to the success of the exercise in generating public support for what would otherwise have

---

[189] For further discussion of these (and other) mechanisms, see L. Pratchett, 'New Fashions in Public Participation: Towards Greater Democracy?' (1999) 52 *Parliamentary Affairs*, 617, especially at 621–8; and in the health context, see J. Abelson, P-G. Forest, J. Eyles *et al.*, 'Deliberations about deliberative methods: issues in the design and evaluation of public participation processes' (2003) 57 *Social Science and Medicine*, 239 at 242–3.

[190] Abelson *et al.*, *ibid.* at 253.

[191] See J. Lenaghan, 'Involving the Public in Rationing Decisions. The Experience of Citizens' juries' (1999) 49 *Health Policy*, 45.

[192] See J. Abelson and F-P. Gauvin, *Engaging Citizens: One Route to Health Care Accountability* (Ottawa: Canadian Policy Research Network, 2004).

[193] See Ham and Coulter, 'Explicit and Implicit Rationing' at 165.

[194] See G. Mooney and S. Blackwell, 'Whose Health Service Is It Anyway? Community Values in Healthcare' (2004) 180 *Medical Journal of Australia*, 76.

[195] See D. Fox and H. Leichter, 'Rationing Care in Oregon: the New Accountability' (1991) 10 *Health Affairs*, 7 at 21.

[196] See R. Klein, P. Day and S. Redmayne, *Managing Scarcity* (Buckingham: Open University Press, 1996) at 113.

been controversial legislative proposals.[197] It is doubtful, however, whether this can be regarded as amounting to genuine deliberative democracy – at best, deliberative mechanisms appear to have been employed to 'shore up' traditional processes of representative democracy.

More recently, in the UK, NICE has shown awareness of the utility of deliberative democratic processes in respect of certain aspects of its work. Recognising that the technical expertise of the scientists, clinicians, health economists and others who are responsible for evaluating the clinical and cost-effectiveness of medical technologies is insufficient basis for legitimate determination of those principles (such as equity) which should underpin the just distribution of healthcare resources,[198] the Institute has established a Citizens' Council to ensure that its judgments on such issues reflect the social values of the public. The Council, which consists of thirty members[199] recruited to be representative of the population in respect of gender, social class, ethnicity, age and disability and which meets twice a year for six days in total, considers topics referred to it by the Institute's Board, such as the relevance of age in decision-making on access to medical treatments, and the role of the 'rule of rescue'. It hears and cross-examines expert witnesses, engages in discussion (including the use of case studies and role play) in plenary and small group sessions and produces its recommendations in the form of a report to the Board. However, notwithstanding the view of the Chairman of the Institute that the Council operates in a deliberative manner,[200] an independent evaluation of its activities has questioned the capacity of the public to deliberate upon broad ethical questions of the type devised by the Institute. The study draws attention to the limited opportunities for integration of the Council's recommendations in the Institute's work given its infrequent meetings, inability to set its own programme, the non-binding nature of its recommendations and the lack of a direct input into the core technology appraisal function performed by the Institute.[201]

---

[197] See L. Jacobs, T. Marmor and J. Oberlander, 'The Oregon Health Plan and the Political Paradox of Rationing: What Advocates and Critics Have Claimed and What Oregon Did' (1999) 24 *Journal of Health Politics, Policy and Law*, 16 at 173.

[198] See M. Rawlins and A. Culyer, 'National Institute for Clinical Excellence and its Value Judgments' (2004) 329 *British Medical Journal*, 224 at 225.

[199] Those employed in the NHS, in private medicine, healthcare industries or patient lobbying organisations are excluded from membership of the Council.

[200] See M. Rawlins, 'Pharmacopolitics and Deliberative Democracy' (2005) 5 *Clinical Medicine*, 471.

[201] See C. Davies, M. Wetherell, E. Barnett *et al.*, *Opening the Box: Evaluating the Citizens' Council of NICE* (Milton Keynes: Open University, 2005).

Conclusion

The problems which emerge in discussions of deliberative democracy and the difficulties of translating theory into practice in the context of health policy (or, for that matter, any other field) are clearly not to be under-estimated. But the goal of this chapter has not been to offer a comprehensive critique of deliberative democracy, nor even – as Daniels and Sabin have sought to do – to construct a theoretical framework for fair decision-making on the allocation of scarce healthcare resources. Rather, the aim is more modest: to offer an account of *the state of current thinking and practice* on how to address a significant policy problem which has emerged in modern health systems. That is, the need to minimise the instability to which explicit forms of rationing give rise, which in turn reflects doubts as to the legitimate moral authority of those responsible for undertaking rationing decisions given a state of ethical pluralism.

From this perspective, it is readily apparent that a procedural approach, in particular one which draws upon the notion of deliberation, has emerged as a leading strategy within the health policy community in recent years. While, as Ham and Coulter have argued,[202] it is somewhat misleading to view this in isolation from other developments in this field – notably, efforts to strengthen the information base upon which rationing decisions may be based through analysis of randomised controlled trials and application of metrics drawn from health economics – it is nonetheless clear that decision-makers continue to regard compliance with norms of procedural justice as being of fundamental significance in the pursuit of legitimacy for rationing choices. This is most evident from the experience of NICE in the UK, which, in addition to its role in gathering and assessing evidence of the clinical and cost-effectiveness of new medical technologies, has publicly avowed its commitment to the 'accountability for reasonableness' model and which, through its Citizens' Council, has sought to integrate deliberative democracy into its decision-making, albeit within limited parameters and with questionable success.

In the context of rationing, therefore, health policy may be said to have taken a distinctive 'procedural turn' as attempts have been made to respond to the problem of legitimacy arising from the implementation of strategies of explicit rationing. What, if anything, is the appropriate role for law within this policy environment? This is the question which the remainder of this book will set out to answer.

---

[202] Ham and Coulter, 'Explicit and Implicit Rationing', especially at 166–7.

5 Rationing and the Courts: Theoretical Perspectives

What's law got to do with it?

The title of a report produced by the Canadian Bar Association[1] neatly captures the attitude of scepticism, prevailing among many who work in this field, towards involvement of the legal process in questions of the rationing of scarce healthcare resources. Law, and in particular litigation, is seen as inimical to the task of establishment of priorities for healthcare expenditure. The consequence is that there has been a failure to consider the potential of legal mechanisms and, specifically, the application of legal principles in an adjudicative setting, to assist in the resolution of the 'legitimacy problem' delineated in the previous chapter. This chapter will canvass the theoretical and jurisprudential arguments for and against an expanded role for law in this context, focussing mainly, but not exclusively, upon the part played by the courts. The three subsequent chapters will consider the degree to which existing case law from England, Canada and South Africa suggests that potential exists to develop an approach to the judicial function in rationing cases along the lines of that which is outlined here.

Mistrust of the legal process

Perhaps the most pointed expression of antipathy towards a perceived intrusion by law into this field of public policy is that of Hunter, who argues baldly that 'there is no place for the courts in rationing healthcare. The law is too blunt a weapon in an area of moral and ethical choices that are heavily contingent upon the circumstances prevailing in a particular case'.[2] A somewhat more measured opinion is voiced by Hall, who

---

[1] Canadian Bar Association Task Force on Health Care, *What's Law Got To Do With It? Health Care Reform in Canada* (Ottawa: Canadian Bar Association, 1994).

[2] D. Hunter, 'Rationing Health Care: the Political Perspective' (1995) 51 *British Medical Bulletin*, 876 at 881.

(writing from the perspective of the market-based US health system) remarks that 'courts appear ill-equipped to stake a middle ground between doing nothing to check insurers and doing too much to protect individual patients',[3] while Mechanic – who, as noted in Chapter 3,[4] argues that explicit forms of rationing will be subject to challenge 'through the mass media and in other ways' – expresses the view that 'litigation is a highly formalized and time-consuming process that involves considerable costs for both the patient and the medical-care system'.[5]

A comparable aversion to legal intervention in matters of rationing is also frequently apparent from media commentary upon specific legal challenges to allocative decisions. Thus, in broadsheet newspaper discussions of the 'Child B' case,[6] it was maintained that 'it is not for courts to interfere with the way health authorities make medical judgments on funding',[7] and that it is 'not for judges to absolve politicians of moral responsibility for choices they make in allocating resources'.[8] Similar views were expressed in response to the decision of the English Court of Appeal in the *Rogers* case,[9] with one broadsheet commenting, under the by-line 'Meddling judges make it worse', that courts:

increasingly have been ready to interfere in the running of the health service, ruling which patients have a right to treatment and which do not. They should desist ... courts should curb their judicial interventions. Judges look at the rights of individuals; health managers have to balance the rights of many different patients. It is as inappropriate for judges to meddle in medicine, as it would be for health managers and medics to sit on the appeal court bench.[10]

The decision of the Canadian Supreme Court in *Chaoulli* also prompted misgivings in the media as to the implications of judicial intervention on issues of allocation of healthcare resources (prompted in part by expressions of uncertainty on the part of the dissenting judges as to the

---

[3] M. Hall, *Making Medical Spending Decisions* (New York: Oxford University Press, 1997) at 73.

[4] Above Chapter 3, n. 58 and accompanying text.

[5] D. Mechanic, *Future Issues in Health Care: Social Policy and the Rationing of Medical Services* (New York: Free Press, 1979) at 118.

[6] *R* v. *Cambridge Health Authority, ex parte B* [1995] 1 WLR 898 ('Child B'), discussed below Chapter 6.

[7] *The Guardian*, 11 March 1995, cited in C. Burgoyne, 'Distributive Justice and Rationing in the NHS: Framing Effects in Press Coverage of a Controversial Decision' (1997) 7 *Journal of Community and Applied Social Psychology*, 119 at 129.

[8] *Sunday Times*, 12 March 1995, cited *ibid.* at 130.

[9] *R (on the application of Rogers)* v. *Swindon NHS Primary Care Trust and Secretary of State for Health* [2006] 1 WLR 2649, discussed below Chapter 6.

[10] *The Guardian*, 13 April 2006. See also 'Appeal Court Tears up the Rules on Prescribing Herceptin', *The Times*, 13 April 2006.

appropriate role for the judiciary in this field).[11] It was accordingly observed that 'the Supreme Court justices have strenuously denied that they are intruding into the political sphere ... Yet, the impact of their decisions has been politically strategic in a most profound way.'[12]

These evaluations suggest that involvement of the legal process is widely seen as antithetical to the task of equitable allocation of scarce healthcare resources. However, they do not speak specifically to the question of legitimacy which, as argued above, raises a particularly acute problem of public policy in modern health systems. Instructive in this regard are the observations of an independent Commission on the NHS, established by the Association of Community Health Councils for England and Wales in 1999 and charged with identifying means of strengthening accountability mechanisms to better serve the public interest. Although developed in a UK context, it is submitted that the analysis of the role of law which is offered by the Commission may be viewed as being of broad applicability to many health systems across the globe:

> For their part, patients and potential patients in the form of the healthy citizen increasingly refuse to be treated as subjects of a paternalistic health service; they want a voice, influence over decisions that affect them, and redress for their grievances. They want the NHS to look out for their individual concerns. There is a growing temptation to turn to the courts and the language of human rights to fill the gap ... it would be a mistake to see reliance on the courts and human rights as a substitute for thinking hard about issues of principle relating to the public interest, and to the proper accountability and therefore the legitimacy of the National Health Service ... It is of course appropriate for individuals to rely on the law to defend themselves from unlawful action by branches of the health service ... It is wrong to castigate the law for having so greatly increased its involvement in the health service in recent years. And it is also wrong to blame individuals and others for turning to the law to further their interests within the health service ... Even a properly functioning health service will attract, possibly frequently, the involvement of the law. All public authorities in the land must adhere to the principles of legality ... What matters is not the principle of the availability of such recourses to law, but the context in which such litigation occurs. At present the perceived secrecy of the NHS and the lack of proper accountability in the system as a whole leads to an over-reliance on law as a means of achieving the responses and the transparency that should be a matter of right. The heavy involvement of the law in a public service is a measure of its failure rather than its success.[13]

It should be readily apparent that the overall tenor of this passage is one of negativity towards (or, at best, a grudging acceptance of) legal

---

[11] *Chaoulli* v. *Québec (Attorney General)* [2005] 1 SCR 791, discussed below Chapter 7.

[12] 'Our Top Court Comes under Scrutiny', *Toronto Star*, 17 June 2005.

[13] The Commission on the NHS chaired by W. Hutton, *New Life for Health* (London: Vintage, 2000) at 31, 60–62.

mechanisms. Involvement of the law in the operation of a health service is a matter which must be tolerated – individuals cannot be prevented from having recourse to the courts – but ideally, it should be minimised as far as possible by strengthening institutional structures to permit greater transparency and accountability, thereby reducing the scope for complaints and disputes, and enabling those which persist to be addressed internally. On this analysis, law does not assist in the achievement of legitimacy. Rather, the increasing likelihood of legal intervention can be linked to declining levels of trust and deference towards the medical profession (or, somewhat more positively, to a desire for a greater 'voice' in healthcare decisions).[14] In short, reliance upon legal mechanisms is symptomatic of systemic instability and represents an (unsatisfactory) *alternative* to devising means to secure accountability and, hence, legitimacy.

The perceived role of law

It is clear, therefore, that many commentators regard law as an unwelcome intruder upon the health policy arena, particularly as regards its involvement in the process of setting priorities for healthcare expenditure. It may, however, be helpful to articulate somewhat more clearly, albeit in brief, the manner in which law is perceived within such analyses.

First, although recourse to legal mechanisms must be condoned, such a tactic should ideally *only be adopted when all else has failed*. This permits the impact of law to be circumscribed as far as possible. Hence, the Commission on the NHS expresses the view that law is 'an important fall-back opportunity for individuals whom the system has grievously failed' and that 'many judicial review applications have been borne out of a desperate sense of hopelessness and out of an inability effectively to penetrate the secrecy with which NHS decisions are currently enshrouded'.[15] It further states its aspiration for 'a properly functioning and democratically accountable health service [which] would be one in which the law would be a tool of last resort to be used reluctantly, rather than the first stop for the (rightly or wrongly) disgruntled that it so often is today'.[16] The language of 'last resort' is deployed by other commentators – for example, New asks: 'is it important that the courts should be used only as a last resort?'[17] Also instructive is the evident anxiety of patients

---

[14] For further discussion of these social trends, see Chapter 2, nn. 145–7 and accompanying text.
[15] Hutton, *New Life for Health* at 62, 61.   [16] *Ibid.* at 62.
[17] B. New, 'The Rationing Agenda in the NHS' (1996) 312 *British Medical Journal*, 1593 at 1597.

(and their legal advisers) who embark upon litigation in response to decisions to deny access to treatment to define such activity as a regrettable necessity. Thus, the solicitors acting for Ann Marie Rogers in the judicial review of the decision to refuse to fund treatment by way of Herceptin commented that 'This legal fight is something she is forced to do',[18] and issued a press release concerning the case entitled 'Christmas cancelled for Breast Cancer patient forced to go to court to fight for life',[19] while the litigant herself maintained that 'I never thought it would go so far and I never wanted to end up in court'.[20] Similarly, another patient seeking treatment with Herceptin, Barbara Clark, explained that her decision to commence legal proceedings 'was spurred on by sheer desperation'.[21]

Secondly, litigation is, in essence, conceived as a *form of intimidation*. Its strategic role is to compel an allocative decision-maker to divert resources towards the aggrieved individual. This is readily apparent from the frequency with which legal action is described as a 'threat',[22] *viz*: 'Barbara Clark had to threaten her local health authority with the European court of human rights';[23] 'all previous legal actions including the cases of Barbara Clark and Elaine Barber have resulted in the PCT reversing their position before judicial proceedings have taken place, following an appeal and threat of High Court action';[24] 'Two other women had threatened to take trusts to court over their refusal to fund Herceptin';[25] 'Bristol breast cancer patient threatens court action to get Herceptin drug'.[26] Correspondingly, any reversal of a decision not to provide funding for treatment is perceived as 'backing down', for example: 'All along, I'd imagined Swindon PCT would back down';[27] 'If it [the

---

[18] Y. Amin, quoted in 'Woman Loses Herceptin Court Bid', *BBC News Online*, 15 February 2006, available at http://news.bbc.co.uk/1/hi/health/4715430.stm (accessed 8 January 2007).

[19] Irwin Mitchell Press Release, 23 December 2005, available at www.irwinmitchell.com/PressOffice/PressReleases (accessed 8 January 2007).

[20] Quoted in 'Herceptin: So Is It Such a Wonder Drug?', *Daily Mail*, 24 May 2005.

[21] Quoted in 'Dying Nurse Sues NHS for Denying Her Cancer Drug', *The Observer*, 18 September 2005.

[22] See further C. Ham and S. McIver, *Contested Decisions* (London: King's Fund, 2000) at 66, referring to the 'threat of legal action'.

[23] 'In the Cancer Lottery, I'm One of the Lucky Ones', *The Guardian*, 7 October 2005.

[24] 'High Court Ruling in Breast Cancer Victim's Fight for Life', Irwin Mitchell Press Release, 21 February 2006, available at www.irwinmitchell.com/PressOffice/PressReleases (accessed 8 January 2007).

[25] 'Judge Orders Health Trust to Fund Interim Course of Herceptin for Cancer Patient', *The Guardian*, 22 December 2005.

[26] Thompsons Solicitors News Story, 19 December 2005, available at www.thompsons.law.co.uk/ntext/rel.php?id=182 (accessed 8 January 2007).

[27] A. M. Rogers, quoted in *Daily Mail*, 24 May 2005.

PCT] does not back down and give Mr. Bould this drug we will go to the High Court for a judicial review challenge against this decision';[28] 'in both cases the trusts backed down'.[29] Also instructive in this regard are descriptions of legal proceedings as a mode of conflict, with the words 'battle' and 'fight' in common usage.[30]

Thirdly, the legal process is seen as a vehicle for the *protection of the individual* and in this regard is juxtaposed to the 'collective' process of allocation of resources which is perceived as being carried out in the interests of the wider community. Once again, media commentary upon the *Rogers* case is revealing here. As noted above, one broadsheet newspaper sought to distinguish the 'judicial function', conceived as being adjudication upon individual claims, from the 'managerial function' of evaluating and weighing the competing interests of a broader community.[31] Another analysis of the case construed it as a 'landmark victory for an individual over a health trust … [and] an important step forward for "patient power"',[32] while a further article highlighted the potentially deleterious consequences of the Court of Appeal's decision for other users of the NHS, asserting that 'Patients will be denied access to drugs at the forefront of medical research after a landmark judgment on the breast cancer treatment Herceptin. The ruling means that trusts will now either have to agree to pay for a new drug for any patient whose doctor recommends it – with serious implications for NHS budgets – or refuse the treatment for the entire population it serves'.[33] It is also worthy of note that the supposed individualistic orientation of the legal process frequently finds expression in the language of rights. This is unsurprising on the occasions where rights legislation is invoked in the (prospective or actual) legal proceedings, as in the cases of Barbara Clark, who stated that 'I am legally challenging the NHS because it is limiting my

---

[28] 'Dying Man Refused Tarceva Cancer Drug to Prolong His Life and Ease his Suffering, Irwin Mitchell Press Release, 8 May 2006, available at www.irwinmitchell.com/PressOffice/PressReleases (accessed 8 January 2007).

[29] *The Guardian*, 22 December 2005.

[30] See e.g. 'Court to Rule in Herceptin Battle', *BBC News Online*, 11 April 2006, available at http://news.bbc.co.uk/1/hi/health/4900674.stm (accessed 8 January 2007); 'Breast Cancer Patient Loses Herceptin Legal Battle', *The Times*, 15 February 2006; 'Cancer Victim Wins Herceptin Battle', *Daily Mirror*, 12 April 2006; 'High Court Ruling', Irwin Mitchell Press Release, above n. 24; 'Cancer Victim Loses Court Fight over Herceptin', *The Independent*, 15 February 2006; 'Patient Wins Legal Fight for "Wonder Drug"', *The Scotsman*, 13 April 2006.

[31] See *The Guardian*, 13 April 2006.

[32] 'Q & A: Herceptin Ruling a Victory for Patient Power', *Times Online* (12 April 2006), available at www.timesonline.co.uk/article/0,8122-2131111,00.html (accessed 8 January 2007).

[33] 'Herceptin Ruling Will Stop Patients Getting Potentially Life-Saving Drugs', *The Times*, 13 April 2006.

right to life by denying me Herceptin',[34] and of Ann Marie Rogers, whose solicitors described the challenge in judicial review as 'the very first time a person's right to receive the drug has reached the courts'.[35] However, litigation is seen more generally as a vehicle for the assertion of individual rights in contradistinction to collective choices, for example in the work of the Commission on the NHS, which argues that 'the assertion of individual rights through litigation is no substitute for voicing the public interest through collective decision-making rooted in democratic choices and thoroughly canvassed social preferences'.[36]

In a number of respects, the preceding perceptions of the contribution which may be made by the legal process in this field of public policy are broadly indicative of the influence of a 'positivist' or 'formalist' reading of the nature and functions of public law.[37] In line with Dicey's seminal analysis of the British constitution,[38] this construes law (with a particular focus upon the role of the courts) as a checking and controlling mechanism designed, in the portentous words of Sir William Wade, 'to keep the powers of government within their legal bounds . . . The powerful engines of authority must be prevented from running amok'.[39] This accounts for the 'intimidatory' quality which litigation appears to possess vis-à-vis allocative decision-makers. And, in acting in this manner, law serves to 'protect the citizen against their abuse' [i.e. that of the 'powers of government']:[40] its role is to safeguard individual autonomy against encroachment by the state, with the consequence that community interests are ascribed an attenuated value within judicial reasoning.

Equally, the reluctance to resort to litigation except as a last resort suggests an understanding of law, redolent of theories of the 'rule of law', as an autonomous social subsystem which is discrete from politics and administration rather than a tool which may be integrated into the decision-making process. Taking legal action is therefore perceived as stepping outside of the proper boundaries of a health system and, in view of the

---

[34] Quoted in *The Observer*, 18 September 2005.

[35] 'First Judicial Proceedings to Take Place in the High Court over a Patient's Right to Herceptin', Irwin Mitchell Press Release, 6 February 2006, available at www.irwinmitchell.com/PressOffice/PressReleases (accessed 8 January 2007).

[36] Hutton, *New Life for Health* at 31.

[37] For a valuable discussion of competing theories of the function of law in the administrative state, see C. Harlow and R. Rawlings, *Law and Administration* (London: Butterworths, 2nd edn, 1997), especially Chapters 1 to 3.

[38] A. Dicey, *Introduction to the Study of the Law of the Constitution* (London: Macmillan, 10th edn, 1959).

[39] H. Wade and C. Forsyth, *Administrative Law* (Oxford: Oxford University Press, 9th edn, 2004) at 5.

[40] *Ibid.* at 5.

widespread support which many publicly funded systems (such as those in the UK and Canada) attract, is a step not to be taken lightly. The influence of a Diceyan approach, in which law is to be divorced from politics, is again apparent here. Interestingly, though, it is also consonant with an alternative 'functionalist' or 'realist' reading of law, which values the involvement of the state as an effective means for the realisation of certain broad-based social goals (such as universal education or healthcare), but which also seeks to minimise the influence of courts and emphasise non-judicial, democratic forms of accountability in pursuit of a more collective notion of the public interest, not least because of the unrepresentative and undemocratic character of the judiciary. Consequently, from either of these perspectives, a certain degree of distrust of judicial involvement may be warranted.

However, the functionalist style of public law does provide a pointer to a more positive role which may be played by law in relation to decision-making by state bodies such as those charged with the allocation of scarce healthcare resources. Operating within this discourse, a school of thought emphasises the capacity of law to function in an *instrumental* or *facilitative* manner, assisting administrators in the discharge of their duties and thus contributing to realisation of the public good.[41] For example, public law mechanisms broadly understood (including internal complaint processes, 'court-alternatives' such as tribunals, inquiries and ombudsmen, and regulatory mechanisms) possess the capacity to articulate a framework of 'principles of good administration' (such as timeliness, reason-giving, transparency, consistency) which can serve to set good standards for decisional processes and thus contribute to their acceptability.[42] As noted above, courts may not be the preferred arenas for the pursuit of such a goal: they have traditionally been regarded as ideologically disinclined to offer support to state organs in the exercise of their functions,[43] and are also seen as undemocratic, costly, slow and inaccessible to the public. Nonetheless, a functionalist analysis might concede that, at least on occasion, courts may play a useful role, particularly as the authority which they carry and the publicity which attends their judgments tend to generate a 'trickle-down' effect on those making decisions of a similar type even if they are not directly involved in the instant case.[44]

---

[41] For general discussion, see M. Loughlin, 'The Functionalist Style in Public Law' (2005) 55 *University of Toronto Law Journal*, 361.

[42] See D. Woodhouse, *In Pursuit of Good Administration: Ministers, Civil Servants and Judges* (Oxford: Clarendon Press, 1997), especially Chapters 7 and 8.

[43] See e.g. H. Laski, 'Judicial Review of Social Policy in England' (1926) 39 *Harvard Law Review*, 832.

[44] For an instructive discussion of the judicial contribution to good administration from a government perspective of government, see Treasury Solicitor's Department, *The Judge over Your Shoulder* (London: The Stationery Office, 4th edn, 2006), especially at 7.

This book's central contention is that the facilitative capabilities of public law have been mistakenly overlooked by those who would seek to develop a publicly acceptable mode of decision-making on the allocation of scarce healthcare resources in light of the suspicion and distrust to which explicit rationing tends to give rise. This has led to the neglect of law, and especially of the processes of public law adjudication, as possible means through which the 'legitimacy problem', identified in the previous chapter, might be addressed. As will be argued subsequently in this chapter, there are significant synergies between the goals and values of public law and those which underpin models of procedural justice in the context of healthcare rationing, such as 'accountability for reasonableness'. It is submitted that this correlation should prompt a reconceptualisation of the potential function for law in this field, although the capability of the courts to realise such a role in practice warrants further examination, which will be the task of the following three chapters.

Nonetheless, any critique of the adoption of an overly narrow conception of the function of law in respect of rationing choices must recognise the weight of two extenuating factors. First, the 'formalist' or 'positivist' conception, which sees the role of the law in negative terms as that of a control mechanism and which apparently prioritises individual autonomy over collective interests, constitutes by far the dominant theoretical understanding of public law,[45] notwithstanding that it is essentially rooted in nineteenth century liberal individualism, *laissez-faire* economics and a limited state. It is therefore unsurprising that accounts of the engagement of law with issues of healthcare resource allocation adopt such a reading, especially if written by non-lawyers with no grounding in alternative approaches. Secondly, and arguably more significantly, there do remain significant weaknesses inherent in public law adjudication which undoubtedly limit its utility as a mechanism through which problems arising from the explicit rationing of healthcare resources may be addressed. These will now be examined.

The limitations of adjudication

Decisions as to the allocation of scarce resources, whether arising in healthcare or other areas of social and economic policy, are sometimes classified as not justiciable.[46] The concept of justiciability expresses the

---

[45] See M. Loughlin, *Public Law and Political Theory* (Oxford: Clarendon Press, 1992) at 181.

[46] See e.g. H. Woolf, J. Jowell and A. Le Sueur, *De Smith, Woolf and Jowell's Principles of Judicial Review* (London: Sweet and Maxwell, 1999) at para. 5–030; D. O'Sullivan, 'The allocation of scarce resources and the right to life under the European Convention on

extent to which a matter is appropriate for determination by courts or similar institutions, that is whether it is 'amenable to the judicial process'.[47] Although it has been criticised as 'inchoate', 'problematic' and 'redundant',[48] justiciability continues to play a role in assessment of the proper limits of judicial scrutiny of administrative decision-making. For example, in *R v. Criminal Injuries Compensation Board, ex parte P*, the English Court of Appeal was obliged to review a decision by the Home Secretary to introduce revised criteria for eligibility for compensation from the Criminal Injuries Compensation Scheme. Neill LJ stated that the decision involved 'a balance of competing claims on the public purse and the allocation of economic resources which the court is ill equipped to deal with',[49] and that accordingly he did not regard it as justiciable.[50]

There are a number of factors which may underpin a judgment by a court that a particular matter is non-justiciable. A useful means of understanding these is by reference to Jowell's classification of judicial competence into 'institutional' and 'constitutional' variants.[51] For Jowell, 'the question of institutional competence involves a practical evaluation of the capacity of decision-making bodies to make certain decisions. It ... focuses not upon the appropriate role of the judge, but upon the inherent limitations of the process of adjudication'.[52] By contrast, 'the question of constitutional competence involves a normative assessment of the proper role of institutions in a democracy',[53] and thus places emphasis upon the extent to which the courts may be viewed as possessing democratic characteristics and their legitimate constitutional functions vis-à-vis the other branches of government.

As regards the institutional capacity of courts, a key consideration is the extent to which the issues involved in allocative decision-making are

Human Rights' [1998] *Public Law*, 389 at 389; J. Jowell, 'Of Vires and Vacuums: The Constitutional Context of Judicial Review' [1999] *Public Law*, 448 at 454. All three of these sources cite allocative decisions in healthcare as illustrations of non-justiciability.

[47] *Council of Civil Service Unions v. Minister for the Civil Service* [1985] 1 AC 374 ('*CCSU*') at 418 (Lord Roskill).

[48] See C. Finn, 'The Justiciability of Administrative Decisions: a Redundant Concept?' [2002] *Federal Law Review*, 9 at 9.

[49] [1995] 1 WLR 845 at 847. See also *CCSU* [1985] 1 AC 374, especially at 407 (Lord Scarman), 412 (Lord Diplock).

[50] But *cf.* the views of Evans and Peter Gibson LJJ in this case, for which see below nn. 71–72 and accompanying text.

[51] Jowell, 'Of Vires and Vacuums' at 451. *Cf.* M. Pieterse, 'Coming to Terms with Judicial Enforcement of Socio-Economic Rights' (2004) *South African Journal on Human Rights*, 383 at 390–96, referring to problems of 'institutional legitimacy' (similar to Jowell's notion of 'constitutional competence') and 'institutional competence'. For further discussion of Pieterse's analysis, see below Chapter 8.

[52] *Ibid.* at 451.   [53] *Ibid.*

polycentric in nature. The classic analysis of polycentric questions is offered by Fuller, who defines the concept largely by way of metaphor and example:

We may visualise this kind of situation by thinking of a spider web. A pull on one strand will distribute tensions after a complicated pattern throughout the web as a whole. Doubling the original pull will, in all likelihood, not simply double each of the resulting tensions but will rather create a different complicated pattern of tensions. This would certainly occur, for example, if the doubled pull caused one or more of the weaker strands to snap. This is a 'polycentric' situation because it is 'many centred' – each crossing of strands is a distinct centre for distributing tensions.[54]

The term therefore refers to situations which are multi-faceted, which may affect large numbers of interested parties, and which carry complex repercussions.

While most matters upon which courts are called upon to adjudicate are, to a greater or lesser extent, polycentric,[55] questions of the allocation of scarce resources – especially in so far as these arise in respect of social policy programmes (such as the provision of healthcare) which have broad societal impact and contrasting and conflicting objectives – may be regarded as being 'preponderantly' so.[56] This was recognised by Fuller, who argued that 'generally speaking, it may be said that problems in the allocation of economic resources present too strong a polycentric aspect to be suitable for adjudication'.[57] As this statement makes clear, polycentricity connects to justiciability. Issues of this type are not suitable for judicial determination because of the nature of the process of litigation. The bivalent character of adversarial adjudication, in which two competing parties present reasoned proofs and arguments in support of their case to a neutral judge who is obliged to respond only to those proofs and arguments, renders a court ill-equipped to evaluate the complex repercussions which arise from polycentric disputes, or to ensure that all affected parties can participate in the decision. On this basis, non-judicial mechanisms (such as those existing within the political process, or administrative institutions such as ombudsmen) may be preferable to courts. Alternatively, reforms to the adversarial system may warrant

---

[54] L. Fuller, 'The Forms and Limits of Adjudication' (1978) 92 *Harvard Law Review*, 353 at 395.

[55] See J. Allison, 'The Procedural Reason for Judicial Restraint' [1994] *Public Law*, 452 at 457.

[56] C. Ngwena, 'Access to Antiretroviral Therapy to Prevent Mother-to-Child Transmission of HIV as a Socio-Economic Right: an Application of Section 27 of the Constitution' (2003) 18 *SA Publiekreg/Public Law*, 83 at 87.

[57] Fuller, 'Forms and Limits of Adjudication' at 400.

consideration to enable courts to better respond to disputes of a poly-centric nature.[58]

Courts may also be considered to lack institutional competence to adjudicate upon disputes turning on the allocation of scarce resources because of a lack of relevant expertise. Legally trained judges may be said not to possess the necessary background skills, knowledge and experience of economics and management to decide matters which carry budgetary implications.[59] This may be a particular obstacle in fields such as health-care where allocative decision-making will frequently be informed by tech-nical and highly specialised disciplines such as epidemiology and health economics.[60] In such circumstances, notwithstanding the availability (at least in some jurisdictions) of procedural mechanisms which may be of assistance in enhancing judicial comprehension of technical questions,[61] courts may concede that the legislature, the executive or an agency with specialist expertise will be better placed to consider the matter.

In the healthcare context, such a conclusion may be expressed in the form of a refusal on the part of the judiciary to countenance that it has any role in 'second guessing' the exercise of judgment by the initial, expert, allocative decision-maker. For example, in the 'Child B' case which is discussed at length in Chapter 6, Sir Thomas Bingham MR opined that the court was '*not fitted* to make any decision favourable to the patient',[62] thereby invoking the notion of justiciability. This view appears to have been formulated on the basis of concerns as to the institutional compe-tence of courts to become engaged in questions of clinical judgment and the management of resources, both of which demanded specialist knowl-edge which was not in the possession of the Court of Appeal.[63] In addition, the judge alluded to the polycentric character of the allocative choice made by the health authority in referring to the need for the latter to determine 'how a limited budget is best allocated to the maximum advantage of the maximum number of patients'.[64]

---

[58] See e.g. Allison, 'Procedural Reason for Judicial Restraint' at 467–73.
[59] See Jowell, 'Of Vires and Vacuums' at 451.
[60] See Chapter 3, nn. 108–9 and accompanying text.
[61] For example, granting rights of third party intervention may increase the amount of information available to the court, while 'Brandeis briefs' permit social and economic data to be admitted. For the former, see below Chapter 7, n. 45 and accompanying text.
[62] *R* v. *Cambridge Health Authority, ex parte B* [1995] 1 WLR 898 at 907. Emphasis added.
[63] Evidence presented to the Court of Appeal indicated that (i) the treatment was consid-ered to be of an 'experimental' nature; (ii) the prospects of successful treatment were between 1% and 4% overall; (iii) the treatment would have debilitating side-effects; and (iv) that the total cost of the treatment could not be justified in light of the prospects of success. See *ibid.* at 901–4
[64] See *ibid.* at 906.

Judicial reluctance to intrude upon allocative decision-making also reflects concerns as to the constitutional competence possessed by courts. In this regard, the judiciary may be seen to exhibit an awareness of the boundaries to adjudication which are imposed by the doctrine of the separation of powers and by broader notions of democratic legitimacy, majoritarianism and judicial accountability.[65] As Pieterse observes, reservations as to the appropriate role for a relatively unaccountable judiciary within a constitutional democracy are not confined to litigation on questions of the allocation of scarce resources (whether in healthcare or other fields of public policy), but surface whenever 'the institution of judicial review seems necessarily to imply the sacrifice of a measure of direct or representative democracy'.[66] The 'counter-majoritarian difficulty of judicial review'[67] is, however, especially acute in the context of resource allocation, which is widely viewed as falling within the province of the 'political' branches of government: indeed, on some definitions, as being the very stuff of politics.[68] Accordingly, rationing choices, particularly at the 'macro' and, to a lesser degree, the 'meso' level, are apt to be viewed by courts as a non-justiciable area of subject matter.[69] In the words of Jowell, 'decisions of social and economic policy are constitutionally allocated to our elected officials and it is not for the courts to engage in matters involving a utilitarian calculus of social good'.[70]

There are, therefore, a number of powerful factors which may incline a court to regard issues of the rationing of scarce resources as non-justiciable. However, notwithstanding the views expressed by Neill LJ in *R* v. *Criminal Injuries Compensation Board, ex parte P*, judges frequently evince an unwillingness to construe such questions as *totally* inappropriate for judicial resolution, seeking instead to reserve some (very limited) scope for scrutiny in cases where the allocative decision reached is egregious in the extreme. Thus, in that particular case, Evans LJ queried whether the evidence in fact demonstrated that the decision had involved a choice between competing claims to scarce resources and noted that, even if there were limits to resources, that this would not 'justify an unfair (irrational) as opposed to a fair distribution under the scheme'.[71] Similarly, Peter Gibson LJ, while

---

[65] See Pieterse, 'Coming to Terms with Judicial Enforcement' at 390.   [66] *Ibid.*

[67] A. Bickel, *The Least Dangerous Branch: the Supreme Court at the Bar of Politics* (New Haven: Yale University Press, 1986) at 16.

[68] See e.g. H. Laswell, *Politics: Who Gets What When and How* (New York: McGraw-Hill, 1936).

[69] For examples, see the discussions of *R* v. *Secretary of State for Social Services, West Midlands Regional Health Authority and Birmingham Area Health Authority (Teaching), ex parte Hincks* (1980) 1 BMLR 93 and *R (on the application of Pfizer Ltd.)* v. *Secretary of State for Health* [2003] 1 CMLR 19 in Chapter 6 below.

[70] Jowell, 'Of Vires and Vacuums' at 454.   [71] [1995] 1 WLR 845 at 861.

concurring with Neill LJ that the court was 'ill-equipped' to decide questions of the type raised by the case, wished to retain jurisdiction to intervene in cases of 'perversity'.[72] As will be noted in Chapter 6, a comparable stance was adopted by judges in early English cases on the allocation of scarce healthcare resources, with courts reserving to themselves the possibility – albeit a remote one – of intervention in such matters where the decision was characterised by extreme unreasonableness or irrationality.[73]

For this reason, it is submitted that it is preferable to regard the judicial approach to questions of the allocation of scarce resources, including those in healthcare, as one which is *deferential* and *restrained*, as distinct from one which turns upon the concept of non-justiciability, with its attendant connotation of absolute immunity from judicial questioning. The notion of 'deference', which has been developed in particular in the context of the proper scope of adjudication upon human rights claims against both executive and legislature, may be said to refer 'to the idea of a court, exceptionally, out of respect for other branches of government and in recognition of their democratic decision-making role, declining to make its own independent judgment on a particular issue'.[74] There is some debate about whether the principle encapsulates notions of lack of both constitutional and institutional competence, or merely the latter,[75] but for present purposes the most significant aspect is that 'the degree of deference which the courts should show will . . . depend on and vary with the context'.[76] Similarly, the idea of judicial restraint, which appears to have evolved in relation to judicial review of administrative action, seeks to capture a willingness on the part of the courts to limit the scope of judicial oversight of decision-making in line with their constitutional and institutional capacity, but may also be operated with greater or lesser intensity as the context demands.[77]

---

[72] *Ibid.* at 863.

[73] See the discussion of *R v. Central Birmingham Health Authority, ex parte Collier* (unreported), Chapter 6 below; and further, *R v. Central Birmingham Health Authority, ex parte Walker* (1987) 3 BMLR 32 at 35 (Sir John Donaldson MR), 'Child B' [1995] 1 WLR 898 at 907 (Sir Stephen Brown P).

[74] Lord Steyn, 'Deference: a Tangled Story' [2005] *Public Law*, 349.

[75] For the view that deference is a matter of institutional capacity alone, see *ibid.* at 352; J. Rivers, 'Proportionality and Variable Intensity of Review' (2006) 65 *Cambridge Law Journal*, 174 at 192; while for the view that it embraces constitutional *and* institutional competence, see Lord Lester and D. Pannick (eds.), *Human Rights Law and Practice* (London: Butterworths, 2nd edn, 2004) at para. 3.19.

[76] Steyn, *ibid.* at 352; see further *International Transport Roth GmbH v. Secretary of State for the Home Department* [2003] QB 728 at paras. 81–7.

[77] See e.g. Lord Irvine of Lairg, 'Judges and Decision-Makers: the Theory and Practice of *Wednesbury* Review' [1996] *Public Law*, 59, writing of 'judicial self-restraint': at 75–8. Note that 'deference' is sometimes distinguished from 'restraint': Rivers, 'Proportionality

It remains clear, however, that where the subject-matter on which the court is asked to adjudicate is one involving the allocation of scarce resources, the judiciary will tend to operate at the higher end of the 'scale' of deference or restraint. That is, while engagement with such issues is not, *a priori* wholly excluded, the courts will show significant respect for the judgment of the original allocative decision-maker and will, in general, decline to become involved. This is likely to be especially true of cases where the impugned decision relates to the rationing of healthcare,[78] given the expert epistemologies upon which this process frequently rests.

Public law and legitimacy

There are therefore important reasons to be wary of the heavy involvement of the law in issues of the allocation of scarce healthcare resources. Nevertheless, it appears likely that increasing resort *will* be had to litigation in situations where individuals are denied access to medical treatments and services. This is, in part, simply a symptom of a more litigious culture within civil society as a whole, a phenomenon which is connected to the decline of deference in, and erosion of trust towards, professional judgment in all fields, as outlined in Chapter 2.[79] However, in the particular context of healthcare, it also follows from the developments which were described in Chapter 3. That is, the increasing public visibility of healthcare rationing as policy-makers implement explicit strategies renders legal action far more likely than was the case under the previous, implicit, mode where awareness of the existence of rationing was much less widespread. As noted by Mechanic,[80] explicit rationing tends towards instability because 'those who care deeply but are denied access will inevitably challenge the explicit judgment through the mass media and other ways' – and one of these 'other ways' is, of course, through the courts. Related to this is the growing impact of pressure groups which may provide support for those individuals seeking to challenge rationing decisions, for example through financial assistance or access to specialist legal advice. Such groups may operate specifically to advance the interests of those suffering from a particular disease,[81] or they may be broader-based

and Variable Intensity' at 192–3 regards the former as deriving from lack of institutional competence and the latter from lack of constitutional competence. No such distinction will be attempted in this text.

[78] See Steyn, 'Deference' at 350.   [79] See Chapter 2, n. 145 and accompanying text.

[80] See Chapter 3, n. 58 and accompanying text.

[81] The Women Fighting for Herceptin group, described in Chapter 1, did not provide financial or legal assistance to Ann Marie Rogers or other women who sought to

groups whose objectives extend beyond the healthcare arena.[82] In either case, however, litigation may prove to be a valuable strategy in advancing the group's campaigning agenda.[83]

The apparent inevitability of law's growing engagement with allocative decision-making in the healthcare context means that arguments that its role should be minimised as far as possible appear to be increasingly out of step with reality. There seems little prospect of 'insulating' this area of public policy from the attentions of the legal process. Yet, is it necessary to adopt an unremittingly negative attitude towards law's involvement in this area of public policy, as so many commentators have done? It is submitted that it would be more profitable for those working within the health policy arena to consider whether the involvement of law can be turned to advantage, rather than seeking to limit its impact. Here, the 'functionalist' style of public law offers some guidance as to the approach to be taken. By channelling and guiding decision-making processes, good administration can be encouraged and facilitated, and this will be to the advantage of a wider community upon whose behalf and in whose interests such administrative decision-making ultimately takes place. On this analysis, therefore, lawyers can most usefully see themselves as 'process architects',[84] engaged (for example) in 'alleviating inconsistencies and structuring effective procedures for decision-making ... ensuring that decisions are taken in a reasoned and justified manner and good standards for decisional processes are developed'.[85]

From the perspective of the argument advanced in the previous chapter, the most valuable contribution which could be made by public law to the enhancement of public administration in this policy field would be to assist in the resolution of the 'legitimacy problem'. That is, attention should be given to the possibilities which law opens up for enhancing the public acceptability of decision-making which has the consequence of denying or restricting access to healthcare as a good of special moral importance, given the existence of incommensurable moral positions in

challenge the refusal to provide Herceptin. Nonetheless, it played an important role as a source of moral support to those involved in litigation. For analysis of the rise of patient groups, see R. Baggott, J. Allsop and K. Jones, *Speaking for Patients and Carers: Health Consumer Groups and the Policy Process* (London: Palgrave Macmillan, 2004).

[82] For example, the trade union Unison funded an application for judicial review by a nurse, Elizabeth Cooke: see www.thompsons.law.co.uk/ntext/thompsons-trade-union-campaign-herceptin.htm (accessed 8 January 2007).

[83] For a valuable discussion of the use of litigation as a campaigning strategy, see C. Harlow and R. Rawlings, *Pressure Through Law* (London: Routledge, 1992).

[84] C. Menkel-Meadow, 'The Lawyer's Role(s) in Deliberative Democracy' (2005) 5 *Nevada Law Journal*, 347 at 352.

[85] D. Longley, *Public Law and Health Service Accountability* (Buckingham: Open University Press, 1993) at 82.

a state of ethical pluralism. The remainder of the argument in this chapter will seek to sketch out the manner in which such a function might be performed, especially by the courts in adjudication upon questions of public law. But it is important to note that the capacity to undertake such a role rests upon the existence of some connection between public law and legitimacy in the exercise of public power, enabling the former to contribute to the alleviation of any deficiency in the latter. To what extent can such a relationship be established?

At first sight, the connection between public law – as that branch of law which is concerned with the exercise and control of governmental power[86] – and legitimacy appears self-evident. The dictionary definition of 'legitimacy' is 'conformity to rule or principle; lawfulness' and, relating specifically to government, 'the condition of being in accordance with law or principle'.[87] On such a definition, legitimacy would seem to correspond to legality. Since, straightforwardly, public law adjudication is fundamentally concerned with appraisal of the legality of decisions and actions undertaken by governmental bodies, a ruling in favour of such a body by a court in the exercise of its public law jurisdiction would appear to be a sufficient (albeit not a necessary) condition of the legitimate exercise of state power.

However, it has been powerfully argued that there is 'nothing inherent or natural about legality [which] makes it conducive to legitimacy'[88] and that it should therefore be considered as distinct from 'mere' legality or lawfulness.[89] This raises the question of how 'legitimacy' should be defined. Regrettably, the concept is not susceptible to simple definition: indeed, it has been described as 'difficult and complex'.[90] Nonetheless, one valuable and widely accepted reading is that of Habermas, who writes that 'Legitimacy means that there are good arguments for a political order's claim to be recognised as right and just; a legitimate order deserves recognition. *Legitimacy means a political order's worthiness to be recognised*'.[91] This captures the understanding of a legitimate system or

---

[86] See Chapter 1, n. 42 and accompanying text.

[87] *Oxford English Dictionary* (Oxford: OUP, 2nd edn, 1989).

[88] J. Ketchen, 'Revisiting Fuller's Critique of Hart – Managerial Control and the Pathology of Legal Systems: the Hart-Weber Nexus' (2003) 53 *University of Toronto Law Journal*, 1 at 18.

[89] See e.g. J. Habermas, 'Law and Morality' in S. McMurrin (ed.) *The Tanner Lectures on Human Values*, Volume 8 (Salt Lake City: University of Utah Press, 1988).

[90] R. Baldwin and C. McCrudden, *Regulation and Public Law* (London: Weidenfeld & Nicolson, 1987) at 32. For fuller discussions of the meaning of the concept, see W. Connolly (ed.), *Legitimacy and the State* (Oxford: Blackwell, 1984), R. Barker, *Political Legitimacy and the State* (Oxford: Clarendon Press, 1990).

[91] J. Habermas, *Communication and the Evolution of Society* (Cambridge: Polity, 1979) at 178. Emphasis in original.

institution as one which is viewed as 'appropriate' or 'right and proper'.[92]

A claim to legitimacy is, therefore, a normative claim to acceptability or validity: a political order, government or institution which issues such a claim is asserting that it *ought* to be willingly obeyed or respected. On some accounts, such as that of Weber, all that is required is that the order, government or institution is itself established through and governed by rules and that those rules are accepted as a valid source of authority.[93] The source of such acceptance is irrelevant: mere compliance with 'right process' will suffice.[94] For others, such as Beetham, 'a given power relationship is not legitimate because people believe in its legitimacy, but because it can be *justified in terms of* their beliefs'.[95] The discourse of legitimacy is thus one in which an action, decision, rule or political order is *explained and justified* – by reference to beliefs shared by dominant and subordinate actors – such that those affected can understand and accept why the exercise of authority is valid.[96] This process of justification need not entail reaching agreement as to the substantive content of all rules, decisions or actions undertaken by a political regime: scarcely any political order would achieve legitimacy if this were required. However, some, such as Fuller, argue that any regime which deserves recognition – i.e. one which lays claim to legitimacy – must comply with the 'internal morality' of law: that is, certain procedural precepts designed to hinder arbitrary, capricious or incoherent exercises of power, such as consistency, transparency and stability.[97]

Two observations may be made in light of this brief analysis of this 'vexing concept'.[98] First, the relevance of the 'accountability for reasonableness' model – and, especially, of its publicity and relevance

---

[92] J. Schaar, 'Legitimacy in the Modern State' in Connolly (ed.), *Legitimacy and the State* at 108–9. See also P. McAuslan and J. McEldowney (eds.), *Law, Legitimacy and the Constitution* (London: Sweet and Maxwell, 1985) at 2, 12; R. Baldwin, *Rules and Government* (Oxford: Clarendon Press, 1995) at 42.

[93] M. Weber, *Economy and Society: An Outline of Interpretive Sociology*, vol. 1 (G. Roth and C. Wittich (eds.)) (Berkeley: University of California Press, 1978) at 215; see further Ketchen, 'Revisiting Fuller's Critique' at 18–22.

[94] *Cf.* also T. Franck, *Fairness in International Law and Institutions* (Oxford: Oxford University Press, 1995) at 26.

[95] D. Beetham, *The Legitimation of Power* (London: Macmillan, 1991) at 11. Emphasis in original.

[96] See further P. Berger and T. Luckmann, *The Social Construction of Reality* (London: Penguin, 1991) at 111; T. Poole, 'Legitimacy, Rights and Judicial Review' (2005) 25 *Oxford Journal of Legal Studies*, 697 at 714.

[97] See L. Fuller, *The Morality of Law* (New Haven: Yale University Press, 1969), especially Chapter II; and further T. Allan, *Constitutional Justice: a Liberal Theory of the Rule of Law* (Oxford: Oxford University Press, 2001) at 73.

[98] C. Ansell, 'Legitimacy: Political' in N. Smelser and P. Bates (eds.), *International Encyclopaedia of the Behavioural and Social Sciences* (Oxford: Elsevier, 2001) at 8704.

conditions – should be immediately apparent. If, as argued, legitimacy is concerned with justification of the exercise of authority by reference to shared beliefs, then a claim to legitimacy by a rationing body is, as Daniels and Sabin contend, likely to hinge upon its capacity to provide reasons for its choices which rest upon evidence, arguments and principles which fair-minded people can agree are relevant (even though, if placed in charge, they might make different choices). The limit-setting body's 'worthiness to be recognised' rests not upon the substance of its decisions (which, in a state of ethical pluralism, will necessarily remain contentious), but rather on the fact that its decisions accord with an accepted norm of fair process.

Secondly, is legitimacy a matter of relevance for lawyers? On a very narrow, positivist reading of law, one might contend that the job of the lawyer is simply that of the exposition, analysis and application of rules: (s)he is not therefore concerned to 'identify those conditions under which an authority is legitimate – the reasons why citizens *ought* to obey'.[99] From this perspective, one might conclude that 'legitimacy is seen as lying beyond, outside the law, even if it has the capacity of occasionally entering its sphere. It is not perceived as the lawyer's concern but as that of the politician, the legislator and the moralist'.[100] Yet, such an outlook surely seriously understates the fundamental linkages between legal and political philosophy – articulated in the claim that 'public law is simply a sophisticated form of political discourse'[101] – which have been brought particularly to our attention by the functionalist approach to public law. Once we move beyond a simple theory of laws as commands backed by sanctions, a fundamental issue which the lawyer must inevitably confront is that of the source of the authoritative force of rules, decisions or actions. The concern is therefore with the extent to which the 'law of a state claims to impose and enforce legal obligations justifiably'.[102] As noted above, such questions of justificatory claims are questions relating to claims to legitimacy.

A better view, therefore, is that public lawyers are centrally concerned with legitimacy for the simple reason that 'the issue of legitimacy goes to the heart of any debate on constitutions and the exercise of public power'.[103] Indeed, the idea of the 'rule of law', which was central to

---

[99] *Ibid.*
[100] D. Georgiev, 'Politics or Rule of Law: Deconstruction and Legitimacy in International Law' (1993) 4 *European Journal of International Law*, 1 at 13.
[101] Loughlin, *Public Law and Political Theory* at 4.
[102] Ketchen, 'Revisiting Fuller's Critique' at 8.
[103] P. McAuslan and J. McEldowney, 'Legitimacy and the Constitution: the Dissonance between Theory and Practice', in McAuslan and McEldowney (eds.), *Law, Legitimacy* at 2.

Dicey's analysis of British constitutional and administrative law in the late Victorian era and which, it scarcely bears stating, has been much debated within jurisprudence and frequently invoked within legal and political discourse ever since,[104] can be regarded as having 'come to encapsulate a complex moral aspiration: the legitimacy of public power'.[105] On this analysis, legitimacy does not derive from the assent of the majority of citizens to particular exercises of public power. Rather, such exercises of public power are regarded as legitimate if they comply with certain formal standards, such as predictability, non-retrospectivity and generality; if they are undertaken in accordance with a constitutionally-ordained procedure for the making of laws and the vesting of executive authority; or (controversially), if they embody certain moral values which are broadly shared within the community.[106]

More recently, Prosser, seeking to move away from the Diceyan paradigm and to reassess the theoretical basis of public law from a 'critical' perspective, has stated that, in addition to the relatively empiricist task of mapping out the interrelationship of public institutions with each other and with private interests, public law should also concern itself with the critique of current institutional arrangements and with proposals for their future design.[107] In this regard, he argues that 'in addition to analysing legitimation offered by the state, it is necessary to develop a theory of legitimacy; a theory of what state action is *actually* legitimate and of how power can be legitimately exercised'.[108] To this end, he identifies two basic concepts around which such a theory can be built, namely

---

[104] See e.g. Preamble to the Universal Declaration of Human Rights 1948; International Congress of Jurists, Declaration of Delhi, 1959; and for further general discussion, A. Hutchinson and P. Monahan (eds.), *The Rule of Law: Ideal or Ideology?* (Toronto: Carswell, 1987); B. Tamahana, *On the Rule of Law: History, Politics, Theory* (Cambridge: Cambridge University Press, 2004).

[105] I. Harden and N. Lewis, *The Noble Lie: The Rule of Law and the British Constitution* (London: Hutchinson, 1986) at 5. See further Ketchen, 'Revisiting Fuller's Critique' at 35 and the discussion of the work of Fuller, above n. 97 and accompanying text.

[106] For a sophisticated modern analysis of the meaning of the rule of law, see Allan, *Constitutional Justice.*

[107] To this end, T. Prosser, 'Democratisation, Accountability and Institutional Design: Reflections on Public Law', in McAuslan and McEldowney (eds.), *Law, Legitimacy* at 172–3 refers with approval to the concept of 'responsive law' as articulated by P. Nonet and P. Selznick, *Law and Society in Transition: Towards Responsive Law* (New York: Harper Torchbooks, 1978) at 106–7: 'legal energies should be devoted to diagnosing institutional problems and redesigning institutional arrangements'; and further to that of 'reflexive law' developed by G. Teubner, 'Substantive and Reflexive Elements in Modern Law' (1983) 17 *Law and Society Review*, 239 at 251: 'legal attention focuses on creating, shaping, correcting and redesigning social institutions that function as self-regulating systems'.

[108] T. Prosser, 'Towards a Critical Public Law' (1982) 9 *Journal of Law and Society*, 1 at 9. Emphasis in original.

accountability and participation. Law provides the means for design of institutions which give effect to these principles, adherence to which enables social learning to take place, providing a basis for the resolution of problems of legitimation.[109] Another approach is that of Poole, who has claimed that a 'rights-based' model of judicial review (in which consideration of the significance of the right in question and the serious-ness of the threatened incursion provide the basis for judicial scrutiny) is inadequate to explain a continuing judicial attention to those 'second order considerations' which reflect general and collective concerns about the functioning of the political and administrative system, such as the appropriate constitutional balance between courts and other branches of government, administrative 'decency' and (which is particularly perti-nent in the context of the allocation of healthcare resources), the signifi-cance of expertise in the conduct of public administration.[110] Instead, he argues that 'judicial review is better understood as a means of trying to ensure legitimacy in the making and application of laws. A decision of a public body is unlawful, on this approach, if it represents an illegitimate exercise of public power, a judgment which may or may not involve considerations of rights'.[111]

Most germane of all to the argument advanced in this book is the analysis of Diane Longley, whose fundamental thesis – that greater attention should be paid to the potential role for (public) law in the shaping of health policy and the management of health services as public organisations – strongly informs the approach which has been taken here. Longley writes of the need to make 'use of the skills and techniques of law as a means of providing the necessary building fabric with which to frame the legitimate exercise of public power and public management',[112] and contends that 'what is per-haps under-emphasised is that law is not just . . . an instrument for achieving goals but is also a means of promoting and ensuring accountability and legitimacy in public decision-making, principles which are fundamental to our ideas of democracy and citizenship'.[113] Her argument, therefore, is that engagement of legal mechanisms with health policy and management is beneficial because 'law may have a vital role to play in developing healthcare provision into a more legitimate and effectively managed service through the innovative design of procedures which seek to promote accountability by a better reflection of public choices and the provision of reasoned justification

---

[109] See Prosser, 'Democratisation, Accountability and Institutional Design', especially at 174.

[110] Poole, 'Legitimacy, Rights' at 709–12.   [111] *Ibid.* at 724.

[112] D. Longley, *Public Law and Health Service Accountability* (Buckingham: Open University Press, 1993) at xi.

[113] *Ibid.* at 4.

for decisions'.[114] The value of accountability (which, it may be recalled,[115] Longley considers to rest upon 'transparency' and 'an obligation on the part of decision-makers to give explanations and justifications for their activities') lies in its capacity to contribute to 'social learning', which in turn will enable legitimacy to be secured:

Learning and social choice require relevant information; consequently a great deal of emphasis needs to be put on the requirement for openness in management processes and professional activity. It is argued that the introduction of norms of conduct for the management of health services, designed to secure acceptance of policy decisions and promote a better understanding of the reasonableness of decisions and the processes of decision-making, might eventually lead to a more stable and satisfactory organisation.[116]

Public accountability necessitates procedures for the open discussion of priorities and objectives before decisions reach a stage where there is no real choice. It also demands justification of policy choices and channels for the expression of dissatisfaction and the redress of grievances. Accountability is an ongoing evaluative process which should provide a vehicle for improvement and change. Such a focus might preclude the provision of any easy answers, but it should frame the questions that could lead to a better understanding of contending issues. Accountability is thus fundamental to an organisation's learning. For this to become a possibility some external direction is required ... the techniques and processes of law can assist in providing that external direction.[117]

These accounts should suffice to demonstrate that the predominantly negative characterisation of law as a bulwark shielding the individual against the arbitrary exercise of power merely captures one possible understanding of its role, and one which may indeed be out of kilter with the collective forms of decision-making demanded within the modern administrative state. At the very least, public law possesses the *capability* to act as a facilitator: to operate instrumentally to assist decision-makers in discharging their tasks in a manner which is conducive to the common good. Specifically, in the context examined here, the synergies which exist between public law and the legitimate exercise of public power (which are to some degree apparent even within the otherwise constraining Diceyan formalist approach) should permit consideration of public law's capacity to 'correct and redesign social institutions' by way of addressing the 'legitimacy problem'. On such an approach, resource allocation would be carried out 'in the shadow of the law', but rather than constituting a scenario to be avoided, this situation would be welcomed as a means of enhancing the 'worthiness to be recognised' of the

---

[114] *Ibid.* at 16.   [115] See Chapter 3, n. 76 and accompanying text.
[116] Longley, *Public Law* at xii.   [117] *Ibid.* at 104–5.

institutions through which, and the process by which, difficult choices as to the allocation of scarce healthcare resources are reached.

'Accountability for reasonableness' and public law

It might be expected that, given their concern with establishing the conditions for the legitimate exercise of public power, and the emphasis which they place upon a transparent and accountable process of decision-making, Daniels and Sabin would be sympathetic to the facilitative role for public law in assuring legitimacy which was delineated in the preceding section. Indeed, it is worthy of note that the underlying objective of the 'accountability for reasonableness' model, that compliance will stimulate 'social learning' about limits and thereby enable a more informed and focussed deliberation upon rationing questions,[118] mirrors the arguments offered by both Prosser and Longley as to the function which may usefully be performed by public law. Furthermore, as will now be outlined, there are strong parallels between the conditions which constitute the 'accountability for reasonableness' model, and principles which are central to public law (and which, in consequence, find frequent articulation in public law jurisprudence).[119]

First, notwithstanding a tradition of judicial discomfiture at imposing a general obligation upon administrative bodies to provide reasons for their decisions,[120] accountability (understood as the provision of justification through reasons)[121] has been identified as a basic foundation of public law theory. As will be seen in the following chapters, recent judicial decisions offer considerable encouragement to those who express the wish that, in relation to decisions on the rationing of healthcare resources, 'the future impact of administrative law will hopefully be to realise the promise of transparency'.[122] It should further be noted that, in offering justification for the imposition of the 'publicity' condition, Daniels and Sabin make explicit reference to the value of building a body of 'case law'. This contributes to legitimacy in so far as it promotes consistent treatment of similar cases and more focused decision-making through 'thoughtful evaluation of these reasons and their foundation within our

---

[118] See above Chapter 4, n. 148 and accompanying text.
[119] For a more extended discussion, see K. Syrett, 'NICE Work? Rationing, Review and the "Legitimacy Problem" in the New NHS' (2002) 10 *Medical Law Review*, 1 at 18–24.
[120] Notably in English law: for analysis, see Craig, above Chapter 4, n. 154.
[121] See Prosser, above Chapter 4, n. 156 and accompanying text.
[122] C. Stewart, 'Tragic Choices and the Role of Administrative Law' (2000) 321 *British Medical Journal*, 105 at 107.

thinking'.[123] Unsurprisingly in view of the analogy to 'case law', such arguments echo those expressed in the legal literature,[124] and to a more limited extent, in court decisions,[125] on the advantages of reason-giving.

Secondly, Daniels' and Sabin's 'relevance' condition, which imposes constraints upon the rationales which can be offered for rationing decisions, bears close resemblance to the grounds upon which the courts may assert control over the exercise of discretion in judicial review of administrative action. In particular, judicial scrutiny of the relevance of considerations taken into account by a decision-maker when engaged in rationing may enable the courts to ensure that the choice which is made 'appeals to reasons, including values and principles, that are accepted as relevant by people who are disposed to finding ways of co-operating with each other on mutually acceptable terms'.[126] Now, it will become apparent from the discussion in subsequent chapters that courts have been somewhat tentative in imposing this requirement upon bodies which are responsible for allocating scarce healthcare resources, and it seems unlikely – notwithstanding the increasing availability of data obtained through health technology assessments undertaken by bodies such as NICE – that they will engage in *detailed* scrutiny of the 'factual presuppositions' which underpin a priority-setting decision, as Daniels and Sabin appear to demand.[127] Nonetheless, the fact that the principles of public law 'include a requirement that ... decisions are rationally based upon a proper consideration of the facts'[128] does offer the courts opportunity to play some part in ensuring that the reasons proffered for decisions to limit access to treatments and services are broadly accepted as relevant. Moreover, it should be noted that they appear more willing to undertake this role in situations where scarcity of resources is not the decisive factor underlying a decision to refuse treatment, as was the case in *Rogers*.[129]

Daniels and Sabin contend that the third requirement of the 'accountability for reasonableness' model, that procedures must exist which

---

[123] N. Daniels and J. Sabin, *Setting Limits Fairly* (New York: Oxford University Press, 2002) at 49.

[124] See e.g. P. Craig, 'The Common Law, Reasons and Administrative Justice' (1994) 53 Cambridge Law Journal, 282 at 283; D. Galligan, *Due Process and Fair Procedures* (Oxford: Clarendon Press 1996) at 431–4.

[125] See e.g. *R* v. *Higher Education Funding Council, ex parte Institute of Dental Surgery* [1994] 1 WLR 241; *R* v. *Ministry of Defence, ex parte Murray* [1998] COD 134.

[126] Daniels and Sabin, *Setting Limits Fairly* at 51.

[127] *Ibid.* at 56–7. See especially the discussion of *Auton* v. *British Columbia (Attorney General)* [2004] 3 SCR 657, below Chapter 7.

[128] *R* v. *North West Lancashire Health Authority, ex parte A, D and G* [2000] 1 WLR 977 at 997 (Buxton LJ).

[129] See below Chapter 6, n. 61 and accompanying text.

enable rationing decisions to be challenged and which permit revision or improvement of policies in the light of new evidence and arguments, is best satisfied by the establishment of an *internal* process of dispute resolution.[130] In this regard, public law adjudication may suffer from the defects that it is focussed upon questions of law rather than of fact, and that revisiting the merits of the original decision (as opposed to its lawfulness) is impermissible.[131] However, judicial involvement is not excluded: as the authors note, it is likely that recourse will be made to litigation if such processes are insufficient to resolve a complaint.[132] In such circumstances, courts may make a useful contribution both by curing any procedural unfairness which has arisen in the original decision-making process or the subsequent internal appeal, and by ensuring that the decision-making body honours any promise to conduct dispute resolution internally, on the basis that an individual has a 'legitimate expectation' that a certain procedure should be followed.[133]

In light of these significant points of congruence, a strong case can be made for law's capacity to contribute to the realisation of 'accountability for reasonableness'. Indeed, public law mechanisms – including, but not necessarily restricted to, the courts – might be seen as very well-suited to fulfilment of Daniels' and Sabin's fourth condition: that there should be voluntary or public regulation of the decision-making process to ensure that the other three conditions are met. To a degree, the proponents of the model recognise this possibility through their expression of support for US state legislation 'governing the behaviour of health plans and other insurers, including restrictions on "gag" orders or other constraints on what physicians may say to patients and often, provision for appeals procedures'.[134]

Yet, taken overall, the attitude of the authors toward law's involvement in decision-making on the allocation of scarce healthcare resources appears to be little more positive than that of the commentators cited in the opening of this chapter. Their views are clearly expressed in the following passage:

The courts are ill-equipped to deliberate about issues of limit setting, especially about the more technical matters involved in assessing efficacy and safety. Court procedures, for example, bring opposing experts to bear, and they leave the final

---

[130] Daniels and Sabin, *Setting Limits Fairly* at 58.
[131] Although it should be noted that the level of scrutiny which obtains in public law cases based upon the alleged violation of human rights is more searching than that in cases of judicial review of administrative action, and comes closer to 'merits-based' review. See below Chapter 6, n. 33.
[132] Daniels and Sabin, *Setting Limits Fairly* at 59.
[133] See e.g. *Attorney General of Hong Kong* v. *Ng Yuen Shiu* [1983] 2 AC 629.
[134] Daniels and Sabin, *Setting Limits Fairly* at 60.

decision up to those – whether judges or juries – with no expertise about technical matters and little understanding of the organisational context within which the issue has arisen. This is simply not the best way to deliberate about these matters, despite its appearance of a democratic input through the opinion of peers.[135]

Consistently with this expression of discomfiture at judicial intervention, and in common with the views outlined previously, Daniels and Sabin see litigation as a 'threat'.[136] It is thus apparent that they also share the conception of the function of adjudication as an *external* mechanism for checking and controlling decision-making by rationing bodies which is invoked to uphold individual interests in situations where mistakes have been made. They remark that 'a well-developed internal dispute resolution mechanism might reduce the degree to which patients or clinicians adversely affected by decisions seek external authorities or institutions to pursue their interests'.[137] From this perspective, therefore, the involvement of law, and particularly of the courts, should ideally be minimised as far as possible, and no consideration is given to the capacity of the judicial process to *assist* decision-makers in carrying out their tasks.

The authors' primary objection to judicial intervention is that of a supposed lack of expertise, 'especially about the more technical matters involved in assessing efficacy and safety', but also because there may be 'little understanding of the organisational context within which the issue has arisen'.[138] While, as noted above, this is a familiar rationale for limiting the involvement of the courts in this field of public policy, it is arguably somewhat surprising in the context of the broader thesis which Daniels and Sabin pursue. As discussed in Chapter 4, the objective of the 'accountability for reasonableness' model is to stimulate 'social learning' to inform a process of deliberation within the institutions of democratic society, including the courts.[139] On this basis, legitimacy for rationing decisions does not, in any event, ultimately derive from the exercise of expert judgment, but arises from informed and democratic deliberation within the wider community. Why, then, is it regarded as problematic that judges and juries are not 'experts'? Is it not possible for the courtroom itself to function as a deliberative arena in which 'social learning' takes place as reasoned argumentation and evidence are presented? One possible response might be to observe that courts are not democratic institutions, an issue which will be addressed below. However, it would

---

[135] *Ibid.* at 59.   [136] *Ibid.* at 58.   [137] *Ibid.* at 59.

[138] It should be noted also that, at least by implication, concern is expressed as regards the procedural suitability of an adversarial process to address polycentric questions: hence, the reference to 'bring[ing] *opposing* experts to bear' (my emphasis).

[139] See above Chapter 4, n. 148 and accompanying text.

appear that Daniels and Sabin do not, in fact, share this concern, given that they argue that litigation has the 'appearance of a democratic input'.

It is submitted that there is space within Daniels' and Sabin's account for development of a rather more nuanced and extensive role for the law (and particularly, for the courts) in addressing the 'legitimacy problem' than is allowed by the authors themselves. From a functionalist perspective, it is possible to agree with the authors that litigation may not be 'the *best* way to deliberate about these matters' [i.e. those relating to rationing],[140] and to therefore look toward the strengthening of internal mechanisms to bring about deliberation. The courts, in short, should not be the first port of call. Nonetheless, the values and principles of public law, notably transparency, accountability and rationality, remain valuable here as a framework within which decision-making must be conducted if it is to stimulate 'social learning' in the manner desired by Daniels and Sabin, thereby feeding into debate within wider democratic society.

However, a functionalist might also concede – as do Daniels and Sabin – that litigation on rationing questions will on occasion be inevitable.[141] It is here that the authors surely understate the potential for law to make a valuable contribution to resolution of the 'legitimacy problem'. Rather than regarding litigation as a 'threat'[142] or, at best, an adjunct to a 'healthy [internal] deliberative process' to be utilised only when the latter has 'failed in some way',[143] it is submitted that courts might be viewed as integral to the process of deliberation on matters of healthcare rationing. In particular, the manner in which courts engage in reasoning and argumentation in a particular case and the open and public nature of their decisions can serve to enhance deliberation upon rationing questions not only in respect of a specific limit-setting decision, but may also act as a stimulus for a broader debate within political institutions and civil society. On such an analysis, and in tune with the role for public law articulated in the work of the legal academics cited in the preceding section, adjudication should not be regarded as antithetical to the pursuit of legitimacy by rationing decision-makers. Rather, it can facilitate attainment of that legitimacy, especially by engendering openness in decision-making which will enable 'social learning' on issues of resource allocation in healthcare to take place, leading to a more informed process of deliberation from which legitimacy may be said ultimately to derive.

It is important, therefore, to ascertain how far the courts have demonstrated a willingness to fashion principles of public law in such a way to enable them to function as deliberative institutions in the context of

---

[140] See above n. 135 and accompanying text. My emphasis.
[141] *Ibid.* at 59.   [142] *Ibid.* at 58.   [143] *Ibid.* at 59.

questions of the rationing of healthcare, and this will be the objective of the next three chapters of this book. However, as a precursor to this discussion, the final section of this chapter will offer a theoretical exploration of the place of the judicial process within deliberative democratic theory.

The place of the courts within a deliberative democracy

The courtroom is not the preferred arena for the development of a deliberative approach to democratic decision-making, for a number of fairly obvious reasons connected to the issues previously explored. Most straightforwardly, the democratic credentials of courts may be questioned,[144] given that judges are both unelected and unrepresentative of the wider population. This appears to be in conflict with deliberative democracy's basic character as 'any one of a family of views according to which *the public deliberation of free and equal citizens* is the core of legitimate decision-making and self-government'.[145] Involvement of a jury may, of course, alleviate this difficulty since this will allow a group of citizens which can be said to reflect a cross-section of the attitudes, beliefs and values held by the public to engage in a collective process of reasoning, argumentation and decision-making which resembles the deliberative model. However, while (as noted in Chapter 4) 'citizens' juries' have been regularly deployed within health service organisations, the public law adjudication which is the subject-matter of this book always takes place in the absence of a jury.

Also problematic is the adversarial nature of adjudication. At root, deliberative theory emphasises the importance of social co-operation and collaboration in decision-making and the resolution of problems, and aims to involve as many citizens as possible in the decision-making process. By contrast, the dialectical nature of adversarial adjudication tends to 'discourage participation, increase exclusion, occlude options, squelch voices',[146] and may be seen as illustrative of a Hobbesian theory of conflict, contest and competition which deliberativists have sought to reject.[147] Of particular practical importance is the impact of adversarial process upon the range of information which is made available for purposes of

---

[144] See e.g. J. Dryzek, 'Legitimacy and Economy in Deliberative Society' (2001) 29 *Political Theory*, 651 at 655, arguing (in response to Rawls, for whose views see further below) that the US Supreme Court is 'most certainly not' a democratic institution.

[145] J. Bohman, 'The Coming of Age of Deliberative Democracy' (1998) 6 *Journal of Political Philosophy*, 400 at 401. Emphasis in original.

[146] R. Talisse, 'Deliberativist responses to activist challenges: a continuation of Young's dialectic' (2005) 31 *Philosophy and Social Criticism*, 423 at 437.

[147] See e.g. J. Mansbridge, *Beyond Adversarial Democracy* (New York: Basic Books, 1980).

deliberation. As noted previously, in the discussion of the 'accountability for reasonableness' model, there is a close connection between democratic deliberation and 'social learning'.[148] That is, the wider the scope of evidence, argumentation and views which are presented, the more likely it is that the eventual deliberation will in fact possess the requisite qualities associated with that process, notably an absence of partiality and self-interest coupled with reasoned reflection and informed communication between participants. However, the adversarial nature of adjudication necessarily limits the available information and evidence to that which serves the interests of the litigating parties, with the consequence that, notwithstanding procedural devices such as third party intervention which serve to broaden the information base available to the court (and thence to the public),[149] the 'social learning' which occurs as a result of the court judgment will inevitably be incomplete.

These factors are sufficiently powerful to incline many theorists to look elsewhere than the courts for the realisation of their deliberative ambitions. As noted in Chapter 4,[150] some seek to move beyond existing institutions of representative democracy altogether by looking to the creation of new social, political and legal forms, while others argue that the judiciary should defer to 'more openly deliberative mechanisms of democracy' within the executive and (especially) legislative branches of government.[151] For example, Sunstein calls for 'judicial minimalism' – the eschewal of broad and general judicial pronouncements and unnecessary dicta – to allow the other branches of government a degree of latitude 'to adapt to future developments, to produce mutually advantageous compromises, and to add new information and perspectives to legal problems'.[152] On this analysis, 'from the standpoint of deliberative democracy ... courts should avoid foreclosing the outcomes of political deliberation if the preconditions for democratic deliberation have been met'.[153] Similarly, Gutmann and Thompson are sceptical of the

---

[148] See above Chapter 4, n. 148 and accompanying text. For further discussion of the 'educative' dimension of deliberation, see M. Cooke, 'Five Arguments for Deliberative Democracy' (2000) 48 *Political Studies*, 947 at 948–49.

[149] See the discussion in Chapter 7 below.

[150] See above Chapter 4, n. 164 and accompanying text.

[151] A. Lynch, 'Dissent: the Rewards and Risks of Judicial Disagreement in the High Court of Australia' [2003] *Melbourne University Law Review*, 724 at 731.

[152] C. Sunstein, 'Foreword: Leaving Things Undecided' (1996) 110 *Harvard Law Review*, 6 at 19; and more generally, C. Sunstein, *Legal Reasoning and Political Conflict* (Oxford: Oxford University Press, 1996).

[153] Sunstein, 'Leaving Things Undecided' at 37. Note, however, that in his later work, Sunstein acknowledges that courts may 'promote', rather than 'pre-empt' deliberation: see the discussion of *Government of the Republic of South Africa v Grootboom* (2001) (1) SA 46, Chapter 7 below.

capability of the judicial process to meet the conditions of deliberation, arguing against certain theorists[154] that it is necessarily superior to the legislative process as a space within which genuine and principled deliberation on moral questions may take place:

Judges review only a small proportion of public policy, and much of what they do consider they accept mostly in the form that it was made by legislators and administrators. Furthermore, the moral reasons and principles to which judges defer do not stand above those of other members of society. Judges find their principles in the experience of their own society, and they must justify those principles to other members of that society. If citizens and their representatives deal only or even primarily in preferences, judges sooner or later will find themselves doing the same, or defending principles that no one else shares . . . [J]udges listen only to citizens who happen to appear as parties in the cases before them. They do not, except incidentally, seek parties who might better speak to the political issues that the cases raise. They are not supposed to listen to voices beyond the instant case because their office seems to require a kind of independence that prevents them from taking into account much of the normal controversy of political life. They are not encouraged to listen because the judicial office protects their judgments from many of the normal challenges of political action, such as the challenge of publicity.[155]

Notwithstanding the potency of these misgivings, other approaches place greater emphasis upon the deliberative contribution which may be made by the courts. Particularly pertinent in this regard is the work of Rawls, who identifies a correspondence between his theories and those of the deliberativists, stating that his model of a 'well ordered constitutional society . . . is understood also as a deliberative democracy'.[156] For Rawls, deliberation takes the form of the exercise of public reason, which follows from the democratic principle which urges citizens to try to reach agreement on shared ends and goals. In view of the fact of reasonable pluralism, and in accordance with the liberal principle of toleration, citizens should appeal to reasons which could in principle be acceptable to all, irrespective of self-interest and partial perspectives (such as religious, metaphysical and philosophical beliefs) which may divide them. The idea of public reason does not apply to all exercises of public power, or to 'non-public reasoning' such as that which takes place in institutions such as churches, universities and other associations making up the background culture of society: *a fortiori* it does not apply to personal reflection

---

[154] The authors cite O. Fiss, 'Foreword: The Forms of Justice' (1979) 93 *Harvard Law Review*, 1 at 10 in this regard.

[155] A. Gutmann and D. Thompson, *Democracy and Disagreement* (Cambridge, Mass: Belknap Press, 1996) at 46–7.

[156] J. Rawls, 'The Idea of Public Reason Revisited' (1997) 94 *University of Chicago Law Review*, 765 at 771–2.

and deliberation on political or non-political questions. Rather, it pertains to all of those political questions which involve 'constitutional essentials' and issues of basic justice.[157] Rawls argues that acceptance of the reasonableness of ideals and principles put forward as justifications in the context of such questions is sufficient to ensure the maintenance of willing political and social co-operation between free and equal citizens,[158] although he acknowledges that it is 'highly desirable' to settle other political questions by invoking the values of public reason.[159] However, the crucial function of political reason is to assure legitimacy, especially in the context of reasonable pluralism, in which differences between citizens may be irreconcilable:

our exercise of political power is proper and hence justifiable only when it is exercised in accordance with a constitution the essentials of which all citizens may reasonably be expected to endorse in the light of principles and ideals acceptable to them as reasonable and rational. This is the liberal principle of legitimacy. And since the exercise of political power itself must be legitimate, the ideal of citizenship imposes a moral, not a legal, duty – the duty of civility – to be able to explain to one another on those fundamental questions how the principles and policies they advocate and vote for can be supported by the political values of public reason. This duty also involves a willingness to listen to others and a fair-mindedness in deciding when accommodations to their views should reasonably be made.[160]

The connection between Rawls' conception of legitimacy, achieved through the exercise of public reason, and Daniels' and Sabin's proposed method of addressing the 'legitimacy problem' through compliance with the model of 'accountability for reasonableness' (particularly, the 'publicity' and 'relevance' conditions) should be readily apparent. This is scarcely surprising given that Daniels draws heavily upon the work of Rawls.

However, what is notable is that there is considerably more space within Rawls' theoretical framework for the process of adjudication – especially constitutional adjudication by the US Supreme Court[161] – than exists within the Daniels and Sabin analysis. Indeed, for Rawls, the

---

[157] J. Rawls, *Political Liberalism* (New York: Columbia University Press, 1993) at 214.
[158] See *ibid*. at 230.   [159] *Ibid*. at 215.
[160] *Ibid*. at 217. See also Rawls, 'The Idea of Public Reason' at 770–1.
[161] The focus of much of the literature upon the US Supreme Court reflects the fact that most theorists of deliberative democracy are American. Clearly, important distinctions exist between the constitutional position of this Court and that of the courts surveyed in Chapters 6, 7 and 8. In particular, the impossibility of legislative override of a Supreme Court ruling absent constitutional amendment gives rise to greater concern as to the Court's lack of democratic credentials than is the case in systems (such as Canada, but not South Africa) where courts do not have the 'last word' on alleged violations of

Supreme Court is 'the exemplar of public reason'.[162] Judicial reasoning can be seen as an exercise of public reason because, in interpreting the constitution, judges are seeking to articulate the 'political ideal of a people to govern itself in a particular way',[163] and 'to prevent that [higher] law from being eroded by the legislation of transient majorities, or more likely, by organised and well-situated narrow interests skilled at getting their way'.[164] It is therefore incumbent upon judges, much more than upon members of the legislative and executive branches,[165] to offer explanations and justifications of their interpretations of the constitution in terms which move beyond self-interest or religious, political or philosophical values held by themselves or certain elements of the community. That is, 'they must appeal to the political values they think belong to the most reasonable understanding of the public conception and its political values of justice and public reason. These are values that they believe in good faith, as the duty of civility requires, that all citizens as reasonable and rational might reasonably be expected to endorse'.[166] Rawls notes that, in undertaking constitutional interpretation and justifying this in terms 'of the public conception of justice or a reasonable variant thereof', the exercise of public reason is fulfilling an 'educative' role.[167] By this he means that Supreme Court judgments on fundamental political questions tend to generate controversy and thus to catalyse deliberation within broader political society, forcing 'political discussion to take a principled form so as to address the constitutional question in line with the political values of justice and public reason. Public discussion becomes more than a contest for power and position. This educates citizens to the use of public reason and its value of justice by focusing their attention on basic constitutional matters'.[168]

Deliberativists who take issue with Rawls' championing of the Supreme Court do so on the basis that this approach is, in essence, elitist (or, perhaps, technocratic) rather than democratic. For example, Dryzek contends that Rawls' theory does not envisage (to utilise Bohman's

constitutional rights. One might therefore plausibly argue that, if a place can be found for a 'US-style' court within deliberative theories of democracy, the task of doing so in systems whose constitutional structure permits of greater possibility of 'dialogue' between courts and other branches of government will necessarily be a more straightforward one. For further discussion, see below Chapter 7.

[162] Rawls, *Political Liberalism* at 231.

[163] *Ibid.* at 232. Articulation of this ideal is described by Rawls as 'the aim of public reason': *ibid.*

[164] *Ibid.* at 233.

[165] However, see Gutmann and Thompson, *Democracy and Disagreement* at 45–6 for the view that the distinction between judges and legislators with regard to reason-giving is empirically and normatively overstated.

[166] Rawls, *Political Liberalism* at 236.   [167] *Ibid.* at 236.   [168] *Ibid.* at 239–40.

definition),[169] the public deliberation of free and equal citizens, but rather that certain individuals – in this case, judges – are better able to reflect than others and therefore are to be entrusted by society with public reason. On this analysis, 'institutions such as the Supreme Court can only contribute to legitimacy to the extent that the public accepts that public reason is indeed singular and that professional experts in the exercise of public reason do indeed know best'.[170] Dryzek also argues that the Rawlsian approach places insufficient emphasis upon the broader social or 'interactive' aspect of deliberation, that is the process of exchange of reasoning and argumentation with the wider political and civil society.[171] Arguably such critiques – which lead Dryzek to label Rawls as 'a deliberative theorist, but not a deliberative democrat'[172] – are overstated, particularly in view of Rawls' identification of the educative function of public reason and the catalytic capacity of the Court, standing at the centre of controversy, 'to give public reason vividness and vitality in the public forum'.[173] Nonetheless, they do reflect the fundamental difficulty, identified at the beginning of this section, of establishing a genuinely *democratic* basis for a judicial contribution to deliberation.

Carlos Nino, who argues that an 'ideal constitution of power' is one which gives effect to deliberative democracy, attempts to respond to these concerns while at the same time acknowledging their weight. Thus, he admits that his 'account of the participatory component of constitutionalism does not appear to leave much room for judicial review',[174] given the 'democratic deficit characterised by the judicial branches of most liberal democracies',[175] with preference being shown for parliamentary forms of government and other institutional arrangements which enable

---

[169] See above n. 145 and accompanying text.
[170] Dryzek, 'Legitimacy and Economy' at 655.   [171] *Ibid.*   [172] *Ibid.*
[173] Rawls, *Political Liberalism* at 237.
[174] C. Nino, *The Constitution of Deliberative Democracy* (New Haven: Yale University Press, 1996) at 219. It should be noted that Nino's discussion of judicial review refers to review of the constitutionality of legislation as undertaken by (inter alia), the US Supreme Court. Nino's model would have less difficulty in accommodating judicial review of administrative action (as traditionally carried out in English law) or a form of rights-based review in which the judicial branch did not have the last word (as under the UK Human Rights Act or the Canadian Charter of Rights and Freedoms). Nevertheless, as discussed above, even where review takes either of these forms, democratic objections to judicial involvement remain highly pertinent in the context of allocative decision making in healthcare, as Nino himself acknowledges: 'If a judge, as a supervisor of the proper working of the democratic process, decides that a citizen must have adequate medical attention, lest her equal and free participation in the democratic process be prejudiced, the judge undoubtedly contributes to the better operation of the democratic process. However, the judge simultaneously takes away from democracy the power to decide how medical resources should be distributed': at 222.
[175] *Ibid.* at 188.

'the transformation of people's interests through the process of participatory discussion and majoritarian decision'.[176] Nonetheless, while he seeks to limit the role of the judicial process, Nino does envisage that a restricted contribution can be made by judicial review. First, to ensure that procedural conditions which maximise the epistemic value of the democratic process (such as freedom of expression, equality and provision of reasons) are met; secondly, to invalidate democratic enactments which are based upon personal moral preferences; and thirdly, to uphold long-standing constitutional practices and understandings. However, perhaps more important than these exceptions to Nino's general denial of a role for judicial review is his articulation of the part which the judiciary can play in stimulating deliberation within the other branches of government and broader civil society. He argues that 'judges can, and should, adopt measures that will promote the process of public deliberation over the issue or a more careful consideration on the part of political bodies'.[177] This can be achieved by institutional measures which promote 'democratic dialogue', such as the 'suspensive veto' which exists within the Canadian Charter of Rights and Freedoms,[178] or a ruling of 'unconstitutionality by omission', whereby a legislature would be required to explain its reasons for failure to implement a constitutional prescription and to outline its plans for remedying the deficiency. Nino contends that 'through such mechanisms, judges would have an active role in contributing to the improvement of the quality of the process of democratic discussion and decision, stimulating public debate and promoting more reflective decisions'.[179] That is, adjudication – underpinned by legal mechanisms which assist the courts in fulfilling such a role – is capable of acting as a catalyst for democratic deliberation in a manner similar to that which is suggested (albeit not comprehensively developed) by Rawls.

A related argument is developed by van Hoecke, who contends that it is possible to legitimate (that is, to establish the societal acceptability of) both judicial review of legislation in particular, and judicial activism more broadly, through 'deliberative communication'.[180] The author explains this in terms of a series of concentric circles, ranging from a process of communication between parties and judge, through further discussion on appeal and the siting of the decision within precedent, through legal and broader media analysis, and finally to discussion within society at large in

---

[176] *Ibid.* at 219.   [177] *Ibid.* at 215.
[178] For discussion of dialogic theory, especially under the Canadian Charter, see further below Chapter 7.
[179] Nino, *Constitution of Deliberative Democracy* at 216.
[180] M. van Hoecke, 'Judicial Review and Deliberative Democracy: a Circular Model of Law Creation and Legitimation' (2001) 14 *Ratio Juris*, 415 at 420.

instances where fundamental ethical or political issues are at stake. On this analysis, adjudication is, in effect, a 'collective endeavour', the product of a 'permanent deliberative community through which new legal concepts, new rules, new principles, new interpretations, new theories are proposed, discussed, elaborated and finally accepted'.[181] Here, too, one may observe the role of adjudication as stimulus to debate, providing an input into the wider processes of deliberative democracy through its capacity to establish that to which van Hoecke refers as a 'public forum'.[182]

From these accounts, one may therefore articulate a response to the contention that judicial activity is antithetical to deliberative democracy because courts suffer from a democratic deficit. Such an approach would indeed concede that democratic deliberation tends to (and perhaps also that it *ought* to) take place in arenas other than the courtroom – for example, in legislative chambers, town hall meetings, citizen juries or even in everyday patterns of communication between individuals. However, it would also recognise that adjudication can nonetheless make a contribution to this deliberative process by functioning as a *catalyst for debate*, operating in an 'educative' manner to inform and stimulate the process of intersubjective reasoning and argumentation between free and equal citizens which characterises deliberative democracy.

In addition to contributing to deliberation elsewhere within political and civil society, it may also be argued that the process of adjudication *is itself deliberative in character*. As was observed at the beginning of this section, the adversarial nature of legal proceedings would seem to contradict the basic precepts of deliberative democracy. However, in various other respects, the judicial process in fact bears strong resemblance to the model espoused by deliberativists. Indeed, to this end it has been claimed that 'the adjudicative process is ... far more "deliberative" than politics typically can be',[183] and that 'the theory of deliberative democracy sketches a model of politics based on models of law and legal decision-making. It aspires to turn political decisions into a form of legal decision-making'.[184]

A number of elements of adjudication may be identified as pertinent in this regard. First, adjudication may be defined as 'a form of decision that

---

[181] *Ibid.* at 422.   [182] *Ibid.* at 421.
[183] C. Peters, 'Assessing the new Judicial Minimism' (2000) 100 *Columbia Law Review*, 1454 at 1498.
[184] C. Schroeder, 'Deliberative Democracy's Attempt to Turn Politics into Law' (2002) 65 *Law and Contemporary Problems*, 95 at 98.

defines the affected party's participation as that of offering proofs and reasoned arguments'.[185] As noted in Chapter 4, the deliberative approach to democracy is likewise premised upon a process of argumentation entailing the marshalling of evidence, the exposition of grounds in favour of a particular position, explanation and interpretation. Crucial to this process, however, is the rejection of reasoning which is based upon self-interest, force and naked preference, and that which is tantamount to coercion, deception and manipulation. Here, perhaps paradoxically, the 'much-maligned isolationism of the law – its insulation from worldly affairs, its persistent formalism, its self-referential reliance only on appropriately pedigreed authorities',[186] achieves a similar result. This is so in so far as, while the arguments presented in court are designed to secure strategic advantage for that party, they are expected to be rooted in legal authority rather than partial interest or personal moral preferences, and 'litigants stand before the bench equal in the eyes of the law, in that their cases are to be judged by legal standards that do not depend upon status, wealth or political influence'.[187] Adjudication may therefore be seen to amount to a realisation of Habermas' call for a process in which 'no force other than that of the better argument is exercised'.[188]

A second correspondence between adjudication and deliberative models of democracy is implicit in the above discussion, but warrants specific emphasis. This is the centrality of reason-giving to both forms of process. The public justification of actions and decisions – captured in the so-called 'publicity' condition – is fundamental to the accounts of both Gutmann and Thompson,[189] and, within the healthcare context, Daniels and Sabin,[190] and it is trite to observe that it is also a key feature of the adjudicative process. Reasoned argument occurs in the courtroom in two forms: first, when parties present their cases, orally and in writing, that relief should be granted; and secondly, (and, from the perspective of the 'catalytic' dimension of the judicial process which was outlined above, more significantly) when judges publicly defend the decision which they have reached on the basis of reason. This process also serves to 'filter out' 'improper' factual, legal and constitutional arguments,[191] that is those which are irrelevant to the disposition of the case or which do not accord with patterns of legal reasoning or understandings of constitutional practice, the relevance of which could accordingly not be expected to be

---

[185] Fuller, *Morality of Law* at 369.   [186] Peters, 'Judicial Minimism' at 1498.
[187] Schroeder, 'Deliberative Democracy's Attempt' at 104.
[188] Above Chapter 4, n. 163 and accompanying text.
[189] See above Chapter 4, n. 171 and accompanying text.
[190] See above Chapter 4, n. 108 and accompanying text.
[191] See Schroeder, 'Deliberative Democracy's Attempt' at 108.

accepted by others. The provision of reasons for decisions therefore enables judges to offer an explanation to (and thus to educate) both the losing side and the wider public in terms which meet the conditions of reciprocity: that is, those which 'fair-minded people' seeking social co-operation can recognise as valid and germane in the light of principles and ideals which they endorse as rational, even if they may disagree on the conclusion reached in the instant case. In this manner, the practice of judicial reason-giving may contribute to legitimacy either through acceptance of the validity of the reasons offered or, more indirectly, through its impact as a stimulus for a further process of public deliberation which can provide the conditions through which such legitimacy may be secured.

A further aspect of adjudication which is worthy of note in this context is the capacity of judges in a multi-member court to dissent from the majority. In line with the discussion to date, this practice may be viewed as deliberative in two senses. First, the presence of a dissenting judgment offers a still greater spur to deliberation within civil and political society upon the issues arising from the case: put simply, the existence of dissent signals that the decision is controversial and, in van Hoecke's terms,[192] will have the effect of broadening the 'communicative circles' created by the court's judgment. Secondly, it demonstrates the deliberative quality of the process of adjudication itself. Since multi-member courts do not insist upon unanimity, the prospect of (deliberatively unacceptable) coercion, manipulation and strategising by judicial brethren in relation to the dissenter is diminished: rather, each judge (and each judgment) is seen to be of equal status. Moreover – though empirical evidence on the process by which courts arrive at decisions is regrettably scanty[193] – the existence of dissent provides a strong pointer to the occurrence of a deliberative exchange of views and reasoned arguments between the judges, especially given that a dissenting judgment must almost inevitably make reference to the views of the majority.[194]

Conclusion

This chapter has sought to call into question the widely held assumption that judicial engagement with issues of healthcare rationing, although

---

[192] See above n. 180 and accompanying text.

[193] However, see D. Dickson (ed.), *The Supreme Court in Conference (1940–1985): the Private Discussions behind nearly 300 Supreme Court Decisions* (New York: Oxford University Press, 2001).

[194] See Lynch, 'Rewards and Risks of Judicial Disagreement' at 735. Indeed, reference to the judgments of others on the panel is not confined to those who are dissenting, suggesting that deliberative exchange between judges is multi-directional.

increasingly prevalent, is a wholly undesirable state of affairs. It should be stressed that there remain a number of powerful reasons to be wary of greater judicial involvement, and it is certainly not the intention of the author to argue that the problems of public acceptability which are generated by explicit strategies of rationing can *best* be resolved in a judicial forum. As commentators such as Daniels and Sabin have recognised, the most crucial steps which can be taken centre upon ensuring that the conditions for procedural justice (especially transparent reason-giving) subsist in internal processes within the institution entrusted with the rationing decision.[195] If such steps are undertaken, it should be possible to minimise the inevitable expense, delay and anxiety which is generated by litigation. This will be in the interest both of those bodies undertaking rationing choices – especially in a publicly funded system where diversion of resources into litigation necessarily reduces the amounts available for the provision of treatments and services to the community – and of patients whose state of health may well be insufficiently robust to endure a lengthy legal case.

Nevertheless, the analysis offered here has sought to demonstrate that there has frequently been too narrow a reading of the possible role which law (and, especially, the process of public law adjudication) might play in this context. An emphasis upon the function of law as an external mechanism for checking and controlling decision-making by public bodies has engendered mistrust of the courts and created a perception that they operate purely in favour of aggrieved individuals, rendering the already difficult task of distributing scarce healthcare resources equitably across the community even more challenging. Such a perspective, however, surely understates the *instrumental* capability of public law principles and values (articulated both through adjudication and, more broadly, within the community of legal thought) to assist in diagnosing and addressing institutional and/or systemic problems and weaknesses. Notably, in this context, the strong correspondence between public law and legitimation would point to the utility of adjudication as a means of responding to the 'legitimacy problem' to which Daniels and Sabin have drawn our attention, notwithstanding the failure of these authors to acknowledge the value of the legal process as a means for ensuring that

---

[195] The work of NICE has been singled out for praise by Daniels and other commentators in this regard. See N. Daniels, 'Accountability for Reasonableness' (2000) 321 *British Medical Journal*, 1300 at 1301; and further, C. Ham and G. Robert (eds.), *Reasonable Rationing* (Buckingham: Open University Press, 2003), Chapter 4. For a more sceptical reading of the claim that NICE takes a deliberative approach to questions of resource allocation, see K. Syrett, 'Deconstructing Deliberation in the Appraisal of Medical Technologies: NICEly does it?' (2006) 69 *Modern Law Review*, 869.

the conditions of 'accountability for reasonableness' are realised. Moreover, insufficient awareness has been shown of the capacity of the judicial process to contribute to the ultimate objective of encouraging wide deliberation within political and civil society upon issues of healthcare rationing. Although the place of courts within deliberative democracy remains a matter of contention for deliberative theorists, two key functions can be drawn from the literature. First, a court case can serve a catalytic purpose, providing information and feeding into a public discussion on the acceptability of healthcare rationing and the criteria which should underpin decision-making, which will take place within political institutions, the media or other public forums. Secondly, the courtroom itself may be seen as a deliberative arena, enabling an exchange of reasoned argumentation to occur between parties and the judge(s) such that those disposed to seek 'fair terms of social co-operation' may come to accept that the particular decision has been fairly based upon relevant considerations even if they disagree with the result reached by the rationing decision-maker.

A strong *theoretical* case can therefore be made for a much more positive, nuanced contribution by the courts upon questions of the rationing of healthcare resources than media and academic commentators within this field of public policy have so far been prepared to allow. But to what extent is there evidence that the courts are, *in practice*, prepared to adopt the type of approach for which this chapter has argued? That is, how far have courts been willing to utilise public law principles to bring about deliberation on matters of the allocation of scarce healthcare resources in a manner which may assist in resolving the 'legitimacy problem'? This is the issue which will be explored in the following chapters, with reference to cases in this field from three jurisdictions.

Introduction: the incidence of legal challenge

In the preceding chapter, it was noted that litigation on questions of healthcare rationing is emerging as an increasingly frequent occurrence in light of evolving social and political trends, coupled with the increasing public visibility of strategies of rationing. In the field of public law, to which the discussion in this text is restricted, a superficial survey of the law reports would seem to bear out the validity of this observation. For example, in England there were very few legal challenges to the allocation of healthcare resources from the establishment of the NHS in 1948 until the 'Child B' case in the mid-1990s, but there have been several more in the ensuing decade (not to mention threats to initiate litigation which have failed to crystallise into a legal case).[2] The impact of human rights law should also be recognised. In both Canada and South Africa – although to a much lesser extent in England – litigants have formulated legal challenges to decisions not to provide medical treatments and services on the basis of the alleged violation of a human right. As will be noted below, this has occurred *indirectly* in the case of the Canadian Charter of Rights and Freedoms, which protects only rights of a civil and political nature, and *directly* in the case of the Constitution of South Africa, which contains a legally enforceable right to access healthcare services.

Yet this trend should not be overstated. It remains relatively rare for decisions on the allocation of scarce healthcare resources to be subject to challenge via mechanisms of public law. Writing on the NHS, Montgomery notes that 'although there is an explicit framework of legal

---

[1] Readers unfamiliar with the structure of the legal process in the United Kingdom may be puzzled by the references in this chapter to *English* law, especially in light of the discussion in preceding chapters of health policy in the UK as a whole. The explanation is that Scotland and Northern Ireland have distinct legal systems from that which exists in England and Wales, and which is commonly referred to as 'English' law.

[2] For example, those relating to the provision of Herceptin which were outlined in Chapter 1: see Chapter 1, n. 27 and accompanying text.

duties to provide health services, attempts to use the law to enforce those duties have proved frustrating for litigants ... There is only limited scope for patients to enforce healthcare rights through public law'.[3] Similarly, it has been argued of Canadian case law that 'there is limited room for a plaintiff to successfully challenge a healthcare resource allocation decision',[4] and that 'Charter actions brought by patients and others have been few in number ... This ... is surprising. Since healthcare affects everyone and is the largest single budget item for provinces, one would expect more litigation'.[5] A comparable assessment is apposite in the case of South Africa. It has been noted that South African courts have adjudicated upon an alleged violation of a right in the context of healthcare in only three cases,[6] and an analysis of South African case law has concluded that 'it would seem to be difficult to use the courts to challenge a particular allocation of healthcare resources'.[7]

The relative paucity of case law relating to the allocation of scarce healthcare resources may, to some extent, reflect factors particular to the political, social and legal cultures of these three jurisdictions. For example, Greschner argues that the relative comprehensiveness of the publicly funded Medicare system in Canada and the fact that the basic principles articulated in the Canada Health Act mirror values of equality and protection of human dignity under the Charter of Rights and Freedoms mean that the latter has been relatively underutilised in this context.[8] However, a key factor in all three systems has undoubtedly been the attitude of the judiciary towards claims of this type. Here, the factors outlined in Chapter 5 have combined to raise questions as to the institutional and constitutional competence of the courts to adjudicate upon issues arising from allocative decision-making in healthcare, with the consequence that (as will be confirmed further below), judges have tended to adopt a restrained and deferential approach towards such

---

[3] J. Montgomery, *Health Care Law* (Oxford: Oxford University Press, 2nd edn, 2003) at 67, 74.

[4] L. Sweatman and D. Woolard, 'Resource Allocation Decisions in Canada's Health Care System: Can these Decisions Be Challenged in a Court of Law?' (2002) 62 *Health Policy*, 275 at 289.

[5] D. Greschner, *How Will the Charter of Rights and Freedoms and Evolving Jurisprudence Affect Health Care Costs? Discussion Paper No. 20* (Ottawa: Commission on the Future of Health Care in Canada, 2002) at 5.

[6] C. Ngwena and R. Cook, 'Rights Concerning Health', Chapter 4 in D. Brand and C. Heyns (eds.), *Socio-Economic Rights in South Africa* (Pretoria: Pretoria University Press, 2005) at 133.

[7] R. Lie, 'Health, Human Rights and Mobilisation of Resources for Health' (2004) 4 *BMC International Health and Human Rights*, available at www.biomedcentral.com/1472-698X/4/4 (accessed 8 January 2007).

[8] Greschner, *Charter of Rights and Freedoms* at 19.

matters when argued before them. It would appear that this has served to dissuade many would-be litigants, who are likely to perceive other channels (such as the political process) as offering greater prospects of success for the venting and redress of their grievances.[9]

If, as argued, litigation in this field of public policy continues to be somewhat sporadic, this serves to underline claims made in the concluding section of the preceding chapter: that public law *alone* does not offer a panacea for the problems of legitimacy which arise from explicit strategies of rationing, and that the courtroom is almost certainly not the *best* arena in which to engage in deliberation on the need for rationing and the principles which should underpin such choices. But it does not follow from this that judicial involvement in this area can be casually dismissed. The publicity which is attendant upon pronouncements by the courts (especially in a field such as allocative decision-making in healthcare which is of significant media and public interest), and the weight which attaches to an authoritative declaration of the legal position, serve to invest public law litigation with a significance which is far greater than its incidence might suggest.[10] In such circumstances, it is perfectly plausible that the courts may make a telling and useful contribution to the process of decision-making on the allocation of healthcare resources, although their capacity to do so will, of course, be contingent upon their readiness to adjust their restrained, deferential approach in the interests of fulfilling the sort of instrumental, facilitative role which was outlined in Chapter 5.

This chapter, and the following two, seek to examine the extent to which the courts in three respective jurisdictions – England, Canada and South Africa – have proceeded in such a manner. The goal is not to present an exhaustive account in which all instances of judicial engagement with questions of the allocation of healthcare resources through the processes of public law are considered. Rather, by drawing upon the jurisprudence in this field, the objective is to reach some general conclusions as to the openness of courts in the three jurisdictions to the employment of public law principles and values in this field of decision-making to bring about a process of deliberation on questions of healthcare rationing. Such an analysis should assist in establishing whether public law adjudication warrants the negative evaluation which it has traditionally received, or whether a reconceptualisation of law's function in this field is merited in view of the potential contribution which it may make.

---

[9] See e.g. Sweatman and Woolard, 'Resource Allocation Decisions' at 289.
[10] See above Chapter 5, n. 44 and accompanying text.

The impact of human rights on English case law

Adjudication on issues of healthcare rationing through public law processes in the English courts has taken place almost entirely through the jurisdiction by means of which courts engage in judicial review of the legality of decisions and actions undertaken by administrative bodies. This procedure focuses upon questions such as whether the body possesses legal power to undertake the decision or action which is at issue, whether that decision or action amounts to an abuse of the discretionary powers with which it has been vested (for example, because relevant factors have been ignored or the decision is utterly absurd or outrageous), and whether the decision-making process adopted by the administrative body is fair. Its primary focus is not upon possible violations of substantive rights which inhere in individual citizens either as a result of case law or by virtue of a legislative or constitutional instrument.

That said, it is true that, following the enactment of the Human Rights Act 1998, some litigants have sought to advance arguments that denial of access to medical treatments and services amounts to a violation of various Convention rights which were given effect in domestic law by that Act.[11] This is so notwithstanding that the European Convention for the Protection of Human Rights and Fundamental Freedoms contains no right of access to healthcare services.[12] However, the courts have, to date – with the notable exception of the High Court judgment in the 'Child B' case (discussed below) – shown little sympathy towards such

---

[11] For example, in *R* v. *North West Lancashire Health Authority, ex parte A, D and G* [2000] 1 WLR 977 ('*A, D and G*'), discussed further below, n. 50 and accompanying text, it was argued that the refusal to provide funding for gender reassignment surgery engaged Articles 3 (right not to be subjected to inhuman or degrading treatment or punishment), 8 (right to respect for private and family life, home and correspondence) and 14 (freedom from discrimination in respect of enjoyment of other rights) of the European Convention; while in the High Court litigation in *R (on the application of Rogers)* v. *Swindon NHS Primary Care Trust and Secretary of State for Health* [2006] EWHC 171 (Admin.) ('*Rogers*'), it was claimed that the refusal to fund the provision of Herceptin engaged Articles 2 (right to life), 3 and 8 of the Convention (although note that the Convention arguments were not further rehearsed in front of the Court of Appeal).

[12] Another source of legal rights which may be relevant to questions of the rationing of scarce healthcare resources is European Community law. In *R (on the application of Watts)* v. *Bedford Primary Care Trust* [2006] QB 667, the European Court of Justice determined that there was a right to reimbursement for medical treatment received abroad if the time spent on a waiting list for treatment in the Member State of residence exceeded a medically acceptable period in light of the patient's particular condition and clinical needs. For discussion of this area of law, see A. Kaczorowska, 'A Review of the Creation by the European Court of Justice of the Right to Effective and Speedy Medical Treatment and its Outcomes' (2006) 12 *European Law Journal*, 345.

arguments,[13] which have been described as 'unfocused', 'unhelpful', 'irresolute' and 'misplaced'.[14] For example, it has been held that a refusal to provide funding for treatment cannot amount to an interference with the right to life,[15] or the right to respect for private and family life, home and correspondence,[16] save where the state has denied treatment to an individual which it has undertaken to make available to the population generally.[17] This unwillingness to extend the ambit of Convention rights to embrace decisions to deny access to medical services and treatments would seem to be in line with the general approach taken by the Convention organs towards issues of resource allocation, which has been mindful of imposing 'an impossible or disproportionate burden' on state authorities which are confronted with 'operational choices which must be made in terms of priorities and resources'.[18]

Collier, Wednesbury and judicial restraint

Commentators on English administrative law, of which judicial review forms an important part, have emphasised that law possesses the capacity both to check and control administrative action, and to facilitate and strengthen the process of decision-making, as discussed in the preceding chapter.[19] However, when presented with questions of the allocation of scarce healthcare resources, the traditional attitude of the English courts

---

[13] An argument based upon violation of Article 8 also succeeded in *R v. North and East Devon Health Authority, ex parte Coughlan* [2001] QB 213, in which a residential care facility for those in need of long-term nursing care had been closed on resource grounds. Here the health authority was already providing a service to the claimant (nursing care within the facility) which it then sought to remove, as distinct from denying or failing to provide a treatment or service in the first instance, as is characteristic of the majority of the rationing decisions considered elsewhere in this text. The case may therefore be better regarded as turning on the existence of a 'legitimate expectation' of continued provision of the home (and the nursing care), especially in view of the promise made by the authority that the claimant would have a 'home for life'. For discussion, see (2000) 8 *Medical Law Review* 145.

[14] *A, D and G* [2000] 1 WLR 977 at 996–7 (Auld LJ). See also *Rogers* [2006] EWHC 171 at paras. 72–5.

[15] *Rogers* [2006] EWHC 171 at para. 72.   [16] *A, D and G* [2000] 1 WLR 977 at 995–6.

[17] *Rogers* [2006] EWHC 171 at para. 72, citing *Nitecki* v. *Poland* (21 March 2002, Application No 65653/01).

[18] *Osman* v. *UK* (2000) 29 EHRR 245 at para. 115. For further discussion of these issues, see D. O'Sullivan, 'The allocation of scarce resources and the right to life under the European Convention on Human Rights' [1998] *Public Law*, 389; E. Haggett, *The Human Rights Act 1998 and Access to NHS Treatments and Services: a Practical Guide* (London: Constitution Unit, University College, 2001); C. Newdick, *Who Should We Treat?* (Oxford: Oxford University Press, 2nd edn, 2004) at 119–20.

[19] For further discussion, see e.g. C. Harlow and R. Rawlings, *Law and Administration* (London: Butterworths, 2nd edn, 1997), especially Chapters 2–3; P. Craig,

was largely to eschew any sort of involvement, significantly constraining their capability to adopt either of these approaches and effectively rendering rationing decisions immune from judicial scrutiny.

This is readily apparent from the first reported case in which litigants sought to challenge the allocation of scarce healthcare resources. In *R* v. *Secretary of State for Social Services, West Midlands Regional Health Authority and Birmingham Area Health Authority (Teaching), ex parte Hincks*,[20] plans for a new orthopaedic unit, which had first been approved in 1971, were subsequently postponed and eventually abandoned. The argument that the Secretary of State had failed in his duty to provide hospital accommodation and medical services under section 3(1) of the National Health Service Act 1977 was rejected by the Court of Appeal. Lord Denning MR held that the statutory obligation must be read as subject to an implied qualification relating to available resources, and concluded that 'the Secretary of State says that he is doing the best he can with the financial resources available to him: and I do not think that he can be faulted in the matter'.[21]

The restrained approach adopted in *Hincks* was endorsed by the Court of Appeal, in the context of a denial of access to treatment to a specified individual, in *R* v. *Central Birmingham Health Authority, ex parte Collier*.[22] Here, the challenge was to a failure to provide intensive care facilities and surgery to a child suffering from a heart defect. The child had been placed at the top of the waiting list for treatment and his clinician had indicated that he was likely to die without it. Notwithstanding the severity of the condition, the Court, following the earlier decision in the factually similar case of *R* v. *Central Birmingham Health Authority, ex parte Walker*,[23] refused to grant an order requiring that the operation be carried out.

As Newdick argues,[24] the judges in *Collier* singularly failed to explore the possibility of utilising public law principles relating to fair process to require the health authority to offer an *explanation* of how its priorities had been established in this case, especially given the nature of the child's condition and the support of his physician. In this regard, there appears to have been a judicial confusion (or, perhaps, a deliberate elision) of review of *decision-making procedure* – which is squarely within the institutional and constitutional competence of the judiciary – with review of the *substance of the decision*, which it is not competent to undertake, except where

Administrative Law (London: Sweet and Maxwell, 5th edn, 2003), Chapter 1; P. Leyland and G. Anthony, *Textbook on Administrative Law* (Oxford: Oxford University Press, 5th edn) at 4–9.

[20] (1980) 1 BMLR 93 (*'Hincks'*).   [21] *Ibid.* at 96.
[22] Unreported, 6 January 1988 (available via Lexis-Nexis) (*'Collier'*).
[23] (1987) 3 BMLR 32.   [24] See Newdick, *Who Should We Treat?* at 99–100.

the decision is so egregious as to be wholly unreasonable or irrational. This is evident from the dictum of Simon Brown LJ, that 'there may be very good reasons why the resources in this case do not allow all the beds in the hospital to be used at this particular time. We have no evidence of that, and indeed ... it is not for this court, or any court, to substitute its own judgment for the judgment of those who are responsible for the allocation of resources'. Similarly, Ralph Gibson LJ observed that 'If I were the father of this child, I think that I would want to be given answers about the supply to, and use of, funds by this health authority. No doubt the health authority would welcome the opportunity to deal with such matters so that they could explain what they are doing and what their problems are. But this court and the High Court have no role of general investigator of social policy and of allocation of resources'.

Ralph Gibson LJ's statement offers an indication of why the highly restrained approach taken in *Collier* may be viewed as problematic. In the absence of explanation and justification, the rationing choice was unlikely to be accepted as legitimate. This would be especially true for those for whom the choice was of an especially 'tragic' nature (notably, the child's parents), as his Lordship implied. However, *public acceptability* of the need for rationing in such a case was also likely to be inhibited since no opportunity had been taken to build understanding as to the need for, and the criteria which underpinned, the decision. Put another way, the refusal of the Court to demand transparency as to the priorities which had been established in this case – even if it was rightly unwilling to interfere with the *substance* of the decision – resulted in the decision failing to meet the conditions of 'accountability for reasonableness', notably the 'publicity' and 'relevance' conditions. In consequence, the case offers no scope for development of a genuine process of deliberation upon the need for rationing, either within the courtroom or more widely. Indeed, Simon Brown LJ appeared expressly to disavow any role for the court as a catalyst for further debate in stating that 'this is not the forum in which a court can properly express opinions upon the way in which national resources are allocated or distributed'.[25] In such circumstances, according to the Daniels and Sabin analysis, a problem of legitimacy appears certain to persist.

---

[25] The judge does allude to the possibility of a wider public and media debate upon the issues raised by the case in stating that 'it may be that it is hoped that the publicity will assist in bringing pressure to bear upon the hospital'. However, he again rejects any role for the Court in bringing this about by remarking that 'this court cannot be concerned with matters of that kind'.

Nevertheless, criticism of the Court of Appeal's decision in *Collier* should perhaps be somewhat tempered by acknowledgement of the health policy and legal context in which it was operating. First, the case was decided in an era when rationing was primarily carried out in implicit fashion and there was consequently no widespread social expectation that rationales would be provided for decisions to deny access to treatment and services. As noted above, the 'legitimacy problem' is much less prevalent in a situation of implicit rationing, as the exercise of clinical judgment serves to obscure the moral conflict inherent in the decision. In *Collier*, however, an issue of legitimacy arose because the clinical support for urgent treatment visibly exposed the resource-driven considerations of the health authority, which sought to delay. This was not, therefore, a 'standard' case of implicit rationing. Nonetheless, it was perhaps forgivable for the Court to treat it as if it had been, given the environment in which the decision was made.

Further, it should be noted that the Court may have been somewhat hamstrung by the limited range of tools (in the form of grounds of judicial review) which were available to it in reviewing the process of decision-making of the health authority. In so far as the weakness of the decision in *Collier* rested upon the failure to require an explanation to be given of the priorities which led the health authority to delay treatment for the child, two aspects are of particular significance. First, at the time when the case was decided, there existed no general common law requirement that administrative bodies should offer reasons for their decisions.[26] Indeed, this principle, in theory at least, remains intact in English law to the present day, although it has been diluted to such an extent that it has been said that 'what were once seen as exceptions to a rule may now be becoming examples of the norm, and the cases where reasons are not required may be taking on the appearance of exceptions'.[27] Secondly, the Court took the view that judicial intervention was only permissible if the decision was 'unreasonable' in the so-called *Wednesbury* sense, that is that it was 'so unreasonable that no unreasonable authority could ever have come to it'.[28] Under this test, a public body is placed under no obligation to explain the decision reached unless the applicant for judicial review can make a case for its irrationality.[29]

---

[26] See e.g. *R* v. *Gaming Board for Great Britain, ex parte Benaim and Khaida* [1970] 2 QB 417 at 431; *McInnes* v. *Onslow-Fane* [1978] 1 WLR 1520 at 1532.

[27] *Stefan* v. *General Medical Council* [2000] HRLR 1 at 10 (Lord Clyde).

[28] *Associated Provincial Picture Houses* v. *Wednesbury Corporation* [1948] 1 KB 223 ('*Wednesbury*') (Lord Greene MR).

[29] The *Wednesbury* test of 'unreasonableness' was reformulated by Lord Diplock in *CCSU* [1985] 1 AC 374 at 410 as 'irrationality', meaning 'a decision which is so outrageous in its defiance of logic or of accepted moral standards that no sensible person who had applied his mind to the question could have arrived at it'.

This represents a much less searching standard of scrutiny than other public law principles, notably proportionality, which requires a court to assess the balance struck between competing interests by the decision-maker and the relative weight accorded to interests and considerations.[30] Necessarily, in undertaking scrutiny according to this latter standard, a court will be required to examine the justifications put forward by the decision-maker as to why it has favoured one interest over another, so that it can establish that interference with the latter is not disproportionate. However, at the date of the decision in *Collier*, this principle did not explicitly form part of English domestic law.[31]

If *Wednesbury* is considered to be the correct basis for judicial intervention in cases of this type, it is difficult to take exception to the Court of Appeal's conclusion. The repeated cancellation of the child's operation may appear to have been both callous and avoidable (had resources been allocated according to a differing set of priorities), but it is surely difficult to make out a case that *no* other health authority *could ever* have come to a similar decision. But it is important to appreciate that the *Wednesbury* test is neither self-executing nor monolithic. Other principles were available to the Court of Appeal which it might have utilised had it wished to oblige the health authority to provide an explanation of the rationing choice in this case.[32] Moreover, courts have applied the test in a much less restrictive manner in other areas of public policy, enabling a far more searching form of judicial scrutiny of decision-making to take place.[33]

In the final analysis, it is difficult to resist the conclusion that the deployment of the *Wednesbury* test in *Collier* and the other early cases in this field was a means of clothing in legal principle a predetermined judicial stance on questions of healthcare rationing: namely, that such matters, while not *wholly* non-justiciable, would in practice only be subject to the most minimal level of oversight in the courts. Such a standpoint

---

[30] See e.g. *R (on the application of Daly)* v. *Secretary of State for the Home Department* [2001] 2 AC 532, especially at para. 27 (Lord Steyn); and further, Chapter 7 below.

[31] In *R* v. *Secretary of State for the Home Department, ex parte Brind* [1991] 1 AC 696, arguments based upon proportionality were rejected by the House of Lords, although its future application in English law was not ruled out. For further discussion, see Craig, *Administrative Law* at 627–28.

[32] For example, a failure to take account of a relevant consideration (the severity of the child's illness), unreasonableness inferred from the absence of reasons, or failure to base a decision on evidential material of a probative value. See e.g. *Padfield* v. *Minister of Agriculture, Fisheries and Food* [1968] AC 997; *Attorney General* v. *Ryan* [1980] AC 718.

[33] In particular, prior to the enactment of the Human Rights Act 1998, the courts developed a more intensive standard of 'anxious scrutiny' in cases in which fundamental rights were at issue. See especially *R* v. *Ministry of Defence, ex parte Smith* [1996] QB 517; and for discussion, M. Fordham, 'What is "anxious scrutiny"?' (1996) 1 *Judicial Review*, 81. *Cf.* the approach taken by Laws J in the 'Child B' case, for which see further below.

was indicative of the weight attached by the English judiciary to the factors militating against judicial involvement in matters of the allocation of healthcare resources, which were explored in Chapter 5. Yet, crucially, it failed to distinguish between unacceptable judicial intervention in the *merits* of an administrative decision – the correct role of the *Wednesbury* principle being to preclude intrusion of this type – and constitutionally proper oversight of the *process* by which decisions were made. In adopting such an approach, therefore, the English courts showed themselves to be unable (or, perhaps, unwilling) to recognise the facilitative role which they might play in this field, notably in utilising public law principles to enforce observance of procedural requirements, compliance with which would facilitate public deliberation on questions of healthcare rationing.

A chink of light? 'Child B'

Speaking extra-judicially in 1992, the English High Court judge, Sir John Laws, argued that the judiciary should develop a variable standard of review of administrative decision-making by reference to the importance of the right or interest which had allegedly been infringed and called for the *Wednesbury* standard to be replaced by an approach in which 'the greater the intrusion proposed by a body possessing public power over the citizen into an area where his fundamental rights are at stake, the greater must be the justification which the public authority must demonstrate'.[34] This could, he believed, be achieved by adoption of the principle of proportionality which would also, he noted, have the effect of recognising 'that decision-makers whose decisions affect fundamental rights must inevitably justify what they do by giving good reasons'.[35] Laws argued that this was particularly appropriate in cases where the legal challenge related to the ordering of priorities by a decision-maker, since it would enable the court to insist that the decision-maker 'accord[s] the first priority to the right in question unless he can show a substantial, objective, public justification for overriding it'.[36]

Almost three years later, the judge had the opportunity to apply this approach in the context of resource allocation in the NHS, in the leading case of *R* v. *Cambridge Health Authority, ex parte B*.[37] Here, the challenge was to a health authority's decision not to fund a form of treatment for a ten-year-old girl's leukaemia. Although he did not phrase his judgment

---

[34] J. Laws, 'Is the High Court the Guardian of Fundamental Constitutional Rights?' [1993] *Public Law*, 59 at 69. The article was based upon a lecture delivered to the Administrative Bar Association in June 1992.
[35] *Ibid.* at 78.   [36] *Ibid.* at 74.   [37] [1995] 1 FLR 1055 (QBD) ('Child B').

explicitly in the language of proportionality, Laws J held that the health authority had acted unlawfully in that it had failed to provide a 'substantial objective justification' for a decision which would have the effect of interfering with the child's right to life. He noted that one of the factors which had underpinned the decision to deny treatment was its cost, which it was estimated could amount to £75,000. In view of the fact that a fundamental right was engaged, Laws J felt that:

> merely to point to the fact that resources are finite tells one nothing about the wisdom, or, what is relevant for my purposes, the legality of a decision to withhold funding in a particular case . . . Where the question is whether the life of a ten year-old child might be saved, by however slim a chance, the responsible authority must in my judgment do more than toll the bell of tight resources. They must explain the priorities which have led them to decline to fund the treatment. They have not adequately done so here.[38]

The Court of Appeal, however, giving judgment on the same day, rejected Laws J's approach and returned to the essentially non-interventionist stance which it had previously adopted in *Collier*. Sir Thomas Bingham MR evaluated the case as an understandable but 'misguided' attempt 'to involve the court in a field of activity where it is not fitted to make any decision favourable to the patient', and suggested that 'it would be totally unrealistic to require the authority to come to court with its accounts and seek to demonstrate that if this treatment were provided for B there would be a patient, C, who would have to go without treatment. No major authority could run its financial affairs in a way which would permit such a demonstration'. In the best-known passage of his judgment, the Master of the Rolls sought to defer to the allocative decision-maker and, in so doing, elided the functions of substantive review of the merits of priority-setting decisions and review of process – particularly, transparency as to the reasons why priorities had been ordered in a certain way – which Laws J had succeeded in disentangling at first instance:

> Difficult and agonising judgments have to be made as to how a limited budget is best allocated to the maximum advantage of the maximum number of patients. That is not a judgment which the court can make. In my judgment it is not something that a health authority such as this authority can be fairly criticised for not advancing before the court.[39]

As in *Collier*, the Court of Appeal decision admitted of no genuine possibility of the development of a deliberative role for the courts on questions of the allocation of scarce healthcare resources. The failure to require the health authority to offer an explanation of its allocative choice,

---

[38] *Ibid.* at 1064–5.   [39] [1995] 1 WLR 898 (CA) at 906.

while justifiable as assisting administrative decision-making (in that it minimised the possible inconvenience of a health authority attending court to account for the priorities which had been established) was, in reality, underpinned by concerns as to the institutional competence of the judiciary ('That is not a judgment which the court can make'; 'it is not fitted to make any decision favourable to the patient'), as noted in Chapter 5.

While such reservations are understandable, the Court thereby over-looked a wider facilitative function which could have been discharged by enhancing the transparency of the decision-making process, thereby assisting in the realisation of legitimacy through the creation of a delib-erative space (both for the parties concerned and the wider public). Indeed, the potential potency of the judicial process as a catalyst for deliberation was amply demonstrated by the 'Child B' case, which attracted very extensive media interest notwithstanding the restrained approach adopted by the Court of Appeal.[40] To a degree, therefore, the court *did* stimulate wider deliberation on healthcare rationing in this case, but it may surely be argued that this deliberation would have been more adequately informed if the rationales underpinning the health authority's establishment of priorities had been articulated in open court. In short, deliberation occurred *in spite of* rather than *because of* the Court of Appeal's judgment.

This stands in stark contrast to the position adopted by Laws J in the High Court, which appeared to meet the conditions of 'accountability for reasonableness' in requiring the health authority to account for its prior-ities ('publicity' condition) with the implication being that any explan-ation provided for failure to treat should be of sufficient weight to justify interference with the child's right to life ('relevance' condition). In ensur-ing that these conditions were satisfied ('enforcement' condition), Laws J thus offered a framework through public law adjudication for creation of the conditions enabling deliberation to take place on the rationing choice in a manner which should have assisted in the resolution of the 'legitimacy problem'.

Similar views have been expressed on the case, albeit in somewhat different terms, by James and Longley, who are critical of the stance taken by the Court of Appeal. They argue that the court failed to realise

---

[40] For discussion, see C. Burgoyne, 'Distributive Justice and Rationing in the NHS: Framing Effects in Press Coverage of a Controversial Decision' (1997) *Journal of Community and Applied Social Psychology*, 119 at 129; V. Entwistle, I. Watt, R. Bradbury and L. Pehl, 'Media Coverage of the Child B case' (1996) 312 *British Medical Journal*, 1587.

its potential to enhance the quality of administration, consequently 'reducing any sense of unfairness':

by highlighting the essentially moral nature of choices inherent in much public administration ... The courts have a part to play in structuring decision-making and ensuring that the policy choice made, even if reasonable, is explained and justified. The public interest in fairness requires the severing of reasons from the shackles of *Wednesbury* when fundamental rights are threatened. This requires not only that all relevant factors are taken into account but also that they are subjected to a rigorous and open analysis before a conclusion is reached.[41]

As Grubb and Jones note,[42] the implications of following the approach taken by Laws J in 'Child B' would have been far-reaching. In effect, the courts would have underpinned a shift to explicit strategies of rationing by requiring explanation of the principles on which allocative decisions were based. Given the innate conservatism of the judiciary, coupled with the continuing weight of the arguments against judicial involvement in such issues, it is perhaps understandable that the Court of Appeal felt unable to take such a step. Yet it is submitted that it is regrettable that the appeal judges did not take the opportunity, which had been presented to them by Laws J's judgment, to respond to the changing policy environment within the NHS. As outlined in Chapter 3, the establishment of the 'internal market' had made allocative decisions more publicly visible and (as theoretical analysis had predicted) had tended to increase instability, reflected in growing media interest in rationing and by the resort to litigation in 'Child B' itself. In such circumstances, a more active judicial engagement with the rationing process would have offered the opportunity to promote public deliberation and thus to diminish the emerging 'legitimacy problem' generated by the increasing explicitness of rationing. Such a role would stop short of a constitutionally improper judicial usurpation of a health authority's discretion on the allocation of resources, but it would ensure that the process of decision-making was transparent, coherent and properly reasoned, thus establishing the conditions for genuine deliberation upon allocative decisions to take place. In this manner, 'the courts would have found for themselves a crucial role. By insisting, in good public law tradition, on the transparency of decisions about resources, they would have become the agent for a development which many consider long overdue, a proper, political discussion about rationing'.[43]

---

[41] See R. James and D. Longley, 'Judicial Review and Tragic Choices: *ex parte B*' [1995] *Public Law*, 367 at 373.

[42] A. Grubb and M. Jones, 'Institutional Liability' in A. Grubb (ed.), *Principles of Medical Law* (Oxford: Oxford University Press, 2nd edn, 2004) at para. 8.73.

[43] *Ibid.* See further the discussion in Chapter 9 below.

After 'Child B': from *Fisher* to *A, D and G*

In the period of just over a decade which has elapsed since 'Child B', the English courts have shown an increasing preparedness to exercise scrutiny over allocative decision-making in healthcare, without ever, perhaps, evolving the fully-fledged role as deliberative spaces on questions of rationing which might have been the consequence of following the approach taken by Laws J.

In *R* v. *North Derbyshire Health Authority, ex parte Fisher*,[44] a challenge to a local health authority's policy on the provision of beta-interferon for treatment of multiple sclerosis was successful. Government guidance recommended that general practitioners should not prescribe the drug themselves, but should refer patients fulfilling the indications for this form of treatment to a hospital neurologist for specialist assessment and, where appropriate, treatment. The health authority, however, adopted a policy whereby funding for treatment with beta-interferon would only be provided for patients participating in a randomised controlled trial, notwithstanding that the date of a proposed national trial had been postponed indefinitely. The authority's policy was held to be unlawful, Dyson J stating that, while it was not obliged to follow the guidance provided by government, clear reasons should have been provided for departure from the guidance.[45]

Subsequently, in *R* v. *Secretary of State for Health, ex parte Pfizer*,[46] the manufacturer of Viagra successfully challenged the legality of a Government circular which indicated that the drug should not be prescribed by general practitioners (a decision which, as noted in Chapter 3, had been taken largely on the basis of the potential cost of the treatment to the NHS), on the basis that their clinical discretion as to which treatments were necessary and appropriate to prescribe should not be overridden without proper explanation as to why this was necessary. Collins J also held that there had been a failure to comply with the terms of Directive 89/105/EEC which required that any decision to exclude a medicinal product from the coverage of a national health system should 'contain a statement of reasons based on objective and verifiable criteria'.[47]

These two cases, therefore, demonstrate that the courts may be willing to impose an explanatory obligation upon decision-makers seeking to deny access to medical treatments and services, and that they possess the available tools, in the form of public law principles, to enable them to carry out such a task. As such, they reflect a preparedness to move beyond

---

[44] (1997) 8 Med LR 327 ('*Fisher*').   [45] *Ibid.* at 336.
[46] [1999] Lloyd's Med Rep 289 ('*Pfizer*').   [47] Article 7(3).

the *Wednesbury* test and to attempt to disentangle procedural from substantive review. However, it is questionable whether either of these decisions affords quite the same scope to engender public deliberation as the judgment of the High Court in 'Child B', as each can be regarded as having been decided on relatively narrow grounds. In *Fisher*, Dyson J expressly stated that unavailability of funds would justify a refusal to treat: he did not indicate that any explanation of the authority's priorities would be required in such a case.[48] Similarly, in *Pfizer*, the unlawfulness arose from the form in which the decision to exclude Viagra had been communicated (mandatory phraseology contained in a document which purported to be advisory). It would have been lawful for government to utilise other measures to exclude Viagra without providing an explanation for the decision.[49]

In a further case, however, the Court of Appeal moved somewhat closer to fulfilling the function which Laws J had outlined in 'Child B'.[50] Here, North West Lancashire Health Authority, unconvinced of either the appropriateness for funding or of the clinical effectiveness of gender reassignment surgery, had placed it low on its list of priorities, alongside other 'marginal' treatments such as varicose vein surgery, tattoo removal and reversal of sterilisation. As noted in Chapter 3,[51] this was a standard form of explicit rationing for health authorities in the NHS during the early to mid-1990s. In this instance, however, it was deemed to be unlawful. In part, the unlawfulness consisted in the fact that the authority's failure to recognise the effectiveness of the treatment (notwithstanding significant medical evidence to the contrary) and thus to provide funding for it meant that there was, in effect, a blanket ban on its availability. In consequence there was an inability to take account of the individual merits of each case, even though the authority's policy ostensibly provided for exceptions in cases of overriding clinical need.

However, most pertinent to the argument advanced here was the Court's judgment that the authority had failed to demonstrate that its decision on the priority to be accorded to treatment for transsexualism

---

[48] See (1997) 8 Med LR 327 at 336.

[49] Following defeat in the High Court, the Secretary of State for Health utilised the powers vested in him by the National Health Service Act 1977 to issue Regulations which added Viagra to the Schedule of drugs whose NHS availability was limited to specified medical conditions or classes of patient (the 'grey list'): see National Health Service (General Medical Services) Amendment (No. 2) Regulations 1999, SI 1999/1627. The Regulation contained no explanation of this decision and it was not subject to debate in Parliament.

[50] *A, D and G* [2000] 1 WLR 977. For further discussion, see K. Syrett (2000) 22 *Journal of Social Welfare and Family Law*, 200.

[51] See above Chapter 3, n. 117 and accompanying text.

had been 'rationally based upon a proper consideration of the facts', in particular its own acknowledgment that transsexualism amounted to an illness, and the weight of medical evidence on the effectiveness of gender reassignment surgery. Adopting language similar to that used by Laws J in 1992,[52] Buxton LJ stated that 'the more important the interest of the citizen that the decision affects, the greater will be the degree of consideration that is required of the decision-maker. A decision that, as is the evidence in this case, seriously affects the citizen's health will require substantial consideration, and be subject to careful scrutiny by the court as to its rationality'.[53] To this end, he contended that the existence of a strong body of medical evidence in support of the effectiveness of the treatment meant that it was not open to a rational health authority 'simply to determine that a procedure has no proven clinical benefit while giving no indication of why it considers that that is so'.[54] In remitting the decision to the health authority for further consideration, he ordered that 'to the extent that such [gender reassignment] procedures continue to be subordinated to other claims on the authority's resources [the consideration should] indicate, at least in broad terms, the reasons for the authority's choice'.[55]

The decision in *A, D and G* arguably lacks the clarity and forcefulness of Laws J's refusal in 'Child B' to accept the 'tolling of the bell of tight resources' and his call for the health authority 'to explain the priorities that have led them to decline to fund the treatment'. Nonetheless, it appears to indicate that the courts have moved on from the passive stance adopted by the Court of Appeal in *Collier* and 'Child B', and that health authorities can expect to be obliged to provide rationales at least for those explicit limit-setting decisions which appear to be inadequately supported by evidence or which are apparently in conflict with their own stated positions. To this extent, the Court's judgment enhances the prospects of deliberation on such choices and, therefore, on the Daniels and Sabin analysis, has the potential to assist in addressing the 'legitimacy problem'.

A note of caution? *Pfizer (No. 2)* and *Rogers*

These cases suggest that there is a gradual but perceptible trend in the English courts towards requiring decision-making on the allocation of scarce healthcare resources to be more transparent, opening up the possibility of the court playing a role as a deliberative space and catalyst. However, the limited parameters and relative fragility of this development

---

[52] See above n. 34 and accompanying text.   [53] [2000] 1 WLR 977 at 997.
[54] *Ibid.* at 998.   [55] *Ibid.* at 1000.

become apparent from consideration of two subsequent decisions of the Court of Appeal.

R (on the application of Pfizer Ltd) v. *Secretary of State for Health*[56] was a challenge by the drug manufacturer under Directive 89/105/EEC, on the basis that the UK Government had failed to provide the statement of reasons based upon objective and verifiable criteria which was required under Article 7(3), since it had merely stated that the forecast aggregate cost of provision of Viagra on the NHS could not be justified. Counsel for the manufacturer had argued that the terms of the Directive required that some form of analysis and explanation of the relative priority of erectile dysfunction vis-à-vis other non-life threatening conditions be undertaken and that failure to do so rendered the decision unlawful. However, the Court disagreed. It held that the function of the Directive was to demonstrate to manufacturers that state imposition of price controls and restrictions on availability of products did not amount to 'disguised' quantitative restrictions on imports. Accordingly, all that was needed was a 'fairly modest'[57] degree of transparency to demonstrate that this was the case, and the Government's statement sufficed for these purposes – no further analysis of competing priorities was needed.

Pfizer (No. 2) might be regarded as a case decided on fairly narrow grounds, namely the meaning of Directive 89/105/EEC. In view of the fact that the funding and structure of national health systems are matters which are primarily to be determined through the laws of the Member States of the Union,[58] it is not surprising that the Court of Appeal took the view that the objectives of the Directive were limited to the regulation of intra-Community trade in medicinal products, and that it did not require explanation of the priorities for allocation of healthcare resources which the Government had established. However, it is instructive that the Court also dismissed any role for English domestic law in this regard. Notably, Simon Brown LJ endorsed the judgment of Lord Bingham MR in the 'Child B' case, stating that the 'making of an overall judgment at to what level of expenditure upon impotence can be justified, in all the circumstances, having regard to (amongst other matters) the competing priorities for finite NHS resources' was 'an essentially political judgment, that is not within the province of a reviewing court'.[59] This meant that all

---

[56] [2003] 1 CMLR 19 (*'Pfizer (No. 2)'*). For further discussion, see K. Syrett, 'Impotence or Importance? Judicial Review in an Era of Explicit NHS Rationing' (2004) 67 *Modern Law Review*, 289.

[57] *Ibid.* at para. 27 (Buxton LJ).

[58] For general discussion, see T. Hervey and J. MacHale, *Health Law and the European Union* (Cambridge: Cambridge University Press, 2004).

[59] *Ibid.* at para. 8.

that was demanded by the court was that the Secretary of State show that the decision was based upon his assessment that Viagra had a lower priority than other calls upon NHS funding. He was not obliged to offer any form of account of how he had determined these priorities, Simon Brown LJ being 'troubled' as to the nature of the reasoning which might be required of the minister.[60]

Similar observations might be made of *Rogers*,[61] notwithstanding that the Court of Appeal in this case ruled in favour of the claimant patient. Here, funding for treatment of the claimant's early-stage breast cancer with Herceptin had been denied. The decision had been taken in pursuance of a policy that drugs which had not yet completed the authorisation and appraisal processes conducted by the EMA and NICE should not be provided, absent proof of exceptional circumstances. Mindful of the Secretary of State's injunction that Herceptin should not be refused on grounds of cost alone,[62] the PCT had been careful to avoid reference to cost in formulating its policy on access to the treatment. This proved to be its undoing. The Court of Appeal determined that the policy adopted by the PCT was unlawful because, in the absence of any indication that available resources to fund the drug were limited, the only possible criterion upon which exceptional circumstances could be established was clinical need; and yet the Trust had not advanced any evidence to suggest that distinctions between patients *could* in fact be made on clinical grounds. Accordingly, it was not possible to envisage any exceptional circumstances which would justify provision of funding for one patient and denial for another. The policy acted, in effect, as a complete denial of funding for Herceptin for all patients within the Trust area, notwithstanding the purported provision for exceptionality.

To a degree, the decision in *Rogers* – like that in *A, D and G* before it – demonstrates that the judiciary is prepared to seek to enhance the transparency of decision-making on access to medical treatments and services. To this end, the court in *Rogers* indicated that a more intensive level of scrutiny would be applied in cases in which the allocative decision-maker specified that sufficient resources existed, since it was to be expected that all of the clinical needs of the population would be met if funds were available for this purpose. Accordingly in these circumstances, any decision to deny access to treatment to a patient in clinical need should be

---

[60] *Ibid.* at para. 12.
[61] *R (on the application of Rogers)* v. *Swindon NHS Primary Care Trust and Secretary of State for Health* [2006] 1 WLR 2649 (CA) ('*Rogers*'). For discussion, see K. Syrett, 'Opening Eyes to the Reality of Scarce Resources? [2006] *Public Law*, 664.
[62] See above Chapter 1, n. 20 and accompanying text.

properly justified by reference to relevant clinical criteria (meeting the 'publicity' and 'relevance' conditions).[63]

Yet the implications of the decision in *Rogers* should not be overstated. Significantly, where financial constraints upon provision of healthcare *have* been acknowledged by the decision-maker – which, given the factors examined in Chapter 2, is likely to be the position in the majority of cases – the Court of Appeal indicated that it would be prepared to permit the latter considerably broader discretion to establish priorities in whichever manner it chose (for example, giving priority to a woman who was responsible for the care of a disabled child).[64] This would be subject only to judicial intervention for irrationality (understood to encompass only the most extreme of decisions) or failure to attend to the merits of individual cases. In such circumstances, it seems (though the matter receives no specific discussion) that *the court would not require the decision-maker to explain how it had arrived at such a set of priorities*, as would undoubtedly have been the preference of Laws J. The case therefore offers an incentive for the open articulation to the parties and public of the fact that pressures on resources necessitate the imposition of limitations on access to treatments and services, through its stipulation that decision-making which recognises the existence of resource limitations will attract a somewhat less intensive standard of judicial scrutiny. However, it is doubtful that the openness required of the decision-maker in this situation need amount to much more than a mere 'tolling of the bell of tight resources', which Laws J viewed as an inadequate level of explanation. Read in this manner, it is therefore unclear that *Rogers* represents a significant advance on the position adopted by the Court of Appeal in 'Child B'.

Conclusion

Both *Pfizer (No. 2)* and *Rogers* suggest that, notwithstanding a gradual retreat from the highly restrained position adopted in *Collier*, the English courts remain generally reluctant to explore the prospects for evolution of a judicial role as deliberative spaces or catalysts in situations where decisions on allocation of health services and treatments are driven by resource considerations. The point is well illustrated by an obiter dictum of Simon Brown LJ in *Pfizer (No. 2)*. Responding to the argument of counsel for the drug manufacturer that the Secretary of State might be obliged to provide an account of his priorities for expenditure on

---

[63] [2006] 1 WLR 2649 at paras. 78–82.   [64] *Ibid.* at para. 77.

healthcare by reference to data on the relative cost-effectiveness of various treatments (for example, in the form of QALYs),[65] the judge indicated that, if there were to be developed in the future a 'comprehensive framework for healthcare prioritisation, underpinned by an explicit set of ethical and rational values to allow the relative costs and benefits of different areas of NHS spending to be comparatively assessed in an informed way',[66] questions of resource allocation might cease to be purely 'political' and, implicitly, would become properly subject to judicial scrutiny.[67]

Given such a scenario, the English courts would be better placed to require compliance with conditions of procedural justice (such as those embodied in the 'accountability for reasonableness' model), on the basis of which public deliberation could take place. But Simon Brown LJ's judgment indicates that any such shift in judicial attitudes is likely only to come about *in response* to developments in public policy elsewhere, especially to a lead taken by government. Since this appears to be an unlikely eventuality in view of the propensity of politicians to engage in strategies of 'blame avoidance' on questions of healthcare rationing,[68] there is scope for other institutions within civil society to seize the initiative in generating wider deliberation on such issues. However, the jurisprudence examined in this chapter suggests that we should not look to the English courts to undertake this task. Put another way, consonant with concerns as to their constitutional and institutional competence in this field – and notwithstanding the promptings of Laws J – the courts regard their role as primarily *reactive* to the wider health policy context. Their capacity to facilitate the attainment of legitimacy through the health system as a whole remains inhibited by such an outlook.

---

[65] [2003] 1 CMLR 19 at para. 12.
[66] This passage is taken from Health Committee, *National Institute for Clinical Excellence*, Second Report, HC 515-I (2001–02) at para. 105.
[67] [2003] 1 CMLR 19 at para. 17.
[68] See above Chapter 3, n. 79 and accompanying text.

7   Rationing in the Courts: Canada

Analysis of the approach of the Canadian courts to issues of the allocation of
scarce healthcare resources offers an opportunity to consider the extent to
which a differing institutional framework for public law and, perhaps more
significantly, a distinct legal culture arising from that framework, may affect
the capacity of the judicial process to develop a role as a deliberative space on
questions of this type. Specifically, does the relative maturity of the Canadian
Charter of Rights and Freedoms, as distinct from the Human Rights Act in
the UK, enhance the potential of the courts to operate in a facilitative
manner in respect of decision-making on the establishment of priorities for
healthcare expenditure? Are the Canadian courts more confident in their
institutional and constitutional competence than their English counterparts,
and has this placed them in a better position to address problems of legitimacy to which the explicit rationing of healthcare resources gives rise?

Clearly, a response to these questions necessitates a close consideration
of cases concerning the allocation of scarce healthcare resources which
the Canadian courts have heard under the Charter, and this will form the
greater part of the discussion below. However, the existence of the
Charter does not preclude challenge to allocative decision-making in
the healthcare context on the basis of principles of administrative law
similar to those utilised by courts in England, and this form of legal
challenge will be examined briefly first.

Judicial review of administrative action

Those seeking to challenge healthcare funding decisions through administrative law mechanisms in the Canadian courts have had mixed success.
In *St Joseph Island Hospital Association* v. *Plummer Memorial Public
Hospital*,[1] a decision to reduce the number of hospital beds was challenged, but the court declined to intervene. In so doing, it articulated
standard arguments of lack of institutional and constitutional

---

[1] (1996) 24 OTC 73.

competence in language strongly reminiscent of that utilised by the English courts in cases such as *Collier* and *Pfizer (No. 2)*:

Funds provided for the operations of hospitals are not infinite. Expenditure of funds for one purpose inevitably means that those funds are not available to be used for some other purpose. Cuts in service which increase risk in one area may be offset by new services which reduce risk in other areas ... Courts are unsuited to the cost benefit analysis which is required to distribute healthcare resources. Absent prima facie entitlement, courts should be loath to embark upon allocation of funds in undertakings as complex as a hospital with, in this case, an annual budget of approximately 90 million dollars. Distribution of healthcare resources throughout the province is a political and not a judicial function.[2]

By contrast, in *Lexogest Inc.* v. *Manitoba (Attorney General)*,[3] the Court of Appeal of Manitoba (albeit by a bare majority), determined that an attempt by the provincial government to restrict the scope of publicly funded healthcare, by issuing regulations which provided that therapeutic abortions performed outside hospitals did not constitute insured services, was unlawful. Huband JA argued that the objective of the Health Services Insurance Act 1987, which provided the statutory framework for the insurance and payment of health services within the province, was to provide necessary and desirable health services, yet to maintain reasonable control over costs. But, since evidence showed that abortion services provided outside of the hospital setting were *cheaper*, the regulations were not consistent with the statutory provisions under which they were made. However, Scott CJM offered a powerful dissent in this case, stating that there was no basis for invalidating the regulations on the grounds of bad faith, improper purpose or irrationality. He counselled against moving beyond the 'judicial domain' and explicitly endorsed the statement that 'much economic and social policy-making is simply beyond the institutional competence of the courts: their role is to protect against incursions on fundamental values, not to second-guess policy decisions'.[4]

---

[2] *Ibid.* at paras. 25–27 (Pardu J). *Cf. Fogo (Town)* v. *Newfoundland* (2000) 23 Admin LR (3d) 138, in which a challenge to a decision on the relocation of a hospital was held to be 'purely and simply dissatisfaction with a government decision' (Easton J at para. 53) and to be a political choice, made by the provincial government in the exercise of its policy and legislative agenda.

[3] (1993) 101 DLR (4th) 523. Note also the almost identical facts in *Prince Edward Island (Minister of Health and Social Services)* v. *Morgentaler* (1996) 139 DLR (4th) 603, in which the Supreme Court of Prince Edward Island held that the relevant provincial legislation was framed in broader discretionary terms than had been the case in *Lexogest* and that, consequently, regulations which effectively denied payment for therapeutic abortion services outside of hospital were lawful.

[4] *Ibid.* at 547–8, citing *Andrews* v. *Law Society of British Columbia* (1989) 56 DLR (4th) 1 at 38 (McIntyre J).

A degree of uncertainty as to the scope of the judicial role in cases of this type was also evident in *Stein* v. *Québec (Tribunal administratif)*.[5] Here, the Supreme Court of Québec held that a refusal to authorise reimbursement for the cost of hospitalisation and surgery of the patient in the United States following cancellation of surgery for his liver cancer in Canada on three separate occasions (entailing a delay well beyond the eight weeks which had been recommended by physicians) was unlawful on account of irrationality. However, notwithstanding the outcome, the Court continued to assert the need for judicial restraint in this field, stating that it would review specialised decision-making with 'caution and deference and will intervene only when the evidence, viewed reasonably, is incapable of supporting the findings of fact or when the tribunal's interpretation of the legislation is patently unreasonable'.[6]

There is little indication within these decisions of any real willingness on the part of the Canadian courts to assume a deliberative function in respect of decisions on the allocation of scarce healthcare resources. Concerns as to institutional and constitutional competence continue to inhibit the adoption of a more facilitative role in respect of priority-setting decisions. The apparent indecision as to the extent of proper judicial engagement – which is evident from the differing conclusions reached in these cases – would seem to limit the utility of administrative law adjudication as a means of responding to the 'legitimacy problem', perhaps even more than has proved to be the case in England.

Human rights cases

As regards the development of a deliberative role for the courts, the more interesting – and potentially fruitful – mode of adjudication in the Canadian context takes place under the Canadian Charter of Rights and Freedoms. Although the Charter upholds civil and political freedoms, and thus contains no right of access to healthcare resources, it has nonetheless provided the legal basis of challenge in a number of cases involving questions of healthcare funding, albeit (as noted above),[7] in fewer than might have been expected. In this context, two rights have been of particular significance. These are section 7 (the right to life, liberty and security of the person) and section 15 (the right to equal protection and equal benefit of the law without discrimination on certain

---

[5] [1999] RJQ 2416.   [6] *Ibid.* at para. 18 (Cohen JCS).
[7] See D. Greschner, *How Will the Charter of Rights and Freedoms and Evolving Jurisprudence Affect Health Care Costs? Discussion Paper No. 20* (Ottawa: Commission on the Future of Health Care in Canada, 2002), above Chapter 6, n. 5 and accompanying text.

enumerated (such as sex, age or mental or physical disability) or analogous grounds).[8]

The first opportunity for the Supreme Court of Canada to consider a claim under the Charter for specific provision of a health-related service came in *Eldridge* v. *British Columbia (Attorney General)*.[9] Here, three deaf patients argued that the failure of the provincial government to provide public funding for sign language interpretation amounted to a violation of their rights under section 15 of the Charter, since it prevented them from communicating effectively with medical personnel. This denied them the equivalent benefit of access to health services which was enjoyed by those who were not deaf. The claim was unanimously upheld by the Supreme Court. In so doing, the Court gave effect to a *substantive* conception of equality, that is, it rejected the notion that equality amounted to identical treatment (here, that neither the deaf nor the hearing were provided with interpretation services), focusing instead upon the adverse impact upon the enumerated or analogous group.[10] The Court also discounted attempts by the provincial government to justify the failure to provide interpretation services under section 1 of the Charter.[11] LaForest J noted that the estimated cost of provision was only Can$150,000, or approximately 0.0025 per cent of the overall provincial healthcare budget,[12] and dismissed arguments – rooted in a polycentric concern as to the potential for the opening of floodgates – that upholding the claim would 'have a ripple effect throughout the healthcare field, forcing governments to spend precious healthcare dollars accommodating the needs of myriad disadvantaged persons'.[13]

As Greschner notes,[14] *Eldridge* was a case in which rationing related to the characteristics of the potential beneficiaries of the health service: that is, not everyone who could benefit from the publicly-funded service could access it. The claimants were not seeking to challenge the government's determination of the 'menu' of funded services. Rather, they were seeking equal access to services which were already available to others. It might be expected that courts would be more sympathetic to claims of discriminatory treatment in such circumstances. Moreover, since the effect of the

---

[8] Section 6 (the right to take up residence and earn a livelihood in any province of Canada) was utilised in a number of challenges in the 1980s and 1990s in relation to policies to achieve equitable geographical distribution of physician services. However, Greschner, *ibid.* at vi considers this line of case law to be 'discredited'.

[9] [1997] 3 SCR 624 ('*Eldridge*').

[10] See M. Jackman, 'Giving Real Effect to Equality: *Eldridge* v. *British Columbia* and *Vriend* v. *Alberta*' (1998) 4 *Review of Constitutional Studies*, 352.

[11] For further discussion of Section 1, see below.

[12] [1997] 3 SCR 624 at para. 87.   [13] *Ibid.* at para. 91.

[14] See Greschner, *Discussion Paper No. 20* at 7.

Court's judgment was not to expand the range of health services offered (a decision which might be regarded as requiring the exercise both of medical expertise and of political judgment), concerns as to institutional and constitutional competence were somewhat diminished.

By contrast, in two further cases in which the subject-matter of the challenge was a decision to ration the scope of available services, claims under section 15 of the Charter ultimately proved unsuccessful. In the first of these, *Cameron v. Nova Scotia (Attorney General)*,[15] the provincial government refused to fund two forms of fertility treatment, in-vitro fertilisation and intra-cytoplasmic sperm injection. The claimants argued that this amounted to a violation of their rights under section 15, since those who were fertile had the benefit of access to publicly funded services to assist reproduction (such as prenatal and childbirth care) while the infertile were denied the opportunity to have children by reason of the denial of funding for these forms of infertility treatment. A majority of the Nova Scotia Court of Appeal ruled that the claim of discrimination under section 15 had been made out, but that the denial of funding was justified under section 1 of the Charter, given the cost of provision of these treatments set against the growing pressures on the provincial budget for healthcare,[16] their limited success rate and the risks involved.[17] Subsequently, in *Auton v. British Columbia (Attorney General)*,[18] a group of parents challenged the decision of the provincial government not to provide public funding for a form of intensive early behavioural intervention for autistic children (Lovaas Applied Behavioural Therapy), which cost between Can$45,000 and Can$60,000 per child per year. Their argument succeeded at first instance and on appeal, the courts holding that the refusal amounted to discriminatory differential treatment (in comparison with non-autistic children or mentally disordered adults) in respect of access to 'medically necessary' services, in violation of section 15 of the Charter. However, the Supreme Court reversed the decisions of the lower courts, holding that the benefit which was being claimed – funding for *all* treatments which might be medically necessary – was not provided by the law. Rather, all that was statutorily required was funding for 'core' (i.e. physician-delivered) services: provinces might also provide full or partial funding for non-core services at their discretion but were not obliged so to do. Thus, the exclusion of this form of treatment from public provision was consistent with the overall

---

[15] (1999) 177 DLR (4th) 611 (*'Cameron'*).
[16] In evidence before the Court, this was estimated at Can$800,000 annually: *ibid.* at para. 227.
[17] For discussion of these factors, see *ibid.* at paras. 22–23.
[18] [2004] 3 SCR 657 (*'Auton'*). For discussion, see K. Syrett, 'Priority-Setting and Public Law: Potential Realised or Unfulfilled?' (2006) 7 *Medical Law International*, 265.

legislative scheme for publicly-funded healthcare and there had accordingly been no discriminatory treatment of the plaintiffs contrary to section 15.[19]

In *Auton*, a claim that the failure to provide Lovaas Therapy amounted to a violation of section 7 of the Charter (in that there would be a likely loss of the benefits of education and the opportunity to make and articulate decisions; a high probability of institutionalisation; loss of physical integrity through self-injurious behaviour and lack of communication skills; and loss of psychological integrity through loss of privacy, disruption of family life and stigmatisation) was rapidly dismissed by the lower courts, Saunders JA in the Court of Appeal observing that claims of this type could not be founded upon the 'underinclusiveness of the health system'.[20] However, section 7 was invoked in much more controversial circumstances in *Chaoulli* v. *Québec (Attorney General)*.[21] The litigants here were a patient who had suffered significant delays in accessing publicly funded treatment in Québec and a physician who had unsuccessfully sought to offer private health services within the province. They argued that provincial statutes which prohibited private health insurance for treatments and services which were covered by the publicly funded system violated section 7 of the Canadian Charter of Rights and Freedoms and section 1 of the Charter of Rights and Freedoms of Québec (which provides that 'every human being has a right to life, and to personal security, inviolability and freedom'). These claims were rejected in the lower courts. Piché J at first instance noted that 'the Québec public health system does not enjoy unlimited and inexhaustible resources ... The same might indeed be said for every health system existing in the world. In such circumstances, it is entirely justifiable for a government, having the best interests of its people at heart, to adopt a health policy solution which is designed to favour the largest possible number of people'.[22] Similarly, Delisle JA in the Court of Appeal stated

---

[19] However, cf. *Newfoundland & Labrador* v. *Sparkes* 2004 NLSCTD 16, in which it was claimed that a delay in the provision of Lovaas Therapy due to the operation of a waiting list was discriminatory (since autistic children had to wait for treatment while those – for example – who suffered from cancer, did not). The Newfoundland and Labrador Supreme Court upheld a decision of the Human Rights Commission that this amounted to a violation of the provincial Human Rights Code, notwithstanding government arguments that waiting lists assisted in resource planning, programme development and evaluation in a situation where available resources were limited.

[20] (2002) 6 BCLR (4th) 201 at para. 73.

[21] [2005] 1 SCR 791 ('*Chaoulli*'). For extensive analysis, see C. Flood, K. Roach and L. Sossin (eds.), *Access to Care, Access to Justice: the Legal Debate over Private Health Insurance in Canada* (Toronto: University of Toronto Press, 2005); and further, J. King, 'Constitutional Rights and Social Welfare: a Comment on the Canadian *Chaoulli* Health Care Decision' (2006) 69 *Modern Law Review*, 631.

[22] [2000] RJQ 786 at para. 262.

concisely that 'section 7 of the Canadian Charter cannot be used to judicially second-guess the appropriateness of a societal choice'.[23]

However, a majority of the seven sitting judges in the Supreme Court of Canada held that the provincial statutes violated the Québec Charter. Deschamps J (with whom three of the other judges concurred, without further explanation, on the Québec issue) considered that, in view of evidence of alternative measures which had been taken both by other Canadian provinces and by OECD countries, it was not necessary to prohibit private insurance in order to preserve the integrity of the publicly funded health system, which she regarded as being the goal of the prohibition.[24] The provincial government had therefore failed to demonstrate that the legislative measures constituted a 'minimal impairment' of the rights protected by section 1 of the Québec Charter, as it was obliged to do in order to demonstrate that the means chosen to achieve the legislative objective were reasonable and demonstrably justifiable in a free and democratic society.[25] The judge declined to consider whether a violation of section 7 of the Canadian Charter had also taken place, although she did indicate that there were important distinctions between the two human rights instruments which might indicate that the right contained in the Québec Charter was less qualified than that in the Canadian Charter.[26] However, three other judges held that section 7 *had* been violated. They concluded – on the basis of evidence from other western countries which they considered to 'refute the government's theoretical contention that a prohibition on private insurance is linked to maintaining quality public healthcare'[27] – that the deprivation of life, liberty and security of the person brought about by the existence of the provincial legislative provisions was not 'in accordance with the principles of fundamental justice' (as required by section 7) because the laws were 'arbitrary'. That is, they bore no relation to, or were inconsistent with, the objective lying behind them.[28] In contrast, the remaining three judges held that no violation of section 7 had taken place. They considered that the provincial legislation was not 'arbitrary', finding the evidence relied upon by the other judges to be both unpersuasive and too readily dismissive of the commitment to healthcare based upon need, rather than wealth and status, which was enshrined in the Canada Health Act.[29] They noted, by contrast, that other evidence showed 'that the introduction of a parallel private health regime would likely increase the

[23] [2002] RJQ 1205 at para. 30.   [24] [2005] 1 SCR 791 at para. 50.
[25] For further discussion of this test in the context of the Canadian Charter, see below.
[26] [2005] 1 SCR 791 at paras. 29–30.   [27] *Ibid.* at para. 149 (McLachlin CJ and Major J).
[28] *Ibid.* at para. 130.   [29] *Ibid.* at paras. 225–32.

overall cost of healthcare to Canadians'.[30] As regards violation of the Québec Charter, the dissenting judges considered that the provincial legislature should be accorded a 'substantial margin of appreciation':

Designing, financing and operating the public health system of a modern democratic society like Québec remains a challenging task. It calls for difficult choices. In the end, we find that the choice made a generation ago by the National Assembly of Québec remains within the range of options that are justifiable ... Shifting the design of the health system to the courts is not a wise choice.[31]

The 3:3 split on the section 7 question meant that the Supreme Court did not declare that legislation prohibiting the provision of private health insurance for services which were covered by the publicly funded system was unconstitutional. Its *legal* effect was therefore limited to invalidation of such legislation within Québec alone. However, following application by the Attorney General of Québec, the Court agreed to stay its judgment for a period of twelve months.[32]

It has been claimed that *Chaoulli* 'may well be the most controversial case yet decided under the Charter'.[33] Clearly, it raises broader questions as to the financing of healthcare: notably, the possible creation of a 'two-tier' health system in Canada, which are well beyond the scope of this text.[34] From the perspective examined here, the importance of *Chaoulli* is that – while the subject-matter of the challenge was somewhat distinct from the cases of rationing considered elsewhere in this book – the case vividly illustrates both the prospects for creation of a deliberative judicial space on questions of healthcare financing which are generated by human rights adjudication under the framework of the Canadian Charter, and the potential pitfalls of the adoption of such a function by the judiciary. Drawing upon the other decisions discussed in this section in addition to *Chaoulli*, these will now be examined in detail.

Charter adjudication and deliberation

The presumptive nature of rights and judicial competence

Let us first return to the question posed above, that is whether the presence of a more mature, embedded framework of constitutionally protected rights within Canada endows the judiciary with more

---

[30] *Ibid.* at para. 255 (Binnie and LeBel JJ).   [31] *Ibid.* at para. 276.
[32] 2005 CarswellQue 579 (4 August 2005).
[33] King, 'Constitutional Rights and Social Welfare' at 632.
[34] For discussion of this issue, see generally Flood, Roach and Sossin (eds.), *Access to Care, Access to Justice*.

confidence in intervening in matters of resource allocation than is characteristic of its English counterpart.

In response, it should be noted that, at least in some instances, courts engaged in Charter adjudication on issues relating to the funding of healthcare remain as mindful of concerns as to institutional and constitutional competence as do those undertaking judicial review of administrative action, whether in Canada or England. This can be seen in the dissenting judgment in *Chaoulli*,[35] and in the observation of LaForest J in *Eldridge* that 'while financial considerations alone may not justify Charter infringements ... governments must be afforded wide latitude to determine the proper distribution of resources in society'.[36] However, the clearest statement of judicial restraint in the face of allocative questions in the healthcare context comes from *Cameron*, in which the court referred to:

evidence [which] makes clear the complexity of the healthcare system and the extremely difficult task confronting those who must allocate the resources among a vast array of competing claims ... The policy-makers require latitude in balancing competing interests in the constrained financial environment. We are simply not equipped to sort out the priorities. We should not second-guess them, except in clear cases of failure on their part to properly balance the Charter rights of individuals against the overall pressing objective of the scheme.[37]

This stance draws upon Supreme Court jurisprudence which suggests that judicial deference to choices made by the elected branches of government is particularly appropriate in cases which turn upon the allocation of scarce resources, protection of vulnerable groups, mediation among groups with competing interests and complex social scientific evidence.[38]

It is nonetheless apparent that the Canadian courts recognise that excessive adherence to a restrained judicial approach may fail to afford meaningful protection to the rights enshrined in the Charter. A clear statement of this position, albeit not in the context of healthcare rationing, was issued by the Supreme Court in *RJR Macdonald Inc.* v. *Canada (Attorney General)*:

... care must be taken not to extend the notion of deference too far. Deference must not be carried to the point of relieving the government of the burden which the Charter places upon it of demonstrating that the limits it has imposed on guaranteed rights are reasonable and justifiable. Parliament has its role: to choose the appropriate response to social problems within the limiting framework of the Constitution. But the courts also have a role: to determine, objectively and

---

[35] See [2005] 1 SCR 791 at para. 276, above n. 31 and accompanying text.
[36] [1997] 3 SCR 624 at para. 85.   [37] (1999) 177 DLR (4th) 611 at 667 (Chipman JA).
[38] See *Irwin Toy Ltd* v. *Québec (Attorney General)* [1989] 1 SCR 927 ('*Irwin Toy*').

impartially, whether Parliament's choice falls within the limiting framework of the Constitution. The courts are no more permitted to abdicate their responsibility than is Parliament. To carry judicial deference to the point of accepting Parliament's view simply on the basis that the problem is serious and the solution difficult, would be to diminish the role of the courts in the constitutional process and to weaken the structure of rights upon which our Constitution and our nation is founded.[39]

In the rationing context, LaForest J noted in *Eldridge* that 'the leeway to be granted to the state is not infinite. Governments must demonstrate that their actions infringe the rights in question no more than is reasonably necessary to achieve their goals',[40] citing in support of this position his judgment in the earlier case of *Tétreault-Gadoury* v. *Canada (Employment and Immigration Commission)*, in which he stated that:

It should go without saying, however, that the deference that will be accorded to the government when legislating in these matters does not give them an unrestricted licence to disregard an individual's Charter rights. Where the government cannot show that it had a reasonable basis for concluding that it has complied with the requirement of minimal impairment in seeking to attain its objectives, the legislation will be struck down.[41]

These passages show the Canadian courts to be less equivocal as to constitutional competence than their English equivalents. Once a substantive basis for engagement with issues of healthcare financing – through sections 7 and/or section 15 – has been established, the judiciary is, in constitutional terms, *obliged* to adjudicate upon any alleged violation of individual rights.[42] In this respect, there is no cause for judicial inhibition on such matters: indeed, as indicated in *RJR Macdonald*, it would be an abnegation of the constitutional role to eschew any involvement. Put another way, the existence of a rights framework enables questions which may be regarded elsewhere (such as in England)[43] as 'political' to be reconceived as 'legal', as Sheldrick has noted:

Conceptualising the question as a rights issue ... gives the court what it lacked in the 'Child B' case; namely, a basis on which to assess the tradeoffs made by the health authority. Rights, then provide the courts with a vehicle for navigating the complex and contradictory world of law, politics and administration ... The existence of a rights discourse ... permits the courts to shift the terrain on which a resource allocation decision is considered. The assessment of costs and benefits

---

[39] [1995] 3 SCR 199 at para. 136 (McLachlin J) ('*RJR Macdonald*').
[40] [1997] SCR 624 at para. 86.   [41] [1991] 2 SCR 22 at 44.
[42] Albeit that a court must, of course, first establish that a given factual situation falls within the scope of the rights protected under the Charter.
[43] Note especially *Pfizer (No. 2)*: above Chapter 6, n. 59 and accompanying text.

must be considered within a rights framework. This permits the courts to assert their authority and expertise over and above the expertise of policymakers.[44]

Steps have also been taken to address problems of lack of institutional competence. Canadian courts, especially the Supreme Court of Canada, have exhibited openness to intervention by third parties in cases with a significant public interest dimension, notably those under the Charter. This phenomenon was apparent both in *Auton*, in which intervener status at Supreme Court level was granted to Autism Society Canada, the Canadian Association for Community Living and Council of Canadians with Disabilities, Disabled Women's Network Canada, Families of Children with Autism, Families for Early Autism Treatment and the Women's Legal Education and Action Fund; and in *Chaoulli*, where the Attorneys General of three provinces other than Québec, ten Senators, twelve organisations seeking to offer medical care on a private basis, and seven interest groups and professional associations were permitted to intervene in the proceedings. As Hannett notes, interventions of this type, which allow parties without a direct discernible pecuniary or material interest in the litigation to make submissions to the court, widen the scope of participation in the adjudication and increase the diversity of information available to the judges.[45] From a deliberative perspective, this would appear to be a welcome development. As noted previously, the engagement of a multiplicity of voices serves to lessen the possibility that the decision will be a manifestation of partial, self-interested views and instead increases the likelihood of genuine reflection and reasoned argumentation. Moreover, in the context of the capacity of the judiciary to respond to the 'legitimacy problem' in the explicit allocation of healthcare resources, it is significant that a key justification which has been advanced for broad third party intervention in litigation is that it may enhance the legitimacy of the eventual decision because 'participation by public interest intervenors in litigation creates a moral obligation on their part to respect the outcome of the litigation'.[46]

Nonetheless, as the passage from *Cameron* suggests, doubts persist as to the capacity of courts to evaluate complex evidence and to accommodate a variety of competing interests. Ultimately, these may incline the court to defer to political choices, accepting that government decisions, policies

---

[44] B. Sheldrick, 'Judicial Review and the Allocation of Health Resources in Canada and the United Kingdom' (2003) 5 *Journal of Comparative Policy Analysis*, 149 at 157.

[45] S. Hannett, 'Third Party Intervention in the Public Interest' [2003] *Public Law*, 128 at 134.

[46] P. Bryden, 'Public Interest Intervention in the Courts' (1987) 66 *Canadian Bar Review*, 490 at 509.

and actions are lawfully based upon a proper analysis of the facts and evaluation of the policy options, as was the case in both *Cameron* and *Auton*. However, in order to enable it to reach such a conclusion, a court engaged in adjudication under the Charter will first demand that the relevant government body offers 'demonstrable justification' of the need to limit rights pursuant to section 1 of the Charter. To what extent does this form of judicial scrutiny open up possibilities of deliberation?

Proportionality, evidence and 'demonstrable justification'

Section 1 operates as a general limitation of the rights protected under the Charter. It provides that the rights are guaranteed 'subject only to such reasonable limits prescribed by law as can be demonstrably justified in a free and democratic society'. The approach to be taken under this provision was set out as a two-stage test in *R* v. *Oakes*.[47] First, the government must establish that the objective of the legislation or policy is pressing and substantial. In practice, this has not proved problematic to demonstrate: in the healthcare context, it has normally entailed arguing that the viability or integrity of the publicly funded system is being protected and its resources used efficiently.[48] Secondly, the court evaluates the government's means for achieving the objective, through the test broadly described as 'proportionality'.[49] This involves three steps: first, that the measure is rationally connected to the objective; secondly, that the measure represents a minimal impairment of the protected right (that is, that there must not be a less drastic means by which to achieve the objective); and, thirdly, that the measure does not have a disproportionately severe effect on those to whom it applies. The section therefore functions to place a burden upon government to introduce evidence to justify the limitations which it has placed upon rights in pursuit of a legitimate and important governmental objective. In this manner, government is compelled to provide rationales for decisions which may have the impact of limiting access to treatment, and, in order to show that alternatives to the policy under scrutiny have been considered, is under an 'obligation to produce evidence in open court about the merits, expense and risks of different healthcare options',[50] possibly involving data on the clinical and

---

[47] [1986] 1 SCR 103.

[48] See Greschner, *Discussion Paper No. 20* at 14; and, for an example of such reasoning, *Chaoulli*, above n. 25 and accompanying text.

[49] Proportionality is more strictly used to refer to the third of the steps which follow: *cf.* P. Craig, *Administrative Law* (London: Sweet & Maxwell, 5th edn, 2003) at 622.

[50] Greschner, *Discussion Paper No. 20* at 16.

cost-effectiveness of treatments together with other relevant factors which were taken into account in arriving at the policy.

The exercise of judicial scrutiny under section 1 appears to offer the opportunity for creation of a deliberative space within the courtroom. The obligation placed upon government to adduce evidence and provide rationales for laws and policies which have an impact upon the funding of, and access to, healthcare services and treatments, would seem to meet the 'publicity' and 'relevance' conditions of the 'accountability for reasonableness' model, as well as Laws J's exhortation in 'Child B' for the provision of a 'substantial objective justification' for any interference with rights and an explanation of how priorities have been established. To this extent, the Canadian courts are better equipped with the necessary tools to bring about deliberation on issues of healthcare rationing than their English counterparts, who remain somewhat reticent to deploy the test of proportionality in cases of this type, especially given the limited impact of the Human Rights Act 1998 to date in this field. However, it does not necessarily follow that, simply because useful mechanisms are available to them, the courts may be regarded as having, in fact, succeeded in creating a deliberative space. To what extent can it be said that the Canadian courts have grasped the opportunity presented by section 1 to initiate genuine deliberation within the courtroom on issues of healthcare financing?

On first impression, the picture appears positive. The application of section 1 analysis facilitates the introduction and scrutiny of a far wider range of evidence than occurs in the English cases, with the consequence that individuals who are affected by the decision are more likely to comprehend its rationale and accept that it was based upon relevant criteria, thus diminishing the 'legitimacy problem'. For example, in *Cameron*, the court considered evidence as to the level of federal and provincial contributions to the health programme in Nova Scotia, the estimated cost of providing fertility treatment throughout the province, the success rate of the treatment, and the overall cost and cost per year of life gained of various other procedures which represented alternative uses for the money which might have been spent on fertility treatment.[51] Similarly, while the evidence considered by the court in *Eldridge* was limited to the likely cost of providing the interpretation service throughout the province,[52] Jackman notes that the judicial process offered considerably greater scope for deliberation upon the issue of funding the service than had been provided by other branches of government. This

---

[51] (1999) 177 DLR (4th) 611 at paras. 227–33.   [52] [1997] 3 SCR 624 at para. 87.

was because, rather than being the product of full legislative consideration, the initial decision had been taken by a committee within the Ministry of Health following a twenty-minute review of a ministerial briefing note and in the absence of any information as to the cost-effectiveness or likely implications of offering the service.[53]

However, further examination suggests that there are reasons to believe that the judicial scrutiny which is undertaken by Canadian courts under section 1 is frequently less than ideal from a deliberative standpoint. It has been argued that 'the Supreme Court in *Eldridge* did not devote any serious attention to the costs of providing [the interpretation] service';[54] rather, it accepted without question an estimate based upon an extrapolation of the costs incurred in provision of the service on a voluntary basis by a private institute in an urban area, without considering the cost implications of offering public funding for this service throughout the less densely populated areas of the province,[55] let alone the implications for other provinces.[56]

Similar criticisms have been voiced of the reasoning of the various courts in *Auton*. In a particularly coruscating analysis of the decisions of the two lower courts, Greschner and Lewis argue that the section 1 'presentation in *Auton* was cursory, and the courts' reasoning was skimpy and barely acknowledged the financial implications'.[57] Thus, neither of the provincial courts engaged in an extensive scrutiny of the clinical effectiveness of Lovaas therapy, merely accepting the parents' affidavits that the children had made significant gains as a result of the treatment and referring in a perfunctory fashion to research findings.[58] For its part, the Supreme Court relied primarily upon the fact that funding had only recently been provided in certain Canadian provinces and US states and was far from universal at the time of trial, as justification for its conclusion that the therapy was of an 'emergent' nature.[59] This, too can be regarded as problematic reasoning in that the decision to provide or withhold funding elsewhere may have been taken for reasons of political expediency (for example, the presence of a particularly vocal patient lobby in

---

[53] Jackman, 'Giving Real Effect to Equality' at 368–9.

[54] C. Manfredi and A. Maioni, 'Courts and Health Policy: Judicial Policy-Making and Publicly Funded Health Care in Canada' (2002) 27 *Journal of Health Politics, Policy and Law*, 213 at 229.

[55] *Ibid.*   [56] Greschner, *Discussion Paper No. 20* at 15.

[57] D. Greschner and S. Lewis, '*Auton* and Evidence-Based Decision-Making: Medicare in the Courts' (2003) 82 *Canadian Bar Review*, 501 at 532. See further Syrett, 'Priority-Setting and Public Law'.

[58] See e.g. (2000) 78 BCLR (3d) 55 (BCSC) at para. 52; (2002) 6 BCLR (4th) 201 (BCCA) at para. 49.

[59] [2004] 3 SCR 657 at para. 55.

some locations and not in others) rather than on the basis of scientific evidence. Nor was the evaluation of evidence on the cost-effectiveness of the treatment much more satisfactory. The courts did not require that the government provide evidence of its evaluation of the treatment in terms of standard health economic metrics, such as the QALY:[60] rather, they appeared to rest content with evidence which can best be described as impressionistic. For example, the judge at first instance stated that 'it is apparent that the costs incurred in paying for effective treatment of autism *may well be more than offset* by the savings achieved by assisting autistic children to develop their educational and societal potential rather than dooming them to a life of isolation and institutionalisation',[61] while the Supreme Court asserted that a failure on the part of the government to meet 'the gold standard of scientific methodology' could not be regarded as decisive in the claimants' favour.[62]

The case which casts most doubt upon the courts' capacity to create a deliberative space within the courtroom by demanding the provision of evidence and reasoned justification for decisions on healthcare funding is *Chaoulli*.[63] Here, the problem did not lie with the quality or quantity of evidence which was presented to the Supreme Court: as King notes, 'the expert testimonies included that of a former Minister of Health of Québec ('the father of Québec Medicare'), and various professors of medicine and public policy who teach and practice and are of generally outstanding reputations. The trial judge found all witnesses credible and that their conclusions withstood cross-examination after weeks of testimony'.[64] Rather, it was the manner in which the judges approached the evidence which was presented which raises questions as to the capacity for deliberation within the courtroom. Perhaps most striking are the following statements:

It is apparent from this summary that for each threat mentioned, no study was produced or discussed in the Superior Court. While it is true that scientific or empirical evidence is not always necessary, witnesses in a case in which the arguments are supposedly based upon logic or common sense should be able to cite

---

[60] See Greschner and Lewis, '*Auton* and Evidence-Based Decision-Making' at 523.
[61] (2000) 78 BCLR (3d) 55 (BCSC) at para. 147 (Allan J). Emphasis added.
[62] [2004] 3 SCR 657 at para. 61 (McLachlin CJC).
[63] Note, however, that the analysis of evidence in this case did not primarily take place within the context of section 1. Deschamps J considered the evidence in connection with section 9.1 of the Québec Charter, which sets out a different standard for justification, while McLachlin CJ and Major J (Bastarche J concurring) analysed it in relation to the question of the arbitrariness of the laws under section 7. However, in both instances a proportionality-type analysis was being employed, with the consequence that the approach taken in *Chaoulli* is relevant to the discussion here.
[64] King, 'Constitutional Rights and Social Welfare' at 637.

specific facts in support of their conclusions. The human reactions described by the experts, many of whom came from outside Québec, do not appear to me to be very convincing, particularly in the context of Québec legislation.[65]

In support of this contention [*viz*: that removal of the prohibition on private insurance would divert resources from the public health system and thus reduce the quality of public care], the government called experts in health administration and policy. Their conclusions were based on the 'common sense' proposition that the improvement of health services depends on exclusivity. They did not profess expertise in waiting times for treatment. Nor did they present economic studies or rely on the experience of other countries. They simply assumed, as a matter of apparent logic, that insurance would make private health services more accessible and that this in turn would undermine the quality of services provided by the public healthcare system.[66]

These dicta are especially controversial because they contradict the findings of the judge at first instance without proper explanation as to how she may have erred. Thus, Wright finds the first of these statements 'utterly inexplicable as the evidence in question, consisting of the published results of specific studies, statements from respected leaders in medicine, and research in prestigious medical journals, convinced the Québec Superior Court to reject Chaoulli's arguments',[67] while Stewart is equally critical of the second, noting (of the expert on healthcare policy called by the government) that:

his qualifications as an expert on health policy issues do not appear to have been challenged, and if those qualifications did not give him 'expertise in waiting times for treatment', it is hard to know what would. His report was not an exercise in speculative common sense but an exercise of his particular expertise. The trial judge largely accepted it, along with similar conclusions reached by other experts, and noted that only one of the expert witnesses had reached the opposing view.[68]

Additionally, Flood, Stabile and Kontic point to a number of 'false conclusions' which are reached by the majority in the light of its consideration of health economics and health policy and the comparative analysis of health systems. Drawing upon studies relating to private health insurance in a number of countries, they argue that the judges demonstrate a 'flawed understanding of the dynamics of public and private financing in healthcare' and that, while it is possible to question the evidence in support of a prohibition on private insurance, the existence

---

[65] [2005] 1 SCR 791 at para. 64 (Deschamps J).
[66] *Ibid.* at para. 136 (McLachlin CJ and Major J).
[67] C. Wright, 'Different Interpretations of "Evidence" and Implications for the Canadian Healthcare System' in Flood, Roach and Sossin (eds.), *Access to Care, Access to Justice* at 223.
[68] H. Stewart, 'Implications of *Chaoulli* for Fact-Finding in Constitutional Cases', in Flood, Roach and Sossin (eds.), *Access to Care, Access to Justice* at 213.

of this conflicting data casts considerable doubt upon the determination of the policy as 'arbitrary'.[69]

As both King[70] and Stewart[71] have noted, the approach taken by the majority in *Chaoulli* to the consideration of expert and social scientific evidence raises significant questions as to the institutional capacity of courts to determine 'legislative facts', that is those which 'involve the use of social and economic data to establish a more general context for policy-making',[72] and which are often not susceptible of proof, even where the relevant evidence is extensive. Yet, even where such facts are at issue (as will inevitably be the case in questions relating to the financing of health-care), it is possible to outline an appropriate role for the courts, which might take the following form. In the presence of inconclusive or conflicting evidence of this type, courts may choose to show greater deference to the decision-maker's policy choices, but will still demand some form of explanation and justification for the choice made by requiring that government show that there is a 'reasonable basis' for concluding that a problem exists, that the means chosen will address it and that these will infringe the right as minimally as possible. As Choudry observes, 'this standard is understood as expecting something less of governments than definitive, scientific proof. But ... an absolute lack of evidence is unacceptable; there must be some factual basis for the public policy'.[73] This approach has, in fact, been adopted in previous Supreme Court cases in which conflicting scientific evidence has been at issue.[74] The failure to utilise such a standard in *Chaoulli* is puzzling.

From a deliberative perspective, the Supreme Court's treatment of evidence in *Chaoulli* gives cause for concern. It is far from clear that – to paraphrase Habermas – only the force of the better argument has been recognised. The apparent readiness to dismiss seemingly cogent evidence and witnesses without adequate explanation as to why this was done does not appear consonant with the careful consideration and weighing of

---

[69] C. Flood, M. Stabile and S. Kontic, 'Finding Health Policy "Arbitrary": the Evidence on Waiting, Dying and Two-Tier Systems' in Flood, Roach and Sossin (eds.), *Access to Care, Access to Justice* at 297.

[70] King, 'Constitutional Rights and Social Welfare' at 636–7.

[71] Stewart, 'Implications of *Chaoulli*' in Flood, Roach and Sossin (eds.) *Access to Care, Access to Justice* at 209.

[72] J. Hagan, 'Social Science Evidence in Constitutional Litigation' in R. Sharpe (ed.) *Charter Litigation* (Toronto: Butterworths, 1987) at 215, following the distinction made in K. Davis, 'An Approach to Problems of Evidence in the Administrative Process' (1942) 55 *Harvard Law Review*, 364 at 402 3.

[73] S. Choudry, 'Worse than *Lochner*?' in Flood, Roach and Sossin (eds.), *Access to Care, Access to Justice* at 95.

[74] See e.g. *Irwin Toy* [1989] 1 SCR 927.

evidence, coupled with reasoned argumentation, which is characteristic of deliberation. Instead, it smacks of the existence of exogenous and fixed judicial preferences, of entrenched views rather than openness to reflection and transformation. Indeed, it has been argued that the decision can best be explained by a pre-existing desire on the Court's part to 'shape the politics of Medicare',[75] and even more strongly, that it may have been a product of class bias.[76] This would not seem to amount to deliberation in the courtroom.

Charter adjudication as catalyst: 'democratic dialogue'

Yet, if *Chaoulli* serves to demonstrate that deliberation within the courtroom may be deficient notwithstanding the existence of legal mechanisms and principles which should facilitate it, it also provides a vivid illustration of the capacity of the legal process to function in the second deliberative manner described in Chapter 5, that is, as a catalyst or stimulus for deliberation within the other political branches and broader civil society.

There was clear recognition within the health policy community that the decision of the Supreme Court would instigate widespread discussion within Canada, both on the specific issue of wait times for treatment and, more broadly, on the appropriate mix between private health insurance and publicly funded healthcare. Academic commentators have written of the decision as 'a shot across the bows of floundering provincial healthcare systems',[77] a 'call to long overdue action on the part of government',[78] and 'a "wake up call" for those Canadians interested in securing an efficient and equitable healthcare system'.[79] Similar language was used by prominent politicians. Notably, two senators responsible for producing highly influential recent reports on the future of healthcare in Canada commented that 'the Court's decision should be a clarion call to all ... to get on with badly needed reforms to Medicare before those clamouring for its destruction gather more momentum',[80] and that the

[75] Choudry, 'Worse than Lochner' in Flood, Roach and Sossin (eds.), *Access to Care, Access to Justice* at 95; A. Hutchinson, '"Condition Critical": the Constitution and Health Care' in Flood, Roach and Sossin (eds.), *Access to Care, Access to Justice* at 111.

[76] See especially Hutchinson, *ibid*.

[77] B. Dickens, 'The *Chaoulli* Judgment: Less than Meets the Eye – Or More?' in Flood, Roach and Sossin (eds.), *Access to Care, Access to Justice* at 19.

[78] Wright, 'Different Interpretations of "Evidence"' in Flood, Roach and Sossin (eds.), *Access to Care, Access to Justice* at 220.

[79] A. Maynard, 'How to Defend a Public Health Care System: Lessons from Abroad' in Flood, Roach and Sossin (eds.), *Access to Care, Access to Justice* at 237.

[80] R. Romanow, 'In Search of a Mandate?' in Flood, Roach and Sossin (eds.), *Access to Care, Access to Justice* at 528. Note also his comment in the book's preface, that 'In its best

judgment was 'anything but a green light for a two-tiered system; it is rather meant to inspire governments and service providers to find a real solution, and fundamentally to reorganise the existing public healthcare system'.[81] The federal Health Minister also acknowledged that the Court had given provincial governments a 'wake-up call'.[82] One might surmise from these statements that a general view persisted that the catalytic impact was a welcome aspect of the of the Supreme Court decision. For example, it has been contended that 'the judgment has triggered a series of timely Canadian debates concerning health services funding… the realisation that the judicial branch of government could add momentum to the movement for improved performance added a dimension of apparent urgency to policy-making',[83] and that:

Perhaps, in its testily divided decision, the Court has done the country a favour. We have not had a national, focused debate on where to draw the line on two-tier healthcare for decades … nor have we carefully and conclusively debated [the] unrealised vision of a genuinely balanced continuum of care … This is not a time for hysteria or fear-mongering, but for self-examination, reflection and choice. How governments respond to this challenge is of course vitally important, and the political exchanges promise to be lively.[84]

The debate triggered by *Chaoulli* took place in a variety of fora. There was extensive discussion of the decision and its implications in the national and provincial media.[85] A number of conferences were organised by universities and professional bodies across Canada.[86] The Canadian

light, the Supreme Court's majority decision … should provide a wake up call to the public and the governments they elect, to get on with badly needed healthcare reforms in an integrated and coherent manner': *ibid.* at ix.

[81] M. Kirby, quoted in D. Low, L. Wakulowsky, G. Moysa, 'Failing on the Fundamentals: the *Chaoulli* Decision', *Law and Governance* (June 2005), available at www.longwoods.com/product.php?productid=17188&page=3. (accessed 8 January 2006).

[82] U. Dosanjh, quoted in 'Ruling may Reshape Medicare: but Government Insists System won't be Undermined', *The StarPhoenix*, 10 June 2005. See also 'Editorial: Medicare Ruling a Wake-Up Call', *The Toronto Star*, 10 June 2005.

[83] Dickens, 'The *Chaolli* Judgment', in Flood, Roach and Sossin (eds.), *Access to Care, Access to Justice* at 25–6. However, for a contrary view, see A. Petter, 'Wealthcare: The Politics of the Charter Revisited' in Flood, Roach and Sossin (eds.), at 119, arguing that 'there has in recent years been no lack of political pressure or commitment regarding the need to reduce wait times … Thus this "wake-up call" came at a time when no one seems to have been asleep'.

[84] S. Lewis, 'Physicians, It's in your Court now' (2005) 173 *Canadian Medical Association Journal*, 275 at 276.

[85] A document produced by the Québec Population Health Research Network lists 1031 articles containing the word 'Chaoulli' in French and English-language Canadian newspapers and journals between 8 June and 8 December 2005. See www.santepop.qc.ca/chaoulli/docs/chaoulli/media_items.pdf (accessed 8 January 2007).

[86] In addition to the conference organised by the University of Toronto (16 September 2005), which is reported in Flood, Roach and Sossin (eds.), *Access to Care, Access to*

Medical Association adopted a motion at its annual meeting in August 2005 which recommended that private health insurance be used to pay for healthcare services where timely access to care could not be provided through the publicly funded scheme – an action which Lemmens and Archibald describe as 'using the *Chaoulli* case as an opportunity to express its view on the state of healthcare in this country and to bring about fundamental change'[87] – and debated a paper on the private/public split at its annual meeting in August 2006.[88]

Deliberation also took place within and at the behest of the legislative and executive branches. This was notably the case in Québec, which was obliged to respond to the finding of a violation of the Charter within twelve months (following the temporary stay issued in August 2005). The province's Premier stated that he wanted public debate on the issue before the government redesigned its healthcare policy,[89] and to this end the government published a consultation paper on healthcare reform in February 2006, in which it invited 'interested groups and citizens to make their views known, thereby contributing to the government's deliberation on new ways of financing our health system'.[90] The document included details of proposals for addressing the decision, which King describes as 'a cautious step forward in expanding the role of private medical insurance'.[91] Other provinces, while not legally required to do so, also acted in the aftermath of *Chaoulli*. For example, the government of Alberta – which was identified as 'the jurisdiction most likely to use the decision as a catalyst for healthcare reform that embraces a larger role for private financing and insurance'[92] – produced a new Health Policy Framework, after public consultation, which emphasised patient choice and the need to define publicly funded

Justice, conferences analysing the case and exploring its implications were also organised, inter alia, by the Ontario Bar Association (19 September 2005), Osgoode Hall Law School (26 October 2005), the Canadian Independent Medical Clinics Association (11–12 November 2005) and Dalhousie University (23–25 February 2006).

[87] T. Lemmens and T. Archibald, 'The CMA's *Chaoulli* Motion and the Myth of Promoting Fair Access to Health Care' in Flood, Roach and Sossin (eds.), *Access to Care, Access to Justice* at 323.

[88] See 'CMA proposes options for private-public split' (2006) 175 *Canadian Medical Association Journal*, 18.

[89] See 'Private care on hold for a year; Québec finds new deadline tight; Public input and new healthcare plan will be Charest's response to June ruling', *The Gazette*, 5 August 2005.

[90] Government of Québec, *Guaranteeing Access* (Montreal: Government of Québec, 2006) at 3. The proposals were given legislative effect in Bill 33 of 2006.

[91] King, 'Constitutional Rights and Social Welfare' at 643. Note also the proposals of the Working Group on Québec's Healthcare System, Press Release, 21 November 2005, available at www.iss.uqam.ca/pages/pdf/CHpress_release.pdf (accessed 8 January 2007).

[92] T. Caulfield and N. Ries, 'Politics and Paradoxes: *Chaoulli* and the Alberta Reaction' in Flood, Roach and Sossin (eds.), *Access to Care, Access to Justice* at 414.

health services.[93] At federal level, the Conservative Party proposed the introduction of a Healthcare Guarantee to ensure that patients received essential medical treatment within clinically acceptable waiting times,[94] the New Democratic Party proposed a legislative amendment which sought to protect publicly funded health care from privatisation,[95] and the Liberal Government sought to remind provinces of an agreement to establish evidence-based benchmarks for medically acceptable wait times, a stance which was seen as having been adopted in response to *Chaoulli*.[96] Given these developments, the claims that the decision was not 'transformative' and that 'on the surface, the decision itself had little impact' appear puzzling.[97] In any event, it has been acknowledged that the decision has stimulated less tangible forms of deliberation within broader civil society, for example by causing a 'big shift in the public debate around healthcare ... What *Chaoulli* did was to open up the playing field to legitimise a wider range of alternatives for the directions of Canada's health system',[98] and broadening the range of inputs from citizens and interested groups.[99]

The catalytic impact of *Chaoulli* is, of course, in large part a function of the decision's highly controversial status.[100] Every instance of judicial engagement with the financing and funding of healthcare services is likely to generate significant interest,[101] especially given the centrality of health policy to a government's agenda and deep-seated public commitment to the principles underlying the provision of healthcare within certain publicly funded systems.[102] However, few legal cases will be perceived to present the fundamental challenge to the basic structure of the health

---

[93] Government of Alberta, *Getting on with Better Health Care* (Calgary: Government of Alberta, 2006).

[94] See 'Harper Pledges Patient Wait Times Guarantee', Conservative Press Release, available at www.conservative.ca/EN/1091/33313 (accessed 8 January 2007).

[95] See 'Layton Outlines *Chaoulli* Response Law to Protect Public Medicare', NDP Press Release, 6 October 2005, available at www.ndp.ca/page/1652 (accessed 8 January 2007).

[96] See 'Private Insurance Won't Hurt Public Healthcare', *The Edmonton Journal*, 17 September 2005.

[97] '*Chaoulli* Decision Resonates One Year Later' (2006) 175 *Canadian Medical Association Journal*, 17 at 17, 18.

[98] A. Maioni, quoted *ibid.* at 18.

[99] See R. Collins Nakai (President of Canadian Medical Association), quoted *ibid* at 18: 'It's wonderful to have different people becoming involved in the debate. It has to be a public debate'.

[100] See King, above n. 33 and accompanying text.

[101] The 'Child B' decision is particularly instructive in this regard. See above Chapter 6, n. 40 and accompanying text.

[102] On public identification with the values of a health system in the UK and Canada respectively, see N. Lawson, *The View From Number 11* (London: Bantam, 1992) at 613: 'the NHS is the closest thing the English (*sic*) have to a religion'; and Commission on the Future of Health Care in Canada, *Building on Values: The Future of Health Care in*

system – or even, to democratic society as a whole – as was *Chaoulli*, at least by some.[103] Nonetheless, that the Supreme Court's decision generated such an extensive process of deliberation may also be attributed to the approach taken by the Canadian judiciary to its role in a constitutional democracy when called upon to adjudicate upon questions of rights.

In seeking to address concerns that rights-based adjudication may be undemocratic because it apparently permits the unelected judiciary to countermand the wishes of elected legislators, one theory which has proved influential – notably in the Canadian context – is that judicial review of alleged violations of rights under instruments such as the Charter of Rights and Freedoms functions as a form of *dialogue* between courts and the other branches of government, particularly legislatures.[104] Dialogic review has been defined as 'any constitutional design that allows rights, as contained in a bill of rights and as interpreted by the courts, to be limited or overridden by the ordinary legislation of a democratically elected legislature'.[105] That is, while courts are constitutionally empowered to adjudicate upon alleged violations of rights and, in so doing, may – at least under certain frameworks[106] – possess the power to strike down offending laws, certain structural features of human rights legislation

Canada, Final Report (Ottawa: National Library of Canada, 2002) at xviii: 'Canadians embrace Medicare as a public good, a national symbol and a defining aspect of their citizenship'.

[103] See e.g. R. Romanow, 'Preface' in Flood, Roach and Sossin (eds.), *Access to Care, Access to Justice* at ix: 'the Court's decision . . . signals a potentially serious disruption of the Canadian balance between the individual and the community, between nation and enterprise'; Hutchinson, '"Condition Criticial"' in Flood Roach and Sossin (eds.), *Access to Care, Access to Justice* at 109: 'the courts have undermined not only the debate on healthcare, but also the democratic foundations of the Canadian polity'. See also 'The New Face of Medicare', *The Globe and Mail*, 10 June 2005: 'Canadian Medicare will Never be the Same'; 'Timely Healthcare a Basic Right, Supreme Court says', *Toronto Star*, 10 June 2005: 'The Supreme Court Has Delivered a Hammer-blow to Medicare'.

[104] The *locus classicus* of dialogue theory is P. Hogg and A. Bushell, 'The Charter Dialogue between Courts and Legislatures (or Perhaps the Charter isn't Such a Bad Thing After All)' (1997) 35 *Osgoode Hall Law Journal*, 75. The theory has been much discussed in subsequent literature. See notably K. Roach, *The Supreme Court on Trial: Judicial Activism or Democratic Dialogue* (Toronto: Irwin Law, 2001). For its use in Supreme Court decisions, in addition to *Chaoulli*, see e.g. *Vriend* v. *Alberta* [1998] 1 SCR 493 at 562–7; *R* v. *Mills* [1999] 3 SCR 668 at 711–13. For application of dialogue theory in another jurisdiction, see R. Clayton, 'Judicial Deference and "Democratic Dialogue": the Legitimacy of Judicial Intervention under the Human Rights Act 1998' [2004] *Public Law*, 33.

[105] K. Roach, 'Dialogic Judicial Review and its Critics' (2004) 23 *Supreme Court Law Review* (2d), 49 at 55.

[106] Striking down legislation which is found to be in violation of constitutionally-protected rights is possible under the Canadian Charter, but not under the UK's Human Rights Act 1998, which provides only that courts may make a 'declaration of incompatibility' with the Act, which 'does not affect the validity, continuing operation or enforcement of the provision in respect of which it is given': section 4(6)(a).

permit the legislature (and, by logical extension, an elected government which is in control of that legislature) to respond to the judicial ruling. This occurs when the legislature places limitations upon and (where it considers it appropriate so to do) overrides the interpretation of rights arrived at by the court. Put simply, under dialogue theory, courts do not have the 'final word' on questions of human rights.[107]

There are a number of features of the Canadian Charter which facilitate dialogue between courts and other branches of government. First, as described above, section 1 requires the government to offer a demonstrable justification of laws which are alleged to violate rights, with the consequence that legislative objectives which satisfy the test of proportionality may lawfully function to limit those rights. Rights under the Charter are therefore relative rather than absolute and, as previously discussed, section 1 analysis imposes an obligation of explanation upon the government (including the introduction of supporting evidence) which 'should promote democratic deliberation and accountability for the limitation of rights'.[108] Secondly, the so-called 'notwithstanding clause' (section 33) enables legislatures to enact legislation for a renewable period of five years for whatsoever objective they select, notwithstanding the existence of the freedoms and rights protected by the Charter and upheld by the courts. Although it has only been used on an infrequent basis,[109] this provision serves a dialogic function in so far as the initial decision to use section 33 and the obligation to renew the derogation after five years will inevitably generate debate between government ministers, within the legislature, and in other political fora, and has the potential to become an election issue.[110] Thirdly, courts engaged in adjudication under the Charter have chosen to exercise their remedial discretion in such a way as to permit governments scope to respond to the judgment and to choose from a range of constitutional options before the remedy takes effect. Here, the most significant instrument is the delayed declaration of invalidity,[111] whereby the court suspends imposition of its final remedy for a period (usually, of between six to eighteen months) to allow time for the formulation of a legislative response which may serve to pre-empt the declaration of invalidity.

The connection between dialogue theory and adjudication as catalyst for deliberation is a relatively straightforward one. Both approaches

---

[107] See Clayton, 'Judicial Deference' [2004] *Public Law*, 33 at 41–2.
[108] Roach, 'Dialogic Judicial Review' at 57.
[109] See Clayton, 'Judicial Deference' [2004] *Public Law*, 33 at 43.
[110] See Roach, 'Dialogic Judicial Review' at 60.
[111] See e.g. *Reference re Manitoba Language Rights* [1985] 1 SCR 721.

centre upon the capacity of court judgments to stimulate a process of broader argumentation and discussion upon the matters which form the subject of the court hearing, and in that sense, to make a contribution to democratic society, notwithstanding the unelected nature of the judiciary. The relationship is readily apparent from the work of Roach, one of the leading dialogic theorists:

Charter decisions can be seen in a mature democracy as a means to manufacture disagreement and to turn complacent majoritarian monologues into democratic, and, at times, divisive dialogues. As a result of controversial court decisions on issues such as gay marriage, we have more not less democratic debate and disputation in Canada and the debate has a sharper and clearer edge. Regardless of whether one agrees with the outcome of the dialogue between courts and legislatures, the Charter has placed such issues as abortion, gay rights, and the rights of the accused on the legislative agenda, and by doing so has improved democracy ... The courts have provoked a more vigorous and open political debate on the issue [gay marriage] than occurred either when Parliament affirmed the traditional definition of marriage or Alberta used the override to preclude Charter litigation of the issue ... Dialogic judicial review can place justice issues on the legislative agenda and can counter the tendency of legislators to duck divisive issues or defer to the status quo. Judicial activism on issues such as abortion and gay marriage should increase rather than decrease meaningful democratic deliberation.[112]

Although dialogue theory places greatest emphasis upon dialogue between courts and *other branches of government*, it nonetheless envisages that the debate will extend more widely, into civil society as a whole.[113] In this regard, the dialogic approach also serves to highlight the educative dimension of adjudication which was previously identified in Chapter 5. For example, Roach writes that 'I think it is both democratic and educational for citizens to think through the possibility that their government could override the court decisions through the use of the override'.[114] Unsurprisingly, given the connection between the two dimensions of deliberation, it should also be noted that dialogue theory reflects the second of the deliberative functions of the legal process which were outlined in Chapter 5, that of the courtroom as an arena for deliberation upon the instant case. This may be seen from the following passage:

Judges write reasons, sometimes overly long reasons, but reasons nevertheless to explain their vote. The reasons should respond to the arguments and evidence

---

[112] Roach, 'Dialogic Judicial Review' at 75, 89, 103–4.
[113] See *ibid.* at 49: 'the Charter contemplates and invites dialogue between courts, legislatures *and the larger society* about the treatment of rights in a free and democratic society'. Emphasis added.
[114] *Ibid.* at 99.

submitted by the parties who have a guaranteed ability to marshal their case and the ability to define the issues and present evidence and argument in support of their case. Pleaders in court do not have to lobby for some face time with the decision-maker and they do not have to worry about other pleaders making secret submissions or having disproportionate time to influence the decision-maker. The pleader in court has a guaranteed right of participation and a right to a reasoned decision that addresses the arguments made in court, as well as the relevant text of the democratically enacted law. The fair process of adjudication and the requirement for reasons help justify why unelected judges should play an important role in our debates about rights and freedoms.[115]

In view of the significant synergies between the dialogic approach and deliberation achieved through adjudication, it would not be inaccurate to regard dialogue theory as *an attempt to justify rights-based judicial review within the context of a deliberative democracy.*

Nonetheless, the precise impact of dialogue theory on the cases previously discussed in this chapter is unclear. The courts made no specific mention of a dialogic approach in any of these cases other than *Chaoulli* (although it is perfectly plausible that the theory constitutes an unacknowledged influence upon those judgments), and even there, its role is ambiguous. As Roach notes,[116] those judges who found that there had been a violation of the Canadian Charter offered no comment on the possibility of government overriding or limiting rights, as might have been expected if they were seeking to encourage dialogue between judiciary and legislature. The Court's decision to suspend its judgment for twelve months is certainly consonant with a dialogic approach, but it is difficult to be certain of the precise rationale of this, as the Court offered no explanation of its decision. This leaves the judgment of Deschamps J as the only direct evidence that the Court was motivated by dialogic considerations in this case. Citing with approval the work of Roach, in which he argues that 'unique attributes of courts include their commitment to allowing structured and guaranteed participation from aggrieved parties; their independence from the executive, and their commitment to giving reasons for their decisions ... Judges can add value to societal debates about justice by listening to claims of injustice and by promoting values and perspectives that may not otherwise be taken seriously in the legislative process',[117] the judge argues that:

The courts are an appropriate forum for a serious and complete debate... The courts have a duty to rise above political debate. They leave it to the legislatures to

---

[115] *Ibid.* at 70.
[116] K. Roach, 'The Courts and Medicare: Too Much or Too Little Judicial Activism?' in Flood, Roach and Sossin (eds.), *Access to Care, Access to Justice* at 198.
[117] Roach, 'Dialogic Judicial Review' at 69, 71.

develop social policy. But when such social policies infringe rights that are protected by the charters, the courts cannot shy away from considering them. The judicial branch plays a role that is not played by the legislative branch. From this perspective, it is through the combined action of legislatures and courts that democratic objectives can be achieved.[118]

As Choudhry has observed, Deschamps J's employment of dialogue theory enables her to adopt the position that 'judicial review should redress the inadequacies of democratic politics'.[119] Her view – expressed in the statement that 'it seems that governments have lost sight of the urgency of taking concrete action. The courts are therefore the last line of defence for citizens'[120] – is that the question of wait times for treatment has been inadequately addressed through the political process (notwithstanding frequent promises by governments to act), and that the courts must therefore step in to fill the breach. Dialogue theory can justify such a stance because one of its primary functions is to act 'as a means of placing important and uncomfortable issues on the legislative agenda'.[121]

Notwithstanding the uncertainty as to the extent of its influence in this instance, critics of the dialogic approach have been quick to point to *Chaoulli* as an illustration of the perceived deficiencies of the theory. Notable amongst these is Petter, who argues that the case demonstrates an unacceptable degree of judicial activism, captured in his claim that the Court relied 'on the Canadian and Québec Charters to pull down a key pillar of Medicare – a program that lies at the heart of Canada's commitment to social justice'.[122] He believes that, in large part, this may be explained by the contribution made by dialogue theory, which he considers to 'provide no normative vision to guide or constrain the Charter enterprise':[123]

the theory has provided judges with a new academically accredited justification for their decisions. And the beauty of the theory from a judicial point of view is that it can be used to justify virtually any decision that the courts choose to make ... Another significant impact of dialogue theory on Charter decision-making results from the reassurance it provides to judges that their judgments are transitory, and that legislatures can remedy or reverse any problems that arise from their Charter decisions ... [this] has encouraged judges to see their Charter role as being advocates rather than arbiters, and their judgments as being missives directed at governments rather than verdicts directed at society. By bolstering the Charter's

[118] [2005] 1 SCR 791 at paras. 89–90.
[119] Choudry, 'Worse than *Lochner*?' in Flood, Roach and Sossin (eds.), *Access to Care, Access to Justice* at 95.
[120] [2005] 1 SCR 791 at para. 96.   [121] Roach, 'Dialogic Judicial Review' at 54.
[122] Petter, 'Wealthcare' in Flood, Roach and Sossin (eds.), *Access to Care, Access to Justice* at 129.
[123] *Ibid.*

ostensible legitimacy, increasing public support for Charter decision-making and encouraging judges to perceive their Charter role as advocates rather than arbiters, dialogue theory has emboldened judges, including those who are prepared to give full expression to the Charter's underlying ideology and regressive tendencies, to be more activist in their Charter decisions.[124]

It is significant that even leading proponents of dialogue theory find *Chaoulli* to be problematic. For example, Roach claims that 'legislative and administrative activism can respond to and head off judicial activism. Consistent with the dialogue model, the fate of Medicare ultimately remains with elected governments and with Canadians'.[125] Nevertheless, he is concerned that, by its apparent bias towards those who are sufficiently wealthy to contract out of the publicly funded health system, the Court has failed to pay sufficient heed to the unique contribution which the judiciary can make in protecting minorities which are vulnerable to discrimination *via* the legislative and administrative processes of government. This is seen as regrettable since, in so doing, the Supreme Court has disregarded one of the key roles which may be played by courts, a role which may serve (contrary to Petter) to provide normative guidance in Charter adjudication. This might have justified judicial input in the dialogue about rights and freedoms as amounting to more than the mere unconstrained exercise of discretion in accordance with predetermined judicial preferences.[126]

A further difficulty with *Chaoulli* from a deliberative/dialogic perspective (not identified by Roach) is that there is a danger that the deficiencies outlined in the previous section – notably, the incomplete and partial treatment of evidence by the Supreme Court – which serve to render the courtroom an unsatisfactory venue for deliberation upon the instant case, may 'spill over' into the wider deliberations of political institutions, the media and public which have been generated by the case. That is, the process of deliberation which the case stimulated may not have been properly informed, given the Court's inadequate explanations of its preference for certain forms of evidence over others. That said, further discussion of the issues outside of the courtroom may have served to remedy the inadequacies in the Court's reading of the evidence and thus to fill any 'information gap'. This would appear to be an accurate characterisation of a number of the academic analyses of the judgment,[127] which have fed into the wider governmental and societal debate triggered by the case.

---

[124] *Ibid.* at 129–30.
[125] Roach, 'The Courts and Medicare' in Flood, Roach and Sossin (eds.), *Access to Care, Access to Justice* at 200.
[126] *Ibid.* at 190.   [127] See, in particular, the works cited above nn. 67–69.

Conclusion

The discomfiture which has been generated by *Chaoulli* suggests that, while rights adjudication on the Canadian model offers vastly greater scope for the development of a deliberative judicial approach to issues relating to the funding of healthcare than does the case law from England, particularly in the light of dialogue theory, there continue to be significant concerns about judicial involvement in questions of this type. Notably, where the question is one of the allocation of scarce healthcare resources in favour of a particular treatment or service, the fear may be that the inherent pliability associated with a dialogic approach will encourage judges to substitute their own views as to how money should be spent for that of the original decision-maker, *rather than* restricting their role to enforcing observance on the part of the decision-maker of procedural conditions which may provide the basis for broader deliberation upon such matters within the other branches of government and wider civil society. There is, therefore, a very narrow margin between a valuable – and constitutionally proper – deliberative judicial function, and improper judicial activism in this field. The task of the next chapter will be to explore whether the balance between the two has been struck more satisfactorily in the final jurisdiction to be surveyed in this book, South Africa.

An exploration of the manner in which the courts in South Africa have dealt with cases involving the allocation of scarce healthcare resources offers an instructive contrast to the two jurisdictions previously considered. The South African constitution protects certain social and economic rights, in addition to those civil and political rights which find expression in human rights instruments in the UK and Canada. One of the rights protected is the right of access to healthcare services, under section 27 of the Republic's Constitution, which provides that:

1. Everyone has the right to have access to
   a. healthcare services, including reproductive healthcare;
   b. sufficient food and water; and
   c. social security, including, if they are unable to support themselves and their dependants, appropriate social assistance.
2. The state must take reasonable legislative and other measures, within its available resources, to achieve the progressive realisation of these rights.
3. No one may be refused emergency medical treatment.

On the face of it, this provision straightforwardly endows South African courts which are charged with interpretation of the Constitution with competence to adjudicate upon cases which turn upon decisions to allocate scarce healthcare resources, at least in so far as such decisions serve to restrict access to services and treatments. In this regard, the South African judiciary can more confidently assert its legitimacy to address such matters than can its counterparts either in England – where such issues are largely treated as exercises of administrative action rather than as potential violations of constitutionally-protected rights – or in Canada, where the courts have succeeded in defining such issues as questions of rights only *indirectly*, largely through section 15 (with some assistance from section 7). For this reason, one might expect courts in South Africa to be less inhibited in identifying and asserting a judicial role in respect of the rationing of scarce healthcare resources.

Even if such a role were assumed it might, of course, reflect the essentially negative Diceyan paradigm of the control and restraint of state action, in the interests of upholding the autonomy of the individual. However, the nature of the South African Constitution and the framework of protection for the rights therein suggest that the courts are likely to assume a more sympathetic and facilitative stance towards government decision-making on the allocation of scarce resources, on the basis of which their function is to work alongside the other branches of government, assisting them in discharging their tasks. This can be deduced in part from the fact that the socio-economic rights which are enshrined in the Constitution are to be realised progressively within the state's available resources, but also from the 'transformative' character of the Constitution. By this is meant that the function of the Constitution (as expressed in particular in its preamble and in section 1)[1] is not only to act as a constraint upon state power, but also to facilitate the use of that power to advance ideals of freedom, equality, dignity and social justice, with a view to 'transforming a country's political and social institutions and power relationships in a democratic, participatory and egalitarian direction. Transformative constitutionalism connotes an enterprise of inducing large-scale social change through non-violent political processes grounded in law'.[2] To this end, socio-economic rights should be interpreted (both by the courts and by other organs of state) in such a way as to secure substantive as well as formal equality. This places a *positive obligation* upon the state to realise access to services within available resources and to take restitutionary or remedial steps to eliminate socio-economic and historical inequalities and disadvantages.[3]

---

[1] Note in particular the following:

> [Preamble] ... We therefore, through our freely elected representatives, adopt this Constitution as the supreme law of the Republic so as to
> Heal the divisions of the past and establish a society based on democratic values, social justice and fundamental human rights;
> Lay the foundations for a democratic and open society in which government is based on the will of the people and every citizen is equally protected by law ...'
> (Section 1) 'The Republic of South Africa is one, sovereign, democratic state founded on the following values:
> a. Human dignity, the achievement of equality and the advancement of human rights and freedoms ...

[2] K. Klare, 'Legal Culture and Transformative Constitutionalism' (1998) 14 *South African Journal on Human Rights*, 146 at 150.

[3] However, Ngwena argues that, while formal equality in access to healthcare services has been realised, substantive equality is much more problematic to achieve given entrenched structural inequalities and high levels of poverty and disease. See C. Ngwena, 'Substantive Equality in South African Health Care: the Limits of Law' (2000) 4 *Medical Law International*, 111.

It should be noted that, prior to the entry into force of the Constitution in 1996, there was lively debate about the appropriateness of an approach of this type to the socio-economic rights contained therein. As Pieterse notes, 'opponents of the justiciable entrenchment of social rights in the Constitution argued that the relative indeterminacy of these rights, their "positive" nature, and their budgetary and policy implications rendered them unfit for judicial deliberation and that their inevitable idealism would place at risk the democratic legitimacy of the Constitution as a whole'.[4] In the *First Certification* case,[5] the Constitutional Court of South Africa was called upon to consider the justiciability of socio-economic rights and their inclusion in the final text of the Constitution. The Court rejected the argument that concerns as to constitutional and institutional competence operated as an impediment to justiciability, observing that difficulties in respect of the separation of powers and implications for the management of expenditure arose in respect of adjudication upon *all* rights, not merely those of a socio-economic nature:

It is true that the inclusion of socio-economic rights may result in courts making orders which have direct implications for budgetary matters. However, even where a court enforces civil and political rights such as equality, freedom of speech and the right to a fair trial, the order it makes will often have such implications ... In our view, it cannot be said that by including socio-economic rights within a bill of rights, a task is conferred upon the courts so different from that ordinarily conferred on them by a bill of rights that it results in a breach of the separation of powers ... We are of the view that these rights are, at least to some extent, justiciable ... The fact that socio-economic rights will almost inevitably give rise to such [budgetary] implications does not seem to us to be a bar to their justiciability.[6]

Having thus set aside arguments against legal enforceability of rights such as those contained in section 27, and with principles of transformative constitutionalism providing legitimation for active judicial participation in a democratic project of bringing about fundamental social change, the South African judiciary appeared well-equipped to undertake the type of deliberative function in respect of allocative decision-making in health-care which has been outlined in this book. Does the case law reveal that the courts have, in fact, proved willing to undertake such a role?

---

[4] M. Pieterse, 'Possibilities and Pitfalls in the Domestic Enforcement of Social Rights: Contemplating the South African Experience' (2004) 26 *Human Rights Quarterly*, 882 at 885.

[5] *Ex parte Chairperson of the Constitutional Assembly: In re Certification of the Constitution of the Republic of South Africa* 1996 (4) SA 744.

[6] *Ibid.* at paras. 77–8.

Soobramoney: judicial restraint?

The first case involving socio-economic rights to be decided by the Constitutional Court was *Soobramoney* v. *Minister of Health, KwaZulu-Natal*.[7] Here, a patient with chronic renal failure (an irreversible condition in which regular renal dialysis is necessary just to keep a person alive) who had exhausted the finances which he had available for private treatment, sought a court order requiring a hospital to provide him with access to state-funded dialysis treatment. He had been refused treatment on the basis of a policy which had been adopted because of a mismatch between the demand for such treatment and the available supply of dialysis machines and attendant nursing care. Under the policy, those patients who were most likely to benefit from treatment were accorded priority. In practice, those suffering from chronic failure would only satisfy the eligibility criteria if they were candidates for a kidney transplant. The patient in this instance was not, since he also suffered from diabetes, peripheral vascular disease and ischaemic heart disease, and had previously suffered a stroke.

The appellant did not base his claim upon the right to have access to healthcare services under section 27(1). Rather, the case was argued as an alleged violation of the right to life (under section 11 of the Constitution) and the right not to be refused emergency medical treatment under section 27(3). The Court rejected the claim that section 27(3) had to be construed consistently with section 11, and stated that the specific provisions dealing with access to healthcare in section 27 should be relied upon. It noted that accepting the appellant's contention would make it more difficult for the state to discharge its obligations to provide access to healthcare to everyone and would have the consequence of prioritising care for terminal diseases over other forms of medical treatment, reducing the resources available for the latter.[8] Chaskalson P held that there had been no violation of section 27(3), since the type of treatment envisaged in that provision was that required by 'a person who suffers a sudden catastrophe which calls for immediate medical attention ... an emergency which calls for immediate remedial treatment',[9] rather than an ongoing medical condition.

Instead, the Court indicated that the case should be determined in accordance with sections 27(1) and 27(2). However, it concluded that no breach of those provisions could be made out. Considering the scope of the state's positive obligation to take measures *within its available resources* to achieve the progressive realisation of the right to access healthcare services, the judge noted the utilitarian calculus upon which the hospital's

---

[7] 1998 (1) SA 765 (*'Soobramoney'*).   [8] *Ibid.* at para. 19.   [9] *Ibid.* at paras. 20, 21.

policy had been based and observed that it had not been suggested that the guidelines which it had adopted were 'unreasonable or that they were not applied fairly and rationally' in reaching a decision on the appellant's request for treatment.[10] The Court also emphasised the polycentric implications of upholding the appellant's claim, expressing concern that imposition of a positive obligation would result in the state having to meet a series of demands which would place unmanageable pressure upon its available resources:

The appellant's case must be seen in the context of the needs which the health services have to meet, for if treatment has to be provided to the appellant it would also have to be provided to all other persons similarly placed. Although the renal clinic could be kept open for longer hours, it would involve additional expense in having to pay the clinic personnel at overtime rates, or in having to employ additional personnel working on a shift basis. It would also put great strain on the existing dialysis machines which are already showing signs of wear. It is estimated that the cost to the state of treating one chronically ill patient by means of renal dialysis provided twice a week at a state hospital is approximately R60,000 per annum. If all the persons in South Africa who suffer from chronic renal failure were to be provided with dialysis treatment – and many of them, as the appellant does, would require treatment three times a week – the cost of doing so would make substantial inroads into the health budget. And if this principle were to be applied to all patients claiming access to expensive medical treatment or expensive drugs, the health budget would have to be dramatically increased to the prejudice of other needs which the state has to meet.[11]

In light of these anxieties, the Court counselled that adjudication upon issues relating to the allocation of scarce healthcare resources necessitated considerable judicial caution, especially in view of concerns as to competence, both of the constitutional and institutional variants:

The provincial administration which is responsible for health services in KwaZulu-Natal has to make decisions about the funding that should be made available for healthcare and how funds should be spent. These choices involve difficult decisions to be taken at the political level in fixing the health budget, and at the functional level in deciding upon the priorities to be met. A court will be slow to interfere with rational decisions taken in good faith by the political organs and medical authorities whose responsibility it is to deal with such matters.[12]

The decision in *Soobramoney* has been strongly criticised on a number of grounds. For example, Ngwena and Cook argue that the case 'did not really lay down any guidelines that could be followed when interpreting socio-economic rights so as to illuminate and indigenise jurisprudence on

---

[10] *Ibid.* at para. 25.   [11] *Ibid.* at para. 28 (Chaskalson P).
[12] *Ibid.* at para. 29 (Chaskalson P).

socio-economic rights, and also to guide lower courts with jurisdiction to determine constitutional matters', identifying in particular the Constitutional Court's failure to engage with the interpretation of the right of access to healthcare under international human rights instruments.[13] However, from the perspective of this book, the key issue is the extent to which the approach taken by the Court facilitated deliberation upon questions of healthcare rationing. In this respect, the judgment does indeed appear to be disappointing. A number of commentators have emphasised that the restraint shown by the Constitutional Court in this case towards review of executive decision-making (at various levels) on allocation of scarce healthcare resources functioned, in effect, to denude the right contained in section 27 of judicial protection.[14] As a corollary of this, the policy on access to treatment and services which had been established by the hospital, which resulted in the patient being denied treatment, was not subject to rigorous scrutiny by the Court. Nor were those who were responsible for decision-making on the allocation of resources placed under a significant obligation to justify, and to provide evidential support for, the priorities which had been established. Thus, Ngwena and Cook conclude that 'there is no promise in the judgment that the Court would be keen to inquire into whether the state and the province were in fact according due priority to the realisation of the right sought, by making available resources which *ought* to be available and utilising such resources effectively. It seems enough for the healthcare provider to "toll the bell of tight resources"'.[15] If this argument is accepted, one might reasonably draw the conclusion that, notwithstanding the constitutional protection afforded to the right of access to healthcare services in South Africa and the transformative nature of the Republic's Constitution, there is *less* scope for development of a judicial space for deliberation on questions of healthcare rationing in this jurisdiction than exists in Canada. It should be noted, however, that the case was decided

---

[13] C. Ngwena and R. Cook, 'Rights Concerning Health' in D. Brand and C. Heyns (eds.), *Socio-Economic Rights in South Africa* (Pretoria: Pretoria University Press, 2005) at 137–8.

[14] See M. Pieterse, 'Coming to Terms with Judicial Enforcement of Socio-Economic Rights' (2004) *South Africa Journal of Human Rights*, 383 at 402, discussing 'fears that the extent of deference suggested by this dictum would strip socio-economic rights of all relevance', and Pieterse, 'Possibilities and Pitfalls' (2004) 26 *Human Rights Quarterly*, 882 at 892, describing the degree of deference shown by the Court as 'exorbitant'. D. Moellendorf, 'Reasoning about Resources: *Soobramoney* and the Future of Socio-Economic Rights Claims' (1998) 14 *South African Journal on Human Rights*, 327 argues that the deference demonstrated by the Court has the effect of making socio-economic rights wholly contingent upon budgetary policies which are adopted by the executive, rendering them 'mere priorities': at 332.

[15] Ngwena and Cook, 'Rights Concerning Health' in Brand and Heyns (eds.), *Socio-Economic Rights in South Africa* at 137. Emphasis in original.

barely a year after the new Constitution had entered into effect, and some degree of unease with the judicial role in respect of socio-economic rights,[16] coupled with acknowledgement that they were to be realised progressively,[17] may explain the stance adopted by the Court.

However, a somewhat more positive reading of *Soobramoney* has been offered by Scott and Alston, who argue that the case does show that the Constitutional Court was willing to subject executive decision-making on allocation of resources to some degree of scrutiny. These authors point out that the Court specifies that it will be slow to interfere when the impugned allocative decisions are 'rational' and 'taken in good faith',[18] and that it sets out a general basis for review when stating that 'it has not been suggested that these guidelines are *unreasonable* or that they were not applied *fairly and rationally*'.[19] While it is not clear precisely what standard of reasonableness was being applied by the Court in this case, Scott and Alston contend that it can best be understood by reference to the limitation clause contained in Section 36 of the Constitution, which provides that:

The rights in the Bill of Rights may be limited only in terms of law of general application to the extent that the limitation is reasonable and justifiable in an open and democratic society based on human dignity, equality and freedom, taking into account all relevant factors, including:
a. the nature of the right;
b. the importance of the purpose of the limitation;
c. the nature and extent of the limitation;
d. the relation between the limitation and its purpose; and
e. less restrictive means to achieve the purpose.

As should be apparent, this provision requires a court to engage in analysis akin to that required under section 1 of the Canadian Charter and, accordingly, if review is conducted on the basis of this section, prospects for deliberation which are comparable to those outlined in the previous chapter open up. Similarly, the authors argue that 'the Court's invocation of "good faith" must be taken seriously as having meaning with a normative bite': specifically, that it relates to 'an inquiry into whether the legislative and executive purposes are consistent with good

---

[16] See Pieterse, 'Coming to Terms with Judicial Enforcement' at 401.
[17] See C. Scott and P. Alston, 'Adjudicating Constitutional Priorities in a Transnational Context: a Comment on *Soobramoney*'s Legacy and *Grootboom*'s Promise' (2000) 16 *South African Journal on Human Rights*, 206 at 243.
[18] See above n. 12 and accompanying text.
[19] See above n. 10 and accompanying text. My emphasis.

faith in the sense of being compatible with a full and sincere *commitment* to realising the constitutional rights in question'.[20]

Understood in this manner – and notwithstanding its explicit invocation of Sir Thomas Bingham MR's well-known dictum on 'difficult and agonising judgments'[21] – the Constitutional Court in *Soobramoney was* seeking more than a mere 'tolling of the bell of tight resources'.[22] Albeit extremely tentatively, it may be viewed as establishing a framework within which scrutiny could be exercised on the basis of the justifications and evidential support proffered by the decision-maker, thereby clearing the path for the creation of a deliberative space within the courtroom, and a potential judicial role as a catalyst for broader public and political deliberation. This reading of the case is also more closely compatible with the earlier decision of the High Court in *B* v. *Minister of Correctional Services*.[23] Although Ngwena regards this decision as 'limited to its facts'[24] and 'of limited value as a precedent' (especially given the failure to refer to any jurisprudence on socio-economic rights or to international law),[25] the Court nonetheless upheld a right to receive 'adequate medical treatment' under section 35(2)(e) of the Constitution for four prisoners who were HIV-positive,[26] on the basis that the Department of Correctional Services had pleaded lack of resources but had failed to submit convincing supporting evidence that the state could not afford to provide the treatment in question.

The *Treatment Action Campaign* case: reasonableness review

Whether *Soobramoney* is viewed positively as laying down (albeit relatively abstract) criteria for judicial scrutiny of priority-setting decisions, or as an instance of excessive deference to the judgment of those charged with

---

[20] Scott and Alston, 'Adjudicating Constitutional Priorities' at 242. Emphasis in original.

[21] In the 'Child B' case: see above Chapter 6, n. 39 and accompanying text, cited in *Soobramoney*, 1998 (1) SA 765 at para. 30. Note also that Sachs J argues that the judgment of Chaskalson P 'does not merely "toll the bell of lack of resources"', on the basis that rationing is integral to a human rights based approach to healthcare: (1998) (1) SA 765 at para. 52 (and see Chapter 9 for further discussion).

[22] *Cf.* Scott and Alston, 'Adjudicating Constitutional Priorities' at 244: 'To read Bingham MR's final sentence – 'That is not a judgment which the court can make' – as relevant in any strong sense to South African constitutional law on priorities in provision of healthcare would be to treat s. 27 of the 1996 Constitution as if it were not there'.

[23] [1997] 6 BCLR 789.   [24] Ngwena, 'Substantive Equality' at 119.

[25] C. Ngwena, 'Access to Antiretroviral to Prevent Mother-to-Child Transmission of HIV as a Socio-Economic Right: an Application of Section 27 of the Constitution' (2003) *SA Publiekreg/Public Law*, 83 at 91.

[26] Section 35 details the rights of arrested, detained and accused persons.

responsibility for the allocation of scarce healthcare resources, it is clear that considerable scope remained for the further development of a deliberative approach to questions of access to healthcare services and treatments, should the courts choose to move in such a direction. In 2002, the Constitutional Court was presented with an opportunity to reconsider its stance in relation to such matters, in *Minister of Health* v. *Treatment Action Campaign (No. 2)*.[27]

In order to comprehend the decision of the Court in *TAC*, it is first necessary briefly to examine the earlier judgment of the same court in *Government of the Republic of South Africa* v. *Grootboom*,[28] in which it was held that a violation of section 26(2) of the Constitution – which imposes an obligation upon the state to achieve the progressive realisation of the right to have access to adequate housing in similar terms to those of section 27(2) – had occurred. Here, the Court moved well beyond the rationality and good faith standards established in *Soobramoney* and applied a more rigorous test of 'reasonableness'. The Court indicated that it would inquire as to the extent to which the measures which the state had devised and implemented to give effect to socio-economic rights were comprehensive and co-ordinated, whether appropriate financial and human resources were made available, and whether the measures were reasonably conceived and implemented, flexible and inclusive (in that they must not exclude a significant segment of society and must respond to the extreme levels of deprivation of people in desperate situations).[29] It should be readily apparent that this represents a much more intensive standard of judicial scrutiny of executive policies and decisions than that employed in *Soobramoney*.

The approach taken in *Grootboom* was followed, and further developed, by the Constitutional Court in *TAC*. In this case, a pressure group for improved access to treatment for HIV/AIDS challenged the South African government's decision to restrict its programme for the prevention of mother-to-child transmission of HIV by means of dispensation of the drug Nevirapine to eighteen pilot (training and research) sites for a period of two years. Although a full treatment for one mother and baby was estimated to cost a mere R10, national government officials argued that the overall cost would be too high.[30] Two further rationales were advanced by government for the restrictions which had been imposed

---

[27] (2002) (5) SA 721 ('*TAC*').   [28] (2001) (1) SA 46 ('*Grootboom*').

[29] *Ibid.* at paras. 39–44. For detailed analysis of the case and its implications, see P. de Vos, '*Grootboom*, the Right of Access to Housing and Substantive Equality as Fairness' (2001) 17 *South African Journal on Human Rights*, 259.

[30] See N. Nattrass, *The Moral Economy of AIDS in South Africa* (Cambridge: Cambridge University Press, 2004) at 47.

upon access. First, concerns as to the drug's safety persuaded the government that further study and monitoring of the treatment was necessary before the programme was extended nationwide. Secondly, government wished to use the pilot sites as a basis for assessing the social, public health and economic implications of providing a comprehensive nationwide programme which would comprise not only the provision of Nevirapine, but also of voluntary HIV testing and counselling services, formula milk where substituted for breastfeeding, antibiotics, vitamin supplements and follow-up services. However, no indication was offered as to when the programme would be extended beyond the pilot sites, and, during this phase of the programme, medical practitioners working outside the pilot facilities were prohibited from prescribing Nevirapine.

The Court found that the government was in breach of sections 27(1) and (2) of the Constitution. The measures taken were not reasonable, and the government had failed to devise and implement a comprehensive and co-ordinated programme for progressive realisation of the right to access healthcare services. This was so in so far as the policy operated inflexibly to deny to mothers and newborn children outside of the pilot sites the opportunity of receiving a single dose of a life-saving drug at the time of birth when it was medically indicated, which could have been administered without harm within the available resources of the state where adequate facilities existed for testing and counselling. Furthermore, the policy had failed to make provision, in hospitals and clinics outside the pilot sites, for training in counselling on the use of nevirapine as a means of reducing the risk of mother-to-child transmission of HIV. The Court accordingly ordered government without delay to remove the restrictions preventing access to nevirapine in public hospitals and clinics outside the pilot sites, to permit and facilitate the use of Nevirapine in public health facilities, to make provision for the training of counsellors in such facilities in the use of Nevirapine, and to take reasonable measures to extend testing and counselling facilities at hospitals and clinics throughout the public sector. Although the order was therefore mandatory in effect, the Court indicated that the government would be permitted to adapt its policy in a manner consistent with the Constitution if equally appropriate or better measures for the prevention of mother-to-child transmission of HIV became available.

The decision in *TAC* is notable for its explicit rejection of the attempt made by the South African Government to 're-litigate the principle of the non-justiciability of socio-economic rights ... in the remedy stage of the case rather than in rights interpretation'.[31] The government had

---

[31] J. Klaaren, 'A Remedial Interpretation of the *Treatment Action Campaign* decision' (2003) 19 *South African Journal on Human Rights*, 455 at 461.

contended that, under the doctrine of the separation of powers, policy-making was the responsibility of the executive branch rather than of the judiciary and that the courts could not make remedial orders 'that have the effect of requiring the executive to pursue a particular policy'.[32] On this analysis, in the event of a finding of unconstitutionality, the only remedy available to a court would have been to issue an order declaring rights, which would leave 'the government free to pay heed to the declaration made and to adapt its policies in so far as this may be necessary to bring them into conformity with the court's judgment'.[33] However, while acknowledging that there were certain matters which primarily fell within the purview of one of the arms of government as opposed to the others, the Court indicated that this did not mean that it could not and should not make remedial orders which might have an impact on policy. It went on to clarify the nature of its constitutional role in this regard:

Where state policy is challenged as inconsistent with the Constitution, courts have to consider whether in formulating and implementing such policy the state has given effect to its constitutional obligations. If it should hold in any given case that the state has failed to do so, it is obliged by the Constitution to say so. In so far as this constitutes an intrusion into the domain of the executive, that is an intrusion mandated by the Constitution itself. There is also no merit in the argument advanced on behalf of the government that a distinction should be drawn between declaratory and mandatory orders against government. Even simple declaratory orders against government or organs of state can affect their policy and may well have budgetary implications. Government is constitutionally bound to give effect to such orders whether or not they affect its policy and has to find the resources to do so ... South African courts have a wide range of powers at their disposal to ensure that the Constitution is upheld ... How they should exercise these powers depends on the circumstances of each particular case. Here due regard must be paid to the roles of the legislature and the executive in a democracy. What must be made clear, however, is that when it is appropriate to do so, courts may – and if need be must – use their wide powers to make orders that affect policy as well as legislation.[34]

This passage signals an unambiguous rejection of the diffident stance towards adjudication on questions of socio-economic rights adopted by the Court in *Soobramoney*. Indeed, Pieterse argues that it represents 'the pivotal moment where the Constitutional Court assumes the power to "decide who decides" on institutional competence and constitutional compliance'.[35] *TAC* confirms that the South African judiciary operates under a *constitutional obligation* to adjudicate upon the lawfulness of legislation and policy within the socio-economic field, including

---

[32] (2002) (5) SA 721 at para. 97.   [33] *Ibid.* at para. 96.   [34] *Ibid.* at paras. 99, 113.
[35] Pieterse, 'Coming to Terms with Judicial Enforcement' at 404.

questions relating to the distribution of healthcare resources. It is, in consequence, clearly endowed with a significantly greater degree of constitutional competence to become involved in issues of the rationing of healthcare than is the case in Canada, and certainly in England.

Yet, it is important to note that, while the Court maintains that 'there are no bright lines that separate the roles of the legislature, the executive and the courts from one another', it remains anxious to avoid undue encroachment upon the other branches of government, in accordance with the principle of the separation of powers. To this end, it observes that 'all arms of government should be sensitive to and respect this separation'.[36] Furthermore, concerns as to institutional competence continue to be apposite in this context. The Court acknowledges that:

in dealing with such [socio-economic] matters the courts are not institutionally equipped to make the wide-ranging factual and political enquiries for determining what the minimum-core standards called for by the first and second amici should be, nor for deciding how public revenues should most effectively be spent. There are many pressing demands on the public purse ... Courts are ill-suited to adjudicate upon issues where court orders could have multiple social and economic consequences for the community.[37]

In view of the potency of these reasons for continued judicial caution, the conclusion which the Court reaches is that 'the Constitution contemplates rather a restrained and focused role for the courts' on socio-economic matters.[38] In so doing, it indicates that the debate has moved beyond the question of whether rights of this type are justiciable at all, to address the 'manner in which the judiciary should exercise their [sic] powers to vindicate social rights while simultaneously remaining sensitive to the realities of the modern executive state and the peculiar strengths and weaknesses of all branches of government'.[39]

The constitutional role identified by the Court is 'to require the state to take measures to meet its constitutional obligations and to subject the reasonableness of those measures to evaluation'.[40] Hence, as in *Grootboom*, 'reasonableness' operates in *TAC* as the standard by which the Court measures compliance by the state with the socio-economic obligations imposed by the Constitution. As noted above, the Court considered that the measures taken by the state to achieve progressive realisation of the right afforded by section 27 of the Constitution were not reasonable. This was because the justification advanced by government for the restricted availability of nevirapine had failed to distinguish

[36] (2002) (5) SA 721 at para. 98.   [37] *Ibid.* at paras. 37–8.   [38] *Ibid.* at para. 38.
[39] Pieterse, 'Coming to Terms with Judicial Enforcement' at 405.
[40] (2002) (5) SA 721 at para. 38.

between its objective of evaluation of the treatment programme and the need to provide access to necessary healthcare services to those who did not have access to the pilot facilities,[41] and also because the policy was insufficiently flexible.[42] The Court also expanded upon the meaning which had been assigned to 'reasonableness' in *Grootboom* by requiring that the contents of a programme conceived and implemented by the state should be properly communicated to those affected by it.[43]

The 'reasonableness' standard which is developed by the Constitutional Court in *Grootboom* and *TAC* has been described as 'relatively abstract and open-ended', although it 'seems essentially to involve an inquiry into the coherence, even-handedness, flexibility, inclusiveness and feasibility of the policy'.[44] Roux has argued that it involves more than an assessment of whether there is any rational basis for a policy (approximating to the *Wednesbury* test in English administrative law), but that it 'stops short . . . of a full-blown proportionality test' (of the type which has been applied by the Canadian courts).[45] Two elements of the inquiry are of particular significance in respect of the 'restrained and focused' role which the South African courts have mapped out for themselves vis-à-vis other branches of government. First, 'reasonableness' does not entail judicial specification to government of the *temporal order* in which competing needs should be met through the policy. Instead, the executive remains free to respond simultaneously to a number of differing needs, rather than necessarily according priority to the needs of the most vulnerable. Secondly, scrutiny of the reasonableness of a policy or programme devised by the state does not necessitate prescription by the courts of the *amount of resources* which need to be allocated to cure the constitutional defect. Again, this means that priority does not have to be accorded to the needs of the most vulnerable before those of others, while it also does not require the state to allocate additional resources to the programme in question. As the Court in *TAC* remarked, 'determinations of reasonableness may in fact have budgetary implications, but are not in themselves directed at rearranging budgets'.[46]

Responses to the Court's deployment of 'reasonableness' as the primary mechanism through which evaluation of compliance with socio-economic obligations is to take place have been mixed. Some commentators regard the 'reasonableness' inquiry as unacceptably broad and

---

[41] *Ibid.* at para. 67.   [42] *Ibid.* at paras. 78, 80.   [43] *Ibid.* at para. 123.
[44] Pieterse, 'Coming to Terms with Judicial Enforcement' at 410.
[45] T. Roux, 'Legitimating Transformation: Political Resource Allocation in the South African Constitutional Court' (2003) 10 *Democratization*, 92 at 96.
[46] (2002) (5) SA 721 at para. 38.

amorphous. For example, Bilchitz comments that 'at present, reason-ableness seems to stand in for whatever the Court regards as desirable features of state policy'.[47] He considers this to be problematic for two reasons. First, because it fails to set clear boundaries upon the judicial role in respect of socio-economic policies implemented by government: 'a clearer enunciation of the principles upon which such litigation is to take place will offer ... a principled statement of the standards the Court is to use in assessing the state's obligations. This will help provide clear reasons for its involvement in these cases, and a clear statement of the important interests involved which would demarcate the scope of its own decision-making powers'.[48] Secondly, because a more concrete content to 'reasonableness' would enable the state to assess its own conduct on matters engaging socio-economic rights against clear bench-marks.[49] On this analysis, the unfortunate consequences of adopting such a nebulous standard are that it fails to accord protection as a matter of priority to those who are in the most vulnerable position,[50] and, more generally, that the socio-economic rights in question may be lacking in tangible effect given that the standard of review is 'essentially formal and procedural' rather than substantive,[51] and that it amounts merely 'to a general expectation on the state to act reasonably in its attempts to realise these rights'.[52] This leads Pieterse to observe that the socio-economic rights entrenched within the Constitution may amount to little more than directive principles of state policy,[53] and that 'doubts may be expressed as to whether, under the Court's "reasonableness approach", social rights offer South Africans entitlements other than those they have always enjoyed under administrative law, which have largely proved fruitless in alleviating the consequences of social deprivation'.[54]

---

[47] D. Bilchitz, 'Towards a Reasonable Approach to the Minimum Core: Laying the Foundations for Future Socio-Economic Rights Jurisprudence' (2003) 19 *South African Journal on Human Rights*, 1 at 10.

[48] *Ibid.* at 10.

[49] See further Pieterse, 'Coming to Terms with Judicial Enforcement' at 470.

[50] A particular problem which has been identified in this regard is the refusal of the Court in both *Grootboom* and *TAC* to acknowledge that sections 26 and 27 of the Constitution should be interpreted to impose a 'minimum core' obligation upon the state akin to that developed under the UN International Covenant on Economic, Social and Cultural Rights, non-compliance with which may only be justified where the state has made every effort to use all resources that are at its disposal to satisfy, as a matter of priority, those minimum obligations. See Pieterse, 'Possibilities and Pitfalls' at 897–8; Bilchitz, 'Towards a Reasonable Approach'.

[51] Pieterse, 'Possibilities and Pitfalls' at 904.   [52] *Ibid.* at 898.

[53] *Ibid.* at 902. For a comparable argument in the context of *Soobramoney*, see Moellendorf, 'Reasoning about Resources' (1998) 14 *South African Journal on Human Rights*, 327.

[54] Pieterse, 'Possibilities and Pitfalls' at 896.

More positive appraisals of the 'reasonableness' standard have been expressed elsewhere. Indeed, Pieterse himself acknowledges that the 'resort to (familiar) principles of administrative law makes sense, especially when keeping in mind that, in many (if not most) legal systems, the review of administrative policy involves striking an appropriate balance between judicial activism and judicial deference'.[55] From this perspective, the deployment of a standard with which the judiciary should be comfortable sends out a signal that adjudication on socio-economic rights is not atypical, but rather an aspect of the normal review function of the courts. Others regard the flexibility inherent in the 'reasonableness' approach, particularly its avoidance of the imposition of temporal or budgetary priorities upon government, as a realistic and sensitive response to the dangers of excessive judicial intrusion upon allocative decision-making by the executive and legislature. Thus, Roux applauds the *Grootboom* judgment for remaining 'respectful of the political branches' primary budget-setting and policy-making powers',[56] while Sunstein (also commenting on *Grootboom*) argues that 'this approach ensures respect for sensible priority-setting and close attention to particular needs, without displacing democratic judgments about how to set priorities'.[57]

Sunstein's contribution is of particular interest because it is developed in the context of a broader exploration of the possibilities of addressing problems of governance through public deliberation. Sunstein seeks to demonstrate that constitutional rules, interpreted and applied by the judiciary, can function to advance the prospects of public deliberation. He regards *Grootboom* not only as clear indication that effective constitutional protection can be accorded to socio-economic rights but also as illustrative of the deliberative possibilities inherent in rights adjudication:

The virtue of the Court's approach is that it is respectful of democratic prerogatives and of the limited nature of public resources, while also requiring special deliberative attention to those whose minimal needs are not being met. The approach of the Constitutional Court stands as a powerful rejoinder to those who have contended that socio-economic rights do not belong in a constitution. It suggests that such rights can serve not to pre-empt democratic deliberation but to ensure democratic attention to important interests that might otherwise be neglected in ordinary debate.[58]

---

[55] *Ibid.* at 893. See also Pieterse, 'Coming to Terms with Judicial Enforcement' at 409.
[56] Roux, 'Legitimating Transformation' at 98.
[57] C. Sunstein, *Designing Democracy* (New York: Oxford University Press, 2001) at 236.
[58] *Ibid.* at 221–2.

If Sunstein's evaluation is correct, the Constitutional Court is undertaking precisely the facilitative role as creator of deliberative space and catalyst for wider deliberation on issues of the allocation of scarce healthcare resources which was outlined above. It is important, therefore, to seek to identify the precise manner in which the approach adopted by the Court in these cases may be said to be deliberative in character.

'Reasonableness', deliberation and a 'constitutional culture of justification'

The deliberative possibilities of adjudication on socio-economic rights under the South African Constitution, including the right to have access to healthcare services under section 27, can best be understood in the context of Mureinik's thesis that the objective of the Bill of Rights contained in the Constitution was to 'spearhead the effort to bring about a culture of justification'.[59] This culture was to be distinguished from the preceding 'culture of authority', resting on the doctrine of parliamentary sovereignty, which allowed government officials to justify their policies and actions simply by reference to their position within a hierarchical command structure, without the need for explanation either to courts or the governed. Such a culture underpinned the apartheid regime. In its place, the new constitutional order was one in which 'every exercise of power is expected to be justified; in which the leadership given by government rests on the cogency of the case offered in defence of its decisions, not the fear inspired by the force at its command. The new order must be a community built on persuasion, not coercion'.[60] The political branches would accordingly be expected to account for their choices by reference to 'reasons that are viewed as cogent in the light of democratic norms and values'.[61]

Central to Mureinik's analysis is the existence of the general limitation clause discussed above. He observes that this provision makes plain that the rights are not to be regarded as absolute principles, on whose content judges are to have ultimate interpretative authority, and which necessarily

---

[59] E. Mureinik, 'A Bridge to Where? Introducing the Interim Bill of Rights' (1994) 10 *South African Journal on Human Rights*, 31 at 32. Note that the thesis originated in relation to the interim Constitution of 1993, but it has subsequently received endorsement as regards the final constitutional settlement of 1996: see D. Dyzenhaus, 'Law as Justification: Etienne Mureinik's Conception of Legal Culture' (1998) 14 *South African Journal on Human Rights*, 11; J. van der Walt and H. Botha, 'Democracy and Rights in South Africa: Beyond a Constitutional Culture of Justification' (2000) 7 *Constellations*, 341.

[60] Mureinik, *ibid*.

[61] van der Walt and Botha, 'Democracy and Rights' at 342.

trump all contravening provisions.[62] Rather, the presence of the limitation clause indicates that, while courts are obliged to determine whether
there has been a prima facie violation of a constitutionally entrenched
right at the first stage of enquiry, the government will then have an
opportunity to demonstrate that the limitation is justifiable and thus
avoid a finding of unconstitutionality. Consequently, the structure of
the Constitution permits to the political branches involvement in the
determination of the content and parameters of constitutional rights, in
that it is possible to enact legislation limiting the scope of rights, provided
that this can be properly justified, if needs be, to a court. On this analysis,
upholding and protecting rights is a task to be undertaken *by all three
branches of government in concert*. The function of the courts is to interpret
the meaning of the rights contained in the Constitution, and should be
seen as 'assisting other branches of government to establish the precise
content of their obligations rather than as an antagonistic mandate from
the judiciary to the legislature and executive'.[63] For their part, the political branches play the important role of balancing individual rights
against the competing rights of others and the interests of the wider
community. There is, in short, 'a complementary relation between
democracy and rights'.[64]

Approached in this way, adjudication upon questions of rights 'should
therefore not be seen as a means to preclude democratic dialogue, but
rather as a way of *facilitating and structuring an inquiry into the justifiability of
official conduct*'.[65] As noted, for Mureinik the general limitation clause is
highly significant in achieving this goal, just as section 1 of the Canadian
Charter (upon which the South African provision is, in part, modelled) is
central to dialogic theory in that jurisdiction. However, it seems apparent
that the 'reasonableness' standard advanced by the Constitutional Court in
Grootboom and *TAC* has the potential to fulfil a comparable justificatory
function, and it has been argued that the 'reasonableness' inquiry might be
rendered less unstructured if it were to draw upon the criteria set out in that
section.[66] On this reading, therefore, courts operating the test of 'reasonableness' are not simply adjudicating upon alleged violations of socio-
economic rights. Rather, they are obliging government to offer reasoned
explanations of the measures which it has taken to achieve progressive
realisation of those rights – together with appropriate supporting evidence

---

[62] Mureinik, 'A Bridge to Where?' 10 *South African Journal on Human Rights*, 31 at 33.
[63] Pieterse, 'Coming to Terms with Judicial Enforcement' at 406.
[64] van der Walt and Botha, 'Democracy and Rights' at 343.
[65] *Ibid.* at 342. My emphasis.
[66] Scott and Alston, 'Adjudicating Constitutional Priorities' at 240.

where necessary – in order to assess whether the policy or programme can be said to be coherent, flexible, even-handed, inclusive, feasible and properly communicated to those whom it affects. That is, litigation offers a space for the presentation of evidence and reasoned argumentation. It thus establishes the conditions for deliberation.

As in the Canadian context, the deliberative opportunities afforded by adjudication upon constitutionally protected rights are of various interlocking types. Deliberation upon the instant case within the courtroom will in turn prompt a wider process of deliberation within the political branches of government, as the 'reasonableness' standard allows the courts to 'engage the political branches in rational discussion over the fairness of the national ... programme, without, however, setting government's priorities for it'.[67] This will extend more broadly into civil society as a result of media coverage of the judicial decision and of the executive and legislative responses to it. Furthermore, it is possible that government will seek to involve certain key groups and organisations in the programmes which are devised to give effect to progressive realisation of the right in question. The court case thus functions as a stimulus for the establishment of a *democratic partnership* between all three branches of government and certain non-governmental bodies and institutions.

The *TAC* case is instructive in demonstrating how far adjudication may have a catalytic effect upon deliberation on issues of access to medical treatments and services. Here, the Constitutional Court demonstrated a clear awareness of the impact which its judgment would have upon public understanding of the problems generated by HIV/AIDS, and its potential to act as a springboard for the evolution of an integrated national response involving a wide range of organisations, both governmental and non-governmental:

The magnitude of the HIV/AIDS challenge facing the country calls for a concerted, co-ordinated and co-operative national effort in which government in each of its three spheres and the panoply of resources and skills of civil society are marshalled, inspired and led ... It is essential that there be a concerted national effort to combat the HIV/AIDS epidemic. The government has committed itself to such an effort. We have held that its policy fails to meet constitutional standards ... This does not mean that everyone can claim access to such treatment, although the ideal ... is to achieve that goal. Every effort must, however, be made to do so as soon as reasonably possible. The increases in the budget to which we have referred will facilitate this. We consider it important that all sectors of society, in particular

---

[67] Roux, 'Legitimating Transformation' at 107. See further J. Fitzpatrick and R. Slye, '*Republic of South Africa* v. *Grootboom and Minister of Health* v. *Treatment Action Campaign*' (2003) 97 *American Journal of International Law*, 669 at 680, referring to the 'intergovernmental dialogue' generated by the court decisions.

civil society, should co-operate in the steps taken to achieve this goal. In our view that will be facilitated by spelling out the steps necessary to comply with the Constitution'.[68]

Indeed, the capacity of rights adjudication to generate deliberation within the other branches of government had already been manifested *prior* to the Constitutional Court's judgment. Heywood comments that, during the period following the first instance decision of the High Court on 14 December 2001, 'politics and law developed an interesting dialectic'.[69] The Department of Health announced that its policy on mother-to-child transmission would be reviewed and that a national consultation of stake-holders would take place 'to share the lessons of the pilot sites and to chart plans for the future on the basis of broad consensus',[70] although no such consultation in fact occurred. Following further discussions between ministers and officials within the Department, the President of the Republic's State of the Nation address to Parliament in February 2002 appeared to signal a shift in policy, with the programme to be rolled out to facilities where capacity for treatment existed or could be created. This was confirmed by a Cabinet statement of 17 April 2002, which promised that the programme would be universally rolled out by December 2002.

Partly in response to these developments, the remedial order imposed by the Constitutional Court in *TAC* differed from that issued by the court at first instance, where Botha J had instructed government to return to the court by 31 March 2002 to present a report detailing the steps taken to implement an effective comprehensive national programme and the further steps which were planned, together with a timeframe for their achievement.[71] The Constitutional Court declined to issue a supervisory order of this type,[72] although the order made was both prescriptive in effect and relatively specific, which assisted the Treatment Action Campaign in monitoring compliance.[73] This may be regarded as unfortunate from a deliberative perspective, since it may be argued that 'through the exercise of supervisory jurisdiction, a dynamic dialogue between the judiciary and the other branches of government on the intricacies of implementation may be initiated'.[74] A supervisory order

---

[68] (2002) (5) SA 721 at paras. 123, 125–6.
[69] M. Heywood, 'Preventing Mother-to-Child HIV Transmission in South Africa: Background, Strategies and Outcomes of the Treatment Action Campaign Case against the Minister of Health' (2003) 19 *South African Journal on Human Rights*, 278 at 304.
[70] Department of Health, Press Release, 19 December 2001.
[71] *Treatment Action Campaign* v. *Minister of Health* 2001 SACLR Lexis, 123 at 87.
[72] (2002) (5) SA 721 at para. 129.
[73] Pieterse, 'Coming to Terms with Judicial Enforcement' at 415.
[74] *Ibid.* at 414; see also Bilchitz, 'Towards a Reasonable Approach' at 25–6.

would accordingly have been more closely in keeping with the spirit of collaboration between the branches of government for which the Constitutional Court argued in *TAC*. As it was, a perception of dilatoriness in implementation of the judgment (reflected, for example, in the failure of the Department of Health to issue a circular to provincial governments explaining their obligations in light of the case),[75] forced the TAC to initiate subsequent contempt proceedings against the national Minister of Health and one of the provincial governments.[76] Such action appears to be somewhat out of step with the deliberative democratic *partnership* which the Constitutional Court's judgment seems to envisage.

Conclusion

The aftermath of the Constitutional Court case suggests that, even where they operate within a 'culture of justification' and in the spirit of transformative constitutionalism, courts may still on occasion find themselves issuing an 'antagonistic mandate' to other branches of government,[77] which is not properly consonant with facilitation of a joint democratic enterprise underpinned by deliberation.

To some extent, this reflects the deliberative shortcomings of the jurisprudence which was developed by the Constitutional Court of South Africa in *TAC*. As noted, the abstract nature of the 'reasonableness' standard prevented the Court both from articulating as clearly as it might have done the proper scope of its role on questions of this type – with the consequence that a penumbra of uncertainty as to judicial competence persisted – and from engaging the political branches in *comprehensive* discussion on appropriate benchmarks, timeframes, etc., thereby permitting government a considerable degree of freedom of manoeuvre in its attempts to progressively realise the right. This was compounded by the refusal to issue a supervisory order, which would have had the impact of obliging government to enter into a dialogue with the judiciary (and, by extension, with civil society as a whole) as regards the steps needed to give effect to the right to have access to treatment. However, surely more problematic was the reluctance of South African government to collaborate fully in addressing the challenge of HIV/AIDS, given the sceptical

---

[75] See M. Heywood, 'Contempt or Compliance? The *TAC* Case after the Constitutional Court Judgment' (2003) 4 *ESR Review*, 7 at 9.
[76] *Treatment Action Campaign* v. *MEC for Health, Mpumalanga and Minister of Health* TPD 35272/02: see further Heywood, *ibid.* at 10.
[77] See above n. 63 and accompanying text.

stance which the governing African National Congress party had taken both upon the significance of the disease and upon the value of anti-retroviral drugs as a form of treatment.[78] The consequence of this was that the scope of deliberation on the issue of access to this form of treatment which was generated by the Court's judgment within the political branches (especially, the executive) was narrower than might have been the case had there been a genuine political willingness to engage with the difficulties presented by the disease.

Such an evaluation serves as a valuable reminder that, even if courts equip themselves to play a more positive, facilitative role in respect of the allocation of healthcare resources than that which has usually been out-lined for them, there remain significant constraints upon their capabilities. Notably, a court is limited to pronouncing judgment on the matter litigated before it. Although judicial obiter dicta may range beyond the question at issue in the case – and may form the basis of future developments in case law, or of legislative or administrative changes – the decision is only legally binding in respect of the particular 'claim of right' asserted by the affected parties.[79] In *TAC*, this related to the constitutionality of the government's programme for addressing the problem of mother-to-child transmission of HIV. As the Constitutional Court itself noted, this was merely 'an aspect of the HIV/AIDS challenge'.[80] Although the Court took the opportunity to make a number of pronouncements upon the governmental response to HIV/AIDS as a whole, the legally binding element of its judgment was limited to the mother-to-child programme. Consequently, it was open to the government to downplay the Court's calls for the evolution of a 'concerted national effort' to combat the wider problem of the disease. Indeed, the national government's response has continued to be subject to widespread criticism, both within South Africa and on an international

---

[78] See Heywood, 'Preventing Mother-to-Child HIV Transmission' at 281–5, discussing the influence of 'AIDS denial' upon the policy of the South African Government. The author cites an anonymous document written by members of the African National Congress, whose 'main argument is that an unholy combination of scientists, AIDS activists and pharmaceutical companies are engaged in a campaign of "scare-mongering that is condemning millions of our own people to ill-health, disability and death ... [t]o sustain a massive political-commercial campaign to promote anti-retroviral drugs"': at 284–5. For a fuller discussion of state policy towards HIV/AIDS in South Africa, see H. Schneider, 'On the Fault-line: the Politics of AIDS Policy in Contemporary South Africa' (2002) 61 *African Studies*, 145; Nattrass, *The Moral Economy of Aids in South Africa*, especially Chapter 2.

[79] The phrase is that of L. Fuller: 'The Forms and Limits of Adjudication' (1978) 92 *Harvard Law Review*, 353 at 368–9.

[80] (2002) (5) SA 721 at para. 2.

level,[81] with 500,000 people estimated still to be in need of urgent access to anti-retroviral drugs in 2006.[82]

Especially in circumstances where one or more of the political branches are relatively unco-operative, there are therefore limits to the catalytic impact which adjudication may have. Nevertheless, the deliberative possibilities generated by the judgment in *TAC* cannot be underestimated. There can be no doubt that the Constitutional Court's decision was a highly significant moment in the history of state management of the HIV/AIDS pandemic in South Africa. The case brought the issue to the forefront of media and public attention, both domestically and internationally. In this regard, however tentative and grudging the government's response to the judgment may have been, adjudication served to place a significant and uncomfortable issue firmly upon the policy agenda. As was noted above, in respect of the dialogic theory of judicial review,[83] this is one of the fundamental functions which public law adjudication can perform, and it was through this means that *TAC* served to initiate a process of political and social deliberation on HIV/AIDS policy, regarded by Nattrass as being of paramount importance.[84]

This should not be surprising. As observed in the discussion of *Chaoulli* in the preceding chapter, it is inevitable that litigation of this type will generate widespread controversy, fuelling a wider debate within political fora, media and broader civil society. Yet, in the Canadian case, much of that debate focused upon the appropriateness and extent of judicial involvement, rather than upon the questions of healthcare financing which the litigation raised. By contrast, in *TAC*, the Constitutional Court of South Africa was at pains to exhibit sensitivity and respect towards the constitutional responsibilities of the executive and legislature – thus

---

[81] See especially the Treatment Action Campaign's call to convene a national meeting to implement an emergency and long-term AIDS plan, and for the sacking of the Health Minister: 'Call to Action', 20 August 2006, available at www.tac.org.za/nl20060820.html (accessed 8 January 2007); and further the keynote address of the UN special envoy for AIDS in Africa to the XVI International AIDS Conference, 18 August 2006: 'It is the only country in Africa . . . whose government is still obtuse, dilatory and negligent about rolling out treatment. It is the only country in Africa whose government continues to propound theories more worthy of a lunatic fringe than of a concerned and compassionate state. Between six and eight hundred people a day die of AIDS in South Africa. The government has a lot to atone for. I'm of the opinion that they can never achieve redemption' available at www.stephenlewisfoundation.org/news_item.cfm?news=1338 (accessed 8 January 2007). The South African government announced a new HIV/AIDS policy in late 2006 based upon an orthodox medical view of the disease: see 'South Africa Ends Long Denial over AIDS Crisis', *The Guardian*, 1 December 2006.

[82] See 'The Drugs Do Work', *The Guardian*, 5 September 2006.

[83] See above Chapter 7, n. 121 and accompanying text.

[84] Nattrass, *The Moral Economy of AIDS in South Africa* at 180.

addressing the concerns of those who express scepticism at judicial involvement in this field of public policy – while simultaneously giving effect to
a meaningful obligation of justification which (notwithstanding certain
limitations) both rendered the courtroom a deliberative space upon the
matter in hand and served to engender further deliberation within the
political branches and wider civil society. In so doing, it commendably
sought to steer a middle course between the largely deferential and non-
interventionist stance adopted by the English judiciary, which admits of
little deliberation on questions of the distribution of healthcare resources,
and the activist approach evident in *Chaoulli*, which was widely regarded
as constitutionally improper.[85]

The question which this raises is whether the approach adopted by the
South African judiciary can offer a model to other jurisdictions for adjudication upon issues of healthcare resource allocation in a manner which
will serve to facilitate deliberation (albeit that, absent political will, the
courts cannot guarantee that deliberation takes place to the fullest possible extent). Alternatively, is this approach specific to this legal and political culture, in particular because of the constitutional entrenchment of
socio-economic rights? The concluding chapter will address this issue, in
the broader context of a summation of the argument which this book has
sought to advance.

---

[85] It is interesting to speculate upon the factors which have influenced the adoption of a
'middle way' by the South African judiciary. That the stance taken is more proactive than
that of the English judiciary is relatively easily explained by the constitutional entrenchment of the right to have access to healthcare services, which, as argued above, accords
constitutional competence on such matters to the judiciary, notwithstanding the initial
debate on the justiciability of socio-economic rights. The employment of the 'reasonableness' standard, however, reflects a degree of continuing unease in this regard. More
difficult to explain is the fact that the Constitutional Court has taken a *less* interventionist
approach than the Supreme Court of Canada, at least in *Chaoulli*, notwithstanding that
the Canadian Charter merely protects rights of the civil and political variety. Aside from
the possibility that the latter judgment is reflective of an ideological preference among the
majority of judges in the Supreme Court for the creation of a 'two-tier' health system in
Canada (in which case *Chaoulli* may be regarded as an 'outlier'), it is submitted that there
are two possible explanations for this seemingly paradoxical position. First, the relative
novelty of the South African constitutional regime and, in particular, its protection of
socio-economic rights, may have led judges to adopt a cautious approach in this field, and
they may be expected to become bolder over time. Secondly, the structure of the
constitutional regime in South Africa which, in contrast to Canada, provides that courts
have the last word on the meaning accorded to rights, may in fact have led the courts to
show *greater* respect and sensitivity towards executive and legislative policies and decisions than has been the case in Canada, where the possibility of legislative override under
section 33 of the Charter may have emboldened the judiciary to adopt an interventionist
stance in the knowledge that the democratic will must ultimately prevail.

9   Conclusion

A role for the courts: a modest proposal

The central contention of this book is that the deliberative possibilities afforded by public law adjudication have been mistakenly overlooked by those who have sought to evolve procedural means to resolve the 'legitimacy problem' which has been generated by the adoption of explicit strategies of rationing.

On one level, the marginalisation of the legal process in the accounts of commentators such as Daniels and Sabin is unsurprising. Increasing resort to litigation on issues of the allocation of scarce healthcare resources is most readily viewed as a symptom of, rather than a solution for, the problem of legitimacy which these authors identify. That is, legal mechanisms are seen as vehicles through which the 'suspicion, distrust and even resistance' which is generated by strategies of explicit rationing may be articulated.[1] The mistrust of law (in general) and courts (in particular) which is evident within the health policy literature (and which is frequently echoed by the media) reflects a commonly held perception that the legal process is profoundly individualistic in nature and that public law functions in an essentially negative manner. On this analysis, public law adjudication acts as an external constraint upon the pursuit of those collective goals of which account must necessarily be taken in reaching decisions on a proper allocation of scarce healthcare resources. For this reason, judicial intervention is to be feared rather than welcomed and may be regarded as an indication of failure in the quest for the legitimate exercise of public power.[2]

Yet, given the apparent inevitability of increased judicial engagement with decision-making in this sphere of public policy, coupled with the apparent impossibility of reversing the trend towards explicit rationing,

---

[1] See Daniels, 'Accountability for Reasonableness in Private and Public Health Insurance' in A. Coulter and C. Ham (eds.) *The Global Challenge of Health Care Rationing* (Buckingham: Open University Press, 2000) at 89.

[2] See especially The Commission on the NHS' chaired by W. Hutton, *New Life for Health* (London: Vintage, 2000) at 31, 60–62.

230

the involvement of the courts cannot simply be 'wished away', as might seemingly be the hope of certain commentators. Instead, it is submitted that it would be more profitable to explore the considerable synergies which exist between the values and principles of public law and the procedural 'solutions' which have been proposed for the 'legitimacy problem', notably the stimulation of deliberation through compliance with the (widely approved) conditions of 'accountability for reasonableness'. In this regard, it is of profound significance that public law is centrally concerned with the design of mechanisms and institutions which will contribute to 'social learning', thereby establishing a foundation for the resolution of problems of legitimation; and that it places particular emphasis upon compliance with norms of procedural fairness, notably transparency and accountability. Once these points of confluence have been identified, it becomes possible to articulate a more positive contribution for public law which focuses upon its capacity to establish the conditions for deliberation, as outlined above. In short, a reconceptualisation of the judicial role within this sphere of decision-making is warranted, which recognises the scope of public law adjudication to function in a *facilitative* manner, assisting in the attainment of legitimacy by engendering deliberation on questions of healthcare rationing. This may be viewed as being of particular significance in light of the limited scope which exists for deliberation through other avenues, as will be discussed below.

It is important to stress the moderation of the argument which is being advanced here. It is emphatically not the objective of this text to contend that courts should take the lead in establishing priorities for the allocation of healthcare resources: that is, that the answer to the question 'who decides?' should be 'judges'.[3] Clearly, powerful concerns as to institutional competence, centred upon the amenability of polycentric questions to resolution through the judicial process and the lack of expertise of judges, would preclude this, even supposing that a lack of democratic legitimacy in respect of such matters could be tolerated. Nor is the claim made that societal deliberation upon the need for rationing and upon the principles which should inform allocative decision-making can *best* be brought about through the adjudicative route. Once again, the preferred mechanisms for realising such a goal are likely to be those of a more democratic character, which are not encumbered by the procedural limitations inherent in adversarial adjudication. However, what *is* argued is that there has been too great a readiness on the part of those working

---

[3] For discussion of this question, see especially M. Hall, *Making Medical Spending Decisions* (New York: Oxford University Press, 1997) at 73.

within the health policy community (mirrored, to some extent, by those working within the academic and professional legal communities) to dismiss judicial scrutiny of allocative decision-making in healthcare as an unwelcome intrusion. What is accordingly required is the development of an awareness of the facilitative dimension of public law which lawyers in this field may already possess,[4] but commentators on health policy do not. It is to be hoped that this book has gone some way towards alleviating this deficiency.

The deliberative possibilities of public law adjudication

The objective of the discussion in the three preceding chapters of this book has been to assess the capacity of the courts to undertake an approach to public law adjudication on disputes turning upon the allocation of scarce healthcare resources which has the potential to facilitate deliberation on rationing. It has been seen that, notwithstanding the theoretical arguments canvassed in Chapter 5 – which suggest that the courtroom may be regarded as a deliberative space and that the judicial decision may serve as a stimulus for further deliberation within and between the political branches of government and within broader civil society – a degree of inhibition persists among the judiciary as to the assumption of any such function. Concerns as to institutional and constitutional competence serve as constraints on the evolution of a more facilitative approach under which the courts might enhance 'social learning' about the need for, and criteria which might underpin, decisions to limit access to healthcare resources. This is manifest in a restrained and deferential stance which, while notionally admitting of the possibility of some limited level of judicial intervention, in reality fails to expose rationing decisions to meaningful scrutiny. In so doing, this effectively renders the courts impotent to give effect to the conditions of the 'accountability for reasonableness' model, thus severely restricting the judiciary's capacity to assist in resolution of the 'legitimacy problem'. Cases such as *Collier, Pfizer (No. 2)* and the decision of the Court of Appeal in 'Child B' in England, and *Soobramoney* in South Africa, afford the most powerful illustrations of this tendency.

However, simply to dismiss the deliberative potential of public law adjudication in this manner would be to ignore a significant number of high-profile decisions in which the judiciary has deployed the principles of public law and constitutional mechanisms in such a way as to render

---

[4] See the discussion of the work of Prosser, Poole and, in particular, Longley, above Chapter 5.

the rationales for decisions on the allocation of scarce healthcare resources considerably more transparent (thus meeting the 'publicity' condition of the 'accountability for reasonableness' model), and has demanded that the decision-maker offer support for its choice by reference to evidence and reasoned justification (thus fulfilling the 'relevance' condition). In cases such as *Eldridge* in Canada (and, more controversially, *Chaoulli*), *TAC* in South Africa and *A, D and G* in England, the courts may be seen to be giving effect to the 'educative function' which Daniels and Sabin identify as a necessary precondition to a process of deliberation upon issues of rationing. They do so both by requiring open articulation of rationales for limit-setting decisions within the courtroom and, in consequence, by providing stimulus for further debate upon such matters within the political branches of government and broader civil society.

These decisions demonstrate that scope exists within the processes and principles of public law for the courts to give effect to an approach to adjudication upon questions of the allocation of scarce healthcare resources which would facilitate broader deliberation on rationing. However, the propensity of the judiciary to act in such a way is likely to be dependant in part upon the nature of the legal framework within which it operates but, more crucially, upon the perspective which it adopts as to the proper function of public law within democratic society. A particular 'judicial mindset' is required if the deliberative possibilities of public law adjudication in this context are to be fully realised. The discussion below seeks both to articulate the nature of this and to consider the feasibility of its development.

Deliberation and rights adjudication

One conclusion which might be drawn from the case law examined in Chapters 6 to 8 is that the deliberative impact of public law is significantly enhanced when litigation on questions of resource allocation in healthcare takes the form of adjudication on alleged violations of rights, as distinct from judicial review of the legality of administrative action. This becomes plain when contrasting the relatively diffident, non-interventionist approach of the English courts, in which human rights arguments have yet to have a significant effect in this field, with the deliberative possibilities which are generated by the judgments of their Canadian and South African counterparts.

The greater willingness of the courts to assert jurisdiction over issues of healthcare rationing in the latter two legal systems can be explained by reference to the notion of judicial competence, particularly of the constitutional variant. Section 27 of the South African Constitution clearly mandates the judiciary to adjudicate upon rationing issues in so far as these are raised under the rubric of the right to have access to healthcare services. As Roux observes, the South African judiciary 'cannot afford the luxury of the classical separation of powers doctrine':[5] it is constitutionally *obliged* to determine the lawfulness of decisions and policies to ration the availability of healthcare resources when these are the subject of litigation.[6] The constitutional mandate of the Canadian courts is rather more problematic to delineate, but the relative maturity of the rights regime in that jurisdiction appears to have endowed the judiciary with the confidence to conceptualise disputes which turn upon the rationing of healthcare resources as raising questions of rights, especially under section 15 of the Charter, with the consequence that allocative choices are considered within a framework of legally enforceable rights rather than as matters of politics.[7] By contrast, the English courts function primarily within the confines of the principles of judicial review of administrative action, the concern of which is not the substance of a decision but the decision-making process. Although, as Jowell observes, it is clear that judicial competence extends to review of the way in which decisions are justified and reasoned and of the grounding of a decision in evidence,[8] the courts remain highly apprehensive of being accused of violation of the separation of powers by exercising an intensive level of scrutiny, especially in an area of allocative decision-making which is patently within the province of the political branches. Accordingly, in the absence of a clear constitutional exhortation to become involved in review of allocative decision-making in the healthcare context, English judges continue to operate in more restrained and deferential manner than their Canadian and South African brethren.

Conceptualisation of disputes as to access to healthcare resources as raising questions of rights thus provides a firmer foundation for judicial willingness to engage in adjudication within this field, which is clearly the necessary first step to assumption of a deliberative function by the courts. However, the prospects for deliberation are significantly enhanced by the structure of human rights instruments and the nature of rights

---

[5] T. Roux, 'Legitimating Transformation: Political Resource Allocation in the South African Constitutional Court' (2003) 10 *Democratization*, 92 at 107.

[6] See M. Pieterse, 'Coming to Terms with Judicial Enforcement of Socio-Economic Rights' (2004) *South African Journal on Human Rights*, 383 at 404.

[7] See especially B. Sheldrick, 'Judicial Review and the Allocation of Health Resources in Canada and the United Kingdom' (2003) 5 *Journal of Comparative Policy Analysis*, 149 at 157.

[8] J. Jowell, 'Of Vires and Vacuums: The Constitutional Context of Judicial Review' [1999] *Public Law*, 448 at 453.

adjudication. Here, an instructive parallel can again be drawn between the approach taken by the English courts and those in Canada and South Africa. The former have struggled to break free of the 'shackles of *Wednesbury* reasonableness',[9] and remain ambivalent as to the degree to which there is scope for the imposition of an obligation to provide the 'substantial objective justification' for which Laws J called in 'Child B'. By contrast, the Canadian courts are empowered to demand 'demonstrable justification' under section 1 of the Charter and – at least to some extent – may seek to promote 'democratic dialogue' with other branches of government. Similarly, the South African judiciary are equipped, by means of the general limitation clause contained in section 36 of the Constitution and the 'reasonableness' standard articulated in *Grootboom* and *TAC*, to make inquiries into the justifiability of government conduct which, as noted in Chapter 8, affords them scope to assume a deliberative role.

If rights adjudication provides the clearest opportunity for development of a judicial approach to questions of rationing which can facilitate democratic deliberation, does it follow that we must look to the constitutional entrenchment of rights of access to healthcare resources, of the type provided by the South African Constitution? Such a development would undoubtedly be highly controversial. Notwithstanding Article 12 of the International Covenant on Economic, Social and Cultural Rights, which provides that everyone has the right 'to the enjoyment of the highest attainable standard of physical and mental health', the legal content of such a right is not yet well established,[10] and a right to health is not generally accepted as a human right by those operating within the 'liberal consensus', which seeks to distinguish positive rights (which require redistribution of resources and which may therefore impose burdens on particular groups within society) from negative rights (which merely require forbearance by all members of society).[11]

From a deliberative perspective, however, certain of the objections to recognition of a right to health (or, more pertinent to the subject-matter of this book, a right to have access to healthcare resources)[12] appear

---

[9] R. James and D. Longley, 'Judicial Review and Tragic Choices': *ex parte B* [1995] *Public Law*, 367 at 373.

[10] United Nations Economic and Social Council, *Economic, Social and Cultural Rights. The Right of Everyone to the Enjoyment of the Highest Attainable Standard of Physical and Mental Health: Report of the Special Rapporteur* (New York, United Nations, 2003) at para. 38.

[11] See T. Evans, 'A Human Right to Health?' (2002) 23 *Third World Quarterly*, 197 at 200.

[12] See C. Newdick, *Who Should We Treat?* (Oxford: Oxford University Press, 2nd edn, 2004) at 10 for discussion of the distinction between a right to health and a right to healthcare; and see further the work of N. Daniels, *Just Health Care* (Cambridge: Cambridge University Press, 1985) at 43 (above Chapter 4, n. 21 and accompanying text).

misplaced. It may be contended that legal enforcement of positive rights, such as those arising in the health context, is problematic because rights act as 'trumps',[13] with the consequence that the interests of the individual will prevail over those of the wider community, a situation which cannot be tolerated in the context of social policy such as the provision of healthcare where the role of the state is to bring about an overall increase in social welfare.[14] Yet, as Feldman notes, although 'historically liberty and rights have usually been espoused by individualists and viewed with suspicion … as hurdles to achieving social goals … rights represent a balance between potentially conflicting interests, some individual, some social'.[15] The need for the judiciary to assess the *balance* which the decision-maker has struck between individual and community interests is inherent to the structure of both the European Convention and the Canadian Charter, but its deliberative possibilities are perhaps best understood against the backdrop of the constitutional 'culture of justification' in South Africa. Within this culture, it has been argued by van der Walt and Botha,[16] that 'rights should not be regarded as simply overriding the will of the democratic majority or trumping policy considerations. Rights are not fixed immutable boundaries, but are standards of justification, the content and meaning of which alter with shifts in the social context'. On this approach, which rejects the 'outdated conception of rights as constraints upon government', 'rights cannot be considered brightline boundaries between the spheres of individual freedom and legitimate state power, but rather constitute a social practice and an occasion for deliberation on vital social issues'.[17]

Viewed in this light, legal enforcement of rights need not necessarily be antithetical to the pursuit of collective social goals or, to put matters another way, individualism will not inevitably trump utilitarianism. Indeed, the assessment of relative weight which is inherent in rights adjudication permits us to consider rationing as an integral element of any human right to access healthcare resources,[18] in that limitations to the availability of treatments and services for particular individuals may be justified as a means of freeing up resources for the provision of

---

[13] See especially R. Dworkin, *Taking Rights Seriously* (London: Duckworth, 1978) at xi.

[14] See Evans, 'A Human Right to Health' at 200–1.

[15] D. Feldman, *Civil Liberties and Human Rights in England and Wales* (Oxford: Oxford University Press, 2nd edn, 2002) at 6.

[16] J. van der Walt and H. Botha, 'Democracy and Rights in South Africa: Beyond a Constitutional Culture of Justification' (2000) 7 *Constellations*, 341 at 343–4.

[17] *Ibid.*

[18] See e.g. the comments of Sachs J in *Soobramoney*, above Chapter 8, n. 21; and *cf.* the view of Daniels, above Chapter 4, nn. 26, 28 and accompanying text.

treatments and services to other members of the community. What is vital, however, is that in adjudicating upon the alleged violation of the right, a court is obliged to require that a reasoned explanation of the rationing choice be presented, in order to ascertain whether the balance which has been struck between individual and community interests can be justified with reference to plausible reasons. It is this process which creates the space for deliberation.

Creating a 'culture of justification'

Nonetheless, it would be out of keeping with the modest proposals outlined here, and well beyond the scope of this text, to argue for the constitutional entrenchment of socio-economic rights such as the right of access to healthcare resources. It suffices to state that the hegemony of the 'liberal consensus' alluded to above makes such a course of action unlikely in a number of states, including the UK and Canada, at least for the foreseeable future. However, it does not follow from this that the South African jurisprudence on the allocation of scarce resources is of no value. On the contrary, it is submitted that the South African example can be applied in other jurisdictions as the basis for a judicial approach to questions of the rationing of healthcare which will serve to facilitate deliberation and thus to assist in resolution of the 'legitimacy problem'.

Such an approach would be centred upon the notion of 'law as justification'.[19] That is, the processes and principles of public law adjudication should not be regarded as vehicles through which individuals contest the legitimacy of exercises of state power and which enable the judiciary to impose constraints upon that power. Rather, and in accordance with the facilitative dimension outlined in this book, public law adjudication should function as a 'mechanism for inquiring into the justifiability of government decisions',[20] by requiring the presentation of reasoned argumentation, justification and evidence for the decision or action which forms the subject-matter of litigation.

While the concept of a constitutional 'culture of justification' arose in the particular political context of post-apartheid South Africa, and finds expression in the judicial enforcement of rights incorporated within the constitutional settlement of 1996, its underlying premise – that the state should be called upon to 'justify its decisions with reference to reasons

---

[19] van der Walt and Botha, 'Democracy and Rights in South Africa' at 344, commenting on E. Mureinik, 'A Bridge to Where? Introducing the Interim Bill of Rights' (1994) 10 *South African Journal of Human Rights*, 11.

[20] *Ibid.* at 343.

that are viewed as cogent in the light of democratic norms and values'[21] – will be highly familiar to public lawyers everywhere. As noted previously, accountability (which centres upon the development of mechanisms which ensure that justifications in the form of reasons are provided for state action) is a foundational principle of public law,[22] and the call for explanation in terms of prevailing democratic norms and values may be regarded as a means of giving effect to the rule of law. Moreover, the existence of a so-called 'crisis of accountability' in modern governance in numerous states,[23] may be said to generate a pressing need for the evolution of institutions and processes (albeit, not necessarily legal in form) through which the justifiability of governmental action and decisions may be scrutinised. Accordingly, the notion of 'law as justification' would appear to be one which can be relatively easily transplanted from its South African environment to perform a useful function in other legal systems.

Nor should it be necessary to undertake radical changes to the structures, processes and principles of public law – such as constitutional protection of socio-economic rights along South African lines – so as to enable adjudication on issues of healthcare rationing to fit the justificatory model. Indeed, it is apparent that the Canadian courts already possess the requisite tools to operate in such a way, in accordance with the 'dialogic approach' to adjudication under the Charter of Rights and Freedoms and notwithstanding the fact that rights of access to healthcare resources are only afforded indirect judicial protection within a rights regime which is civil and political in nature. It is therefore unsurprising that van der Walt and Botha acknowledge the justificatory character of Charter adjudication by the Canadian courts.[24]

The English case is clearly more problematic. The National Health Service Act 1977, which forms the statutory basis for the organisation of the NHS, expresses the issue of access to healthcare resources as a generalised 'target' duty imposed upon government, rather than as a matter of individual rights. This, coupled with two factors previously noted, namely the relative lack of impact of human rights jurisprudence upon this area (at least to date) and the absence of a general administrative law duty for decision-makers to provide reasons, renders the English courts less likely to approach questions of healthcare rationing from a

---

[21] *Ibid.* at 342.
[22] See especially T. Prosser, 'Towards a Critical Public Law' (1982) 9 *Journal of Law and Society*, 1 at 11.
[23] See e.g. M. Dowdle (ed.), *Public Accountability: Designs, Dilemmas and Experiences* (New York: Cambridge University Press, 2006) at 1.
[24] van der Walt and Botha, 'Democracy and Rights in South Africa' at 346.

perspective of 'law as justification' which has developed primarily in the context of rights adjudication. However, the basis for some progression in such a direction exists within English law, as Laws J's judgment in 'Child B' indicates. Two related developments, noted both in Chapter 6 and by Newdick,[25] are of particular significance in this regard. First, in cases such as *Fisher, Pfizer* and *A, D and G*, the courts have shown a willingness to undertake a more intensive, 'harder look' form of scrutiny of resource allocation, under which some degree of explanation may be expected of the decision-maker. Secondly, it appears at the very least possible that proportionality will replace *Wednesbury* as a ground of judicial review of administrative action, even outside of the human rights context.[26] As previously discussed, in assessing whether the means adopted by government are the least intrusive necessary to achieve particular policy objectives, a court will inevitably demand some form of articulation of the rationales which led the decision-maker to pursue the objective to the detriment of the right or interest which has been infringed, and of the relative weight which has been attached to competing interests and considerations. While judicial application of this test may well stop short of 'requiring a strongly evidence-based cost-benefit analysis',[27] it is undoubtedly more congruent with a justificatory approach than *Wednesbury* – as witness the endorsement of proportionality by both Laws[28] and van der Walt and Botha[29] – and, to that extent, it offers at least a springboard for the English courts to assume a role in facilitating deliberation on rationing.

Approached in this way, 'law as justification' need not be contingent upon conceptualisation of issues of healthcare rationing in the form of legally enforceable rights. Although the jurisprudential framework of rights-based adjudication may afford an easier path to the development of a role for the courts in facilitating deliberation, in particular because of the explanatory obligation upon decision-makers which is inherent in rights instruments such as the South African Constitution and the Canadian Charter, the key to this approach is the *attitude of the judiciary to its role in adjudication upon allocative questions in healthcare*. If judges are willing to regard the function of adjudication in such cases as a 'mechanism for inquiring into the justifiability of government decisions', it becomes incumbent upon them to utilise or further develop those

---

[25] Newdick, *Who Should We Treat?* at 100–107, 121–5.
[26] For discussion, see P. Craig, *Administrative Law* (London: Sweet & Maxwell, 5th edn, 2003) at 630–2.
[27] P. Cane, *Administrative Law* (Oxford: Oxford University Press, 4th edn., 2003) at 258.
[28] See above Chapter 6, nn. 34–36 and accompanying text.
[29] van der Walt and Botha, 'Democracy and Rights in South Africa' at 346.

principles of public law which already exist, so as to impose requirements of reason-giving and relevance upon decision-makers which mirror the conditions of 'accountability for reasonableness'. In such a manner, even in the absence of a rights framework, the courts may significantly contribute to the creation of a deliberative space on issues of healthcare rationing, and hence to the resolution of the 'legitimacy problem'.

The continuing need for judicial restraint and focus

However, such a thesis must confront the potent arguments for judicial restraint and deference which follow from the concerns as to institutional and constitutional competence which were articulated in Chapter 5. That is, 'the demonstration that courts can play a vital role in building a democratic culture of justification does not tell us where to draw the line between legitimate exercises of the review power and the judicial usurpation of the legislative and/or executive function'.[30]

The difficulties inherent in drawing such a line are amply illustrated by the *Chaoulli* case, in which the Supreme Court of Canada was widely acknowledged to have transgressed the constitutional boundaries established by the doctrine of the separation of powers and thus to have operated in a manner which was democratically illegitimate. Opponents of an enhanced judicial role in respect of questions of healthcare financing can accordingly point to this decision as affording strong support for their position. How, then, might a supporter of the justificatory approach which is outlined here respond to such a critique?

Once again, it is submitted that a way forward is offered by the jurisprudence of the South African Constitutional Court. It was noted in Chapter 8 that the Court outlined a 'restrained and focused' role for the judiciary in its judgment in *TAC*, which was sensitive to the relative competences of the judicial, executive and legislative branches of government. It is therefore clear that a degree of judicial deference remains appropriate, but that this should not be carried to the extent of absolving the court of its constitutional obligation of adjudicating upon those disputes which are within its jurisdiction.

Pieterse offers a valuable analysis of the balance which must be struck by the courts in cases of this type. He observes that a degree of discretion must be accorded by the judiciary to the political branches to select a policy option from a range of alternatives. However, a 'culture of justification' requires that where there has been a prima facie infringement of

---

[30] *Ibid.* at 344.

an interest or right, the policy choice which is made is justified to the court and that it is demonstrated to be the least intrusive means necessary to achieve that (justifiable) objective. For Pieterse, 'insisting on justification while at the same time deferring from substituting (duly chosen and implemented) policy with seemingly equally valid (but judicially pre-ferred) options would simultaneously allow government to go about its business while having the 'directive principle'-like benefit of inspiring government to pay attention to its constitutional obligations in policy-formulation'.[31] He therefore argues that:

It is integral not to lose sight of the fact that a matter does not *become* one of policy or of budgeting merely because it requires that policy or budgetary evidence be scrutinised. Opponents to judicial review in social rights matters typically attempt to shield budgets and/or policies from scrutiny by claiming that courts are ill-equipped to decide *matters of* budgets or policy ... The fact is that courts are not ill-equipped to *scrutinise or evaluate* budgets or policies just because they are ill-equipped to *engage in* budgeting or policy-making. In reality, the matter remains one concerning the realisation of a constitutional right and the accompanying satisfaction of a constitutional duty. Budgetary evidence or policy are merely scrutinised in order to reach answers to those questions of right and obligation.[32]

Although developed in a context of constitutional protection of socio-economic rights, it is submitted that Pieterse's account of the parameters of the 'restrained and focused' judicial role is apposite to public law adjudication upon issues of healthcare rationing in other jurisdictions. It serves to remind us that the function of the courts in such cases is not the substitution of judicially determined priorities on healthcare expen-diture for those established by the allocative decision-maker – which would, indeed, be beyond the constitutional competence of the judiciary – but rather, the scrutiny of *process*, that is, that which 'deals with the way decisions are justified or reasoned, or the factors taken into account *en route* to a decision'.[33] This latter clearly does lie within constitutional competence. The political branches of government remain free to allo-cate scarce resources in whatsoever manner they choose, but if the law-fulness of such an allocation is challenged in judicial review proceedings, they can expect to be rendered accountable to the court in that an explanation will be demanded of the choice made and of the weight attached by the decision-maker to competing interests, so as to satisfy the court that interests and/or rights have been interfered with by the least intrusive means possible. Should the court consider that the explanation advanced does not afford adequate justification for infringement of the

[31] Pieterse, 'Coming to Terms with Judicial Enforcement' at 409.
[32] *Ibid.* at 408–9. Emphasis in original.   [33] Jowell, 'Of Vires and Vacuums' at 453.

right/interest, it may of course declare the decision to be unlawful. But such an outcome in no way precludes the allocative decision-maker from reaching the same conclusion (that is, ordering of priorities) again, provided that, if challenged for a second time, it is able to proffer an explanation which satisfies the court that the right/interest is not being infringed to a disproportionate degree.

Understood in this way, a judicial approach to rationing issues which is grounded in 'law as justification' is appropriately constitutionally circumscribed. This is not to claim that a respect for the limits to the proper judicial role in such cases thereby renders the latter uncontroversial. As Pieterse states, adjudication on such matters is 'likely to involve judicial scrutiny of actual executive policies and the manner of their implementation, as well as of evidence on resource-availability (directly or indirectly implicating budgets)'.[34] Since this process of scrutiny may raise substantive concerns, for example as to the plausibility of justifications and the grounding of rationales in evidence, it is likely on occasion to generate significant tensions between the judicial and political branches of government. Moreover, in exercising scrutiny, courts may frequently be obliged to concede that those other branches possess greater expertise in the evaluation of the evidence upon which allocative decisions are grounded, or that they are procedurally better-suited to assess the multifaceted implications of those decisions and the variety of interests which may be affected. In such instances, it would seem appropriate for the courts to approach the task of scrutiny on the basis that considerable respect should be paid to the judgments reached by the allocative decision-maker. In large part, it was the failure of the Supreme Court of Canada to accord such respect to the evaluation of evidence, data and policy arguments which formed the basis of the provincial government's legislative choice in *Chaoulli* which made this case so problematic, especially in view of the relative lack of explanation advanced by the Court as to why the justification grounded in such evidence was unsatisfactory.

It is therefore clear, as acknowledged by the South African Constitutional Court in *TAC*, that it is incumbent upon the judiciary to remain acutely 'sensitive to the realities of the modern executive state and the peculiar strengths and weaknesses of all branches of government' in adjudicating upon questions of healthcare rationing.[35] This will be no easy task, and failure to exhibit the correct degree of sensitivity, as in *Chaoulli*, may carry highly deleterious consequences for the legitimacy of the judiciary within democratic society. But, equally, courts cannot shirk

[34] Pieterse, 'Coming to Terms with Judicial Enforcement' at 408.
[35] *Ibid.* at 405. See above Chapter 8, nn. 36 to 39 and accompanying text.

their constitutional obligations. Operation of a standard of scrutiny which is restrained and deferential to the degree that no obligation of justification at all is imposed upon allocative decision-makers amounts to an abdication of the essential democratic function of the judiciary: that is, to secure legal accountability for decisions which are alleged to impinge upon constitutionally-protected rights or to amount to unlawful exercises of administrative power. The Constitutional Court is to be commended for its recognition of this fact in *TAC*.

Prospects for deliberation outside the courts

The difficulties inherent in adoption of an appropriately sensitive, restrained and focused judicial role on questions of healthcare rationing serve to underline a point made earlier in this chapter. Although the notion of 'law as justification' provides a basis upon which the judiciary can build a facilitative approach to public law adjudication and thus offer stimulus to political and public processes of deliberation on rationing from which legitimacy for such choices may ultimately be derived, the democratic and institutional limitations of courts mean that they are not the ideal institutions to bring about such deliberation. Undoubtedly, it would be preferable if the impetus for societal deliberation upon the need for rationing of healthcare and upon the criteria which should inform allocative decision-making arose from democratic political processes. However, aside from the relatively small-scale experimentation with deliberative mechanisms (such as citizens' juries) which was outlined in Chapter 4, and leaving aside the Oregon experiment, there seems little likelihood of government encouraging such deliberation to take place.

The explanation for this reticence lies in the nature of healthcare rationing as a 'hot potato' of public policy. As noted in Chapter 2, government politicians consistently engage in blame avoidance and blame diffusion strategies in this field and deploy the more neutral discourse of 'priority-setting' to avoid the political and electoral discomfiture which would be attendant upon an open acknowledgement of the inevitability of rationing. This remains the case notwithstanding the shift towards more explicit strategies of rationing, with the consequence that there is a disjuncture between political rhetoric and the realities of resource allocation. Accordingly, there is no realistic prospect of public deliberation on healthcare rationing being encouraged by government, while opposition politicians (whose political interests may be served by such a debate) are hamstrung by government's control of the policy and legislative agenda.

Yet there can be little doubt that a widespread demand exists for some form of debate upon the acceptability of limitations on the availability of treatments and services within healthcare systems. For example, in the UK, within the first six months of 2006 alone, a poll of doctors showed that 96 per cent believed that it was 'time for an open debate on rationing',[36] and spokespersons for respected thinktanks at various ends of the political spectrum argued that 'the public must become more aware of, and involved in, "rationing"; in making decisions about trade-offs, and what they want from a cost-constrained health service',[37] demanding 'a proper national debate on the long-term future' of NHS funding.[38] Similarly, newspaper articles asserted that 'a sober, considered debate about rationing has never been more badly needed'[39] and that 'the time has come for a frank debate on how the cash-strapped NHS allocates its limited resources among competing demands',[40] while an independent MP contended that 'perhaps the most important thing is to have an open debate on health care rationing and on what people would be prepared to pay and what sort of NHS charges are realistic'.[41] The frequency and potency of these pleas reflect the growing perception that budgets for healthcare are coming under increasing and irreversible strain, and that a growing mismatch between the demand for and supply of available resources necessitates urgent action.[42]

Viewed from this perspective, the arguments which this book has made for a more positive attitude to judicial engagement in issues of healthcare rationing are, indeed, modest. Litigation on such matters can never comprehensively substitute for a process of broad public deliberation upon the achievable and appropriate parameters of expenditure within a health system.

Nonetheless, the contribution which the courts can make should not be overlooked or dismissed, as has all too frequently been the case. As Parkin notes in relation to the 'Child B' case, the claim 'that the court [is] ill-equipped to answer the question [as to how scarce healthcare resources are to be allocated], misses the point; everyone will remain ill-equipped to answer the question unless steps are taken to bring it, and the process by which it is considered, into the public domain'.[43] In the absence of any

---

[36] 'Doctors want Debate on Rationing of Treatment', *The Guardian*, 3 February 2006.

[37] 'Rationing is only Rational' (J. Allan, Institute for Public Policy Research), *The Guardian*, 25 April 2006.

[38] 'New ideas needed to revive the NHS' (K. Sikora, Reform), *The Times*, 20 February 2006.

[39] 'Find the Balance', *The Times*, 27 May 2006.

[40] 'Why We Need to Face Facts on Drug Costs', *Sunday Express*, 20 February 2006.

[41] *House of Commons Debates*, vol. 444, col. 104 (20 March 2006) (R. Taylor).

[42] For an important earlier call for debate, see R. Smith 'Rationing: the Debate We Have to Have' (1995) 310 *British Medical Journal*, 686.

[43] A. Parkin, 'Allocating Healthcare Resources in an Imperfect World' (1995) 58 *Modern Law Review*, 867 at 876.

meaningful political will, the courts represent one of the few avenues through which (to paraphrase the argument of Roach)[44] such uncomfortable matters can be placed upon the political and public agenda. In this manner, by approaching public law adjudication as a means of building a 'culture of justification', they possess the capacity to enhance political and societal debate on rationing choices. Hence, though they remain imperfect mechanisms, the courts surely warrant closer consideration (as befits the inevitability of their continued engagement with allocative decision-making in healthcare), and a more positive evaluation than they have previously been accorded in analysis of this hugely contentious area of modern public policy.

[44] See above Chapter 7, n. 121 and accompanying text.

Index

Notes: 1. In this Index entries in **Bold** denote main entries.
2. The following abbreviations are used:

ECHR   European Convention for the Protection of Human Rights
        and Fundamental Freedoms
EMA   European Medicines Agency
NHS   National Health Service
NICE   National Institute for Health and Clinical Excellence
OECD   Organization for Economic Cooperation and Development
PCT   Primary Care Trust
QALY   Quality Adjusted Life Year
TAC   Treatment Action Campaign
UK   United Kingdom
USA   United States of America